“Right Development”

"Right Development"

The Santi Asoke Buddhist Reform Movement of Thailand

Juliana Essen

LEXINGTON BOOKS
Lanham • Boulder • New York • Toronto • Oxford

LEXINGTON BOOKS

Published in the United States of America
by Lexington Books
An imprint of The Rowman & Littlefield Publishing Group, Inc.
4501 Forbes Boulevard, Suite 200, Lanham, Maryland 20706

PO Box 317
Oxford
OX2 9RU, UK

British Library Cataloguing in Publication Information Available

Library of Congress Cataloging-in-Publication Data

Essen, Juliana, 1970-
"Right development" : the Santi Asoke Buddhist reform movement of Thailand / Juliana Essen.
p. cm.
Includes bibliographical references and index.
ISBN: 978-0-7391-0937-3
1. Santi 'Asåok (Organization) 2. Economics—Religious aspects—Buddhism. 3. Religious life—Buddhism. 4. Buddhism—Doctrines. 5. Buddhism—Social aspects—Thailand. I. Title. II. Title: Santi Asoke Buddhist reform movement of Thailand.
BQ9800.S252E88 2005
294.3'373'09593—dc22 2005002242

Printed in the United States of America

The paper used in this publication meets the minimum requirements of American National Standard for Information Sciences—Permanence of Paper for Printed Library Materials, ANSI/NISO Z39.48–1992.

For my parents and Jon

Contents

Illustrations

Acknowledgments

This research was funded through an International Field Research Predissertation Grant and a Doctoral Field Research Grant from the MacArthur Interdisciplinary Program on Global Change, Sustainability, and Justice; a Block Grant from the University of Minnesota Department of Anthropology; a Doctoral Special Grant from the University of Minnesota Graduate School; and a Foreign Language and Area Studies (FLAS) Grant from the Southeast Asian Studies Summer Institute, University of Oregon. Many thanks to these organizations for their generosity.

At the University of Minnesota, my gratitude goes to Kathleen Barlow, Stephen Gudeman, and Delane Welsch as well as to the MacArthur Interdisciplinary Program on Global Change, Sustainability, and Justice for helping to shape my research.

In Thailand, I thank the National Research Council of Thailand as well as Dr. Apinya Fuengfusakul at Chiang Mai University. To members of the Santi Asoke Buddhist Reform Movement, particularly the residents of Srisa Asoke, I offer my utmost appreciation for such kindness that I can never repay. I hope this research will make some small contribution to their endeavors.

At home, I am indebted to my parents for a lifetime of support and encouragement and to Jon, my loudest cheerleader and most thorough critic.

Last but not least, thanks to the folks at Lexington Books for their efforts to bring this work to a larger audience.

Chapter 1: Introduction

"Right Development" The Santi Asoke Buddhist Reform Movement of Thailand

One day King Mahajanaka visited the Royal Park where he tasted the sweet fruit of a mango tree. When he passed the tree later, he found it had been plundered and uprooted by greedy people scrambling for its delicious fruit.

His Majesty the King of Thailand uses this traditional Buddhist riddle in his recent book to teach his kingdom lessons about sustainable development. Prominent Thai scholars such as Dr. Prawase Wasi interpret it as an analogy for "development driven by greed." Dr. Prawase[1] laments, "We are short-sighted. . . When people struggle only for economic gain, society and the environment are destroyed" (*Bangkok Post*, September 13, 1999). Indeed, after more than three decades of promoting rapid economic growth via capital-intensive industrialization, Thailand faces a widening socioeconomic gap, environmental devastation, and decline of Buddhist values. The 1997 economic crisis in Southeast Asia thus marks a critical moment in Thailand's history. Now, many Thais pause to re-evaluate their nation's development path and to consider other options for a primarily Buddhist, agrarian society.

The Santi Asoke Buddhist Reform Movement in Thailand offers one such alternative. The Asoke group's aim is not a Western ideal—to accumulate high levels of material comfort—but a Buddhist ideal—to release attachment to the material world and attain spiritual freedom. The fact that the seven Asoke communities have continued to thrive throughout the nation's economic troubles is a testament to the movement's success in raising the quality of life for ordinary people. This book draws on ethnographic research at one community, the Srisa Asoke Buddhist Center, to illustrate Asoke beliefs and practices that foster material and spiritual development on three levels: individual, community, and society.

The research sprang from a fundamental critique of the mainstream development paradigm that promotes economic growth through monetary and technical aid. Anthropologists and other social scientists have exposed Western development models as historically and culturally constructed, which thus cannot be reproduced globally with consistently satisfying results. These scholars further criticize the overemphasis on economic growth, not only for failing to "trickle down" to improve ordinary people's lives, but for in fact worsening their existence through the burdens of structural adjustment programs and environmental ruin.

Avoiding the common academic trap of deconstructing without rebuilding, this project is also part of an ongoing quest for alternatives to the conventional development approach. While numerous "alternative" development strategies have been proposed over the years such as alternative technology and participatory development, these too frequently fall short of their ideals. Many social scientists maintain that what makes a development approach "alternative" is not merely its *content* but its ability to increase local control of processes of change. Moreover, the work of such social scientists highlights how individuals and social groups can reshape the way development is conceived and enacted in diverse contexts.

The Santi Asoke Buddhist Reform Movement enters here, not only offering a contextually appropriate alternative to development programs driven by Western models, but also exemplifying a generalizable "right development" approach that raises the quality of life for ordinary people.[2] To do so, I argue that development must be culturally/locally situated, focused on livelihoods rather than macroeconomic growth, environmentally "sustainable," and endogenously inspired, implemented, and maintained. How the Asoke way of life represents such an approach will unfold through the ethnographic description and the final analysis.

Methodology

Ethnographic research for this project took place primarily at the Srisa Asoke Buddhist Center, Srisaket Province, Northeast Thailand, in September and October 1999 and between September 2000 and July 2001. The community members welcomed this six-foot tall, Scandinavian-American, Christian[3] *cum* Buddhist sympathizer as a fellow practitioner and did everything imaginable to aid my research. For my part, I endeavored to be the least disruptive as possible. This meant behaving as a Srisa Asoke community member: keeping the five Buddhist precepts (abstain from killing, stealing, sexual misconduct, lying, and sense-altering substances) and abstaining from *abayamook* (the six vices: alcohol, drugs including cigarettes, gambling, nighttime entertainment, laziness, and sexual playing), sleeping on a grass mat on the floor of a small wooden house, rising at 3:30 a.m. to chant and listen to sermons at the Common Hall, contributing my labor to community work, sharing vegetarian meals, chatting with neighbors, minding children, attending committee meetings or evening programs, and retiring early. Through these activities, I came to understand not only how Asoke beliefs and practices contribute to development, but more deeply, what it means to call oneself *chao asoke* (Asoke People).

By participating in community life and observing actual material and social conditions, ethnographers are in a unique position to analyze prevailing beliefs and practices in a given society, as well as to explore the interplay of agency and structure. Sherry Ortner (1984) states that the participant observer's position "on the ground" allows her to see people not as passive reactors to the dictates of dominant social forms, but as active agents in their own history. In the case of the Asoke movement, my engagement in life at Srisa Asoke made it possible to study how individuals interpret, internalize, negotiate, and transform the established national Asoke ideals.

Gudeman and Rivera reflect critically on the nature of participant-observation, anthropology's methodological cornerstone:

> We have also come to doubt the accepted wisdom that the ethnographer is both a participant and an observer. This conceit—which must raise questions about what anthropologists actually are doing, because each task appears to exclude the other—is closely tied to a post-Cartesian theory of knowledge which is dominant only in certain cultures. We would replace the two dualities by seeing anthropologists as artisans fashioning ethnographies by forming communities and making conversations. (1995:243)

The idea that ethnography is a joint project—that ethnography does not represent the observations and intellect of the anthropologist alone, but is created through conversations between people—resonates with recent disciplinary concern over power and authority. Moreover, the perspective that field research is not so much a set of techniques as "a way of doing" (244) or "a way of learning and conversing" (245) allows ethnographic research to be more flexible and less contrived.

That said, this study's primary ethnographic method of participant-observation was fortified with the following other techniques of data collection:

1. Archival research on the national Asoke movement at the main Asoke library, Santi Asoke Buddhist Center, Bangkok;[4]
2. Demographic surveys of a random sample totaling half the regular Srisa Asoke residents;
3. Structured interviews with twenty-four Srisa Asoke community members representative of community-wide distribution in gender and age; and

4. A participatory method in which twenty residents took photographs and wrote explanatory captions illustrating their own impressions of "What Is Most Important about Srisa Asoke Community?"

This mix of research methods demonstrates the difference between formal group rhetoric and individual interpretations, diversifies data by revealing gender-, class-, ethnic-, and age-based dimensions of experience, aids in cross-checking information, and mitigates power differentials and researcher bias.

Readers may find more direct quotes in this book than they are accustomed to. This is another participatory technique that allows people to speak for themselves and provides a richer description than simple summary and analysis. I did not use a translator but relied on my own fluency developed though two years as a US Peace Corps volunteer in Thailand and formal advanced study at the Southeast Asian Studies Summer Institute (made possible by a FLAS grant from the University of Oregon) as well as my familiarity with the research context and participants. I endeavored to remain true to the actual words as they were spoken—including the speaker's speech patterns and interjections. However, spoken language is often vague and imprecise. The people engaged in dialogue may know the other's meaning within the context of the conversation, but the reader merely catches snippets of this conversation. Therefore, I have inserted words in brackets where meaning may be unclear. Some Thai and Pali or Sanskrit (Buddhist scriptural language)[5] terms remain untranslated not only because they may have no direct English equivalent, but also because language is a significant part of culture. These terms are listed in the glossary for quick reference.

Despite such efforts to mediate power, some feminists and post-modernists (e.g., Stacey 1988) maintain that ethnographic research is by nature exploitative as it takes knowledge from others for personal gain (a degree or tenure). Conversely, I believe that reciprocity—giving something back to the research participants—can help balance the exchange between researcher and informant as well as build genuine rapport. Realistically, there may be no way to repay Srisa Asoke members for their immense generosity. Still, I labored four hours a day for one meal as was expected of all community residents. My main work included the Three Professions to Save the Nation—natural farming, composting, and waste management. In addition, I taught English occasionally to classes of boarding school students and four nights a week to a handful of adults. I also taught my research methods to Asoke university students who wanted to conduct research on their own community. They considered my methods more thorough—and more fun—than the paper surveys brought by other researchers. When I left, I gave these budding ethnographers my Polaroid camera and leftover supplies. Lastly, reciprocity may be found in our mutual appreciation for a simple lifestyle, spicy food, and shady trees; satisfaction in doing meaningful work; and endeavors to make ourselves better people.

Chapter Summaries

The remainder of this book is organized as follows. Chapter 2 provides background on diverse forms of lay and monastic Buddhism in Thailand and sketches the social, economic, and environmental conditions that gave rise to expressions of "engaged Buddhism" in Thailand. This chapter establishes a context for the emergence of the Santi Asoke Buddhist Reform Movement. Chapter 3 introduces the research setting of Srisa Asoke Buddhist Center: its physical setting, the history of the community, and community targets, as well as the results from the "What Is Most Important about Srisa Asoke Community?" photo activity.

The next three chapters present ethnographic data about beliefs and practices that form Asoke's trilevel development model: Building the Individual, Community, and Society. Like other Buddhist approaches to development, the Asoke movement asserts that development must begin with the individual. Chapter 4 considers what the Asoke group means by "building the individual" and details four strategies for individual-level development: 1) refining morality by following the Buddhist precepts; 2) enacting the Asoke slogan "Consume Little, Work Hard, and Give the Rest to Society"; 3) educating 200 students at Srisa Asoke; and 4) attending special events such as the "Intensive Human Development" training seminar. Chapter 5, "Building the Community," illustrates the ways in which individual development fosters development at the community level. This chapter then examines obstacles to community building as well as proposed and attempted solutions. Chapter 6, "Building (Thai) Society," describes the activities through which the Asoke movement and Srisa Asoke in particular help "outside" Thai society. Their methods are grouped here into three categories: spiritual and material aid, cultural preservation, and political reform. Since "development" implies some sort of goal, this chapter also considers what makes an ideal society, both in formal Asoke rhetoric and in the imaginations of Srisa Asoke residents.

For chapter 7, "A Day in the Life of Four Women," I accompanied four different women of Srisa Asoke, each throughout a single day. This ethnographic narration illuminates everyday life in Srisa Asoke Community and, in doing so, provides another vantage point to view how Asoke beliefs and practices build the individual, community, and, to a lesser extent, society. In addition, detailing the lives of women in an Asoke community reveals a greater degree of gender equality in Asoke lay and monastic life than in "outside" Thai society where women are expected to follow the path of marriage, not religion. This chapter opens with background on how women and gender are perceived in Thailand, Buddhism, and the Asoke movement.

The final chapter moves to the abstract plane to situate Asoke-style development within contemporary development discourse. The objective of chapter 8 is to argue for an alternative "right development" approach that is culturally/locally situated, focused on livelihoods, environmentally "sustainable," and endogenously inspired, implemented, and maintained.

Notes

1. Thais refer to themselves and others by given names preceded by the appropriate honorific or kinship title, even in scholarly citations. This practice is followed here.

2. What makes for a "good life" is culturally relative; at the very least, one must be able to fulfill basic needs in food, shelter, clothing, and medicine with minimal struggle, consistently sustain the base year after year, and have some resources (including time) left over to pursue other activities not directly related to the provisioning of needs.

3. Being a Christian did not hinder my acceptance in the Asoke community since contemporary Buddhism encourages dialogue between all religions, viewing them as having essentially the same purpose—to teach people to be "good."

4. This center houses a library of Asoke publications, videos, news clippings, and external and internal research about the Asoke group, as well as assorted literature on Buddhism, Thai culture, natural farming, vegetarianism, and other subjects related to the Asoke way of life. The majority of this literature is written in Thai.

5. Theravada Buddhist texts tend to use romanized Pali; however, I have used the more familiar Sanskrit forms of *nirvana, Dharma,* and *karma*, rather than the Pali *nibbana, Dhamma,* and *kamma.*

Chapter 2

Context: Thai Buddhism(s)

The Santi Asoke Buddhist Reform Movement is chiefly concerned with the practice and propagation of Buddhism in a nation that is 95 percent Buddhist. As such, background on Thai Buddhist traditions and responses to modern problems will facilitate a deeper understanding of the Asoke movement's foundational principles and its significance within the wider Thai context. While much acclaimed literature on Buddhism in Thailand[1] focuses on the relationship between Buddhism and the state, this political level of analysis gives only a partial picture. Thus, this chapter aims to give a fuller sense of the diverse beliefs and practices that make up Buddhism in Thailand.

Elementary Buddhism

But first, a brief overview of elementary Buddhist tenets may be helpful to the less familiar reader. There are many schools of Buddhist thought and innumerable forms of practice, yet these variations maintain certain common principles. Buddhism is non-theistic; that is, the Buddha is an exemplar and teacher, not a god. A Buddhist vows to take refuge in the Three Jewels: Buddha, Dharma (meaning the Buddha's teachings, duty, and the laws of nature), and Sangha (traditionally the hierarchical order of monks, but more loosely understood as the Buddhist community). The Buddha's central doctrine, the Four Noble Truths, teaches that there is suffering (*dukkha*), the cause of suffering is craving or desire (*tanha)*, there is an end to suffering, and the Way to end suffering is the Eightfold Path (also known as the Middle Way). According to the Buddha, the negative craving that causes suffering stems from the delusion that there is a separate, permanent self. In fact, the three basic moral defilements (*kilesa*)—

greed, anger, and delusion—are tied to the self. Buddhism therefore teaches *anatta* (non-self), the release of attachment to ideas of "me" and "mine" (Swearer 1989). When the Buddha spoke of enlightenment, *nirvana*, he was referring to the absolute understanding of these Truths that ends suffering.

Buddhism has been labeled individualistic because—at least for the Theravada school of Buddhism—the individual is solely responsible for his or her own salvation without interference from a supernatural power. To attain salvation, *nirvana*, individuals must practice the Eightfold Path according to their own capabilities and prove the validity of this Path for themselves. The eight aspects of the Path are right view, right effort, right thought, right speech, right action, right livelihood, right mindfulness, and right concentration. These eight components are practiced simultaneously and aim to promote and perfect the three divisions of Buddhist training: morality (*sila*), concentration (*samãdhi*), and wisdom (*paññã*). There are great differences in opinion between and within the various schools of Buddhism as to which of these three aspects is most important as well as what particular practices are most effective for attaining enlightenment.

Monasticism in Thailand

Though monasticism is not emphasized in this book, it requires mention since monks, who are the only ones capable of enlightenment in the Theravada tradition, are central figures in Thai Buddhism. Writings on Thai State Buddhism"tend to represent the Thai monkhood as having close ties to Bangkok, seeking advancement in the institutional hierarchy, and promoting government ideology and objectives in their religious activities. While this is true of some monks in the Thai Sangha, there are also scholarly monks, forest monks who focus on reclusive contemplation, and monks who reside in rural villages. This latter category comprises the majority of monks in Thailand but it has received the least attention in the literature. By nature of their position within a community, village monks are unable to devote themselves to meditative, scholastic, or political pursuits. Instead, they are called to address the needs of their community. Traditionally, village monks in Thailand have been active in lay life as educators, arbitrators in minor disputes, counselors in domestic affairs, practitioners of traditional medicine, architects, fortune-tellers, and astrologists (Mulder 1996:118). While the expansion of government social services has diminished the importance of many such secular functions, contemporary problems have urged monks into new roles of "development monk" and "environmental monk" in service to their communities, as detailed below.

The common political analysis of Thai Buddhism also obscures varied motivations for ordination. Few individuals make a lifelong commitment to religious pursuits. Of those that do, many were sent to the temple as young boys by their impoverished families in order to be fed, clothed, and educated. More commonly, young Thai men may become monks following custom to ordain for one Lenten period[2] as a rite of passage between adolescence and marriage. It is hoped that young men will improve their characters through higher training in Buddhist wisdom, morality, and meditation. It is also custom for eldest sons to ordain for a short time as an act of filial piety, to make merit for their mothers.

Monks are highly revered in Thailand; however, escalating instances of moral defilement and materialism weaken the Sangha's credibility. Stories of "lust-tainted corruption" within the Sangha appear regularly in the national and international press. These cases range from the disregard of basic vows to illegal activity: 1) a raid on one monk's secret love pad where police found women's underwear, pornographic magazines, and flasks of whiskey; 2) the astounding exploits of two monks carousing in karaoke bars, wearing wigs to hide their shaven heads (*Associated Press*, October 27, 2000); and 3) the arrest of the abbot of a large temple near Bangkok who was charged with sexually assaulting young hill tribe girls (*London Times*, June 21, 1998).

Materialism and commercialism in Thai Buddhist temples is also rising. Donations are often mismanaged or squandered on elaborate and ornate temple facilities. Moreover, it is common in even the remotest temples to find air conditioners, refrigerators, TVs, and other modern conveniences that violate monastic vows of poverty. Like sex scandals, money-related scandals are splashed across the media. For instance, at Wat Lat Phrao, a temple in the prosperous eastern suburbs of Bangkok, street vendors seeking funeral rites for a family member were turned away because they could not meet the monk's high fee *(London Times*, June 21, 1998). The most sensational case of monastic materialism is the Dhammakaya temple in Bangkok, which has made news for its "pre-packaged" worship and the arrest of its abbot for possessing hundreds of *rai*[3] of land that rightfully belonged in the temple's name. Aside from punishing those involved in extreme cases, the Thai Sangha's Council of Elders has done little in terms of overall reform.

Lay Buddhism

Anthropologist Niels Mulder observes, "To conventional believers, who constitute the vast majority, Buddhism is a way of life, an identity, and the key to primordial 'Thai-ness'" (1996:129). Since monks are but a small minority of the Thai Buddhist populace, what then of the laity? The central question is "how a lay public rooted in this world can adhere to a religion committed to the renunciation of the world" (Tambiah 1968:41). To resolve this paradox, it is necessary to explore both theoretical and actual options for lay Buddhist practice.

Max Weber's (1958) solution to this paradox is a "religion of the masses" that develops alongside the official doctrine. Following Weber and Robert Redfield (1956), Gananath Obeyesekere explains, "In orthodox doctrine, the prescriptions for the layman are very inadequate so that under pressure of mass

ments of which have no doctrinal justification" (Obeyesekere 1968:26). Thus, Obeyesekere propounds that in doctrinal Buddhism, individuals desiring salvation follow the monastic path, while in practical Buddhism, individuals limit the effects of bad karma[4] by using magic or appealing to the appropriate deities.

Tambiah contends that the "spirit cult" in Thailand is more complicated than this categorization might suggest:

> It is a phenomenon which some writers have called "animism"[5] and which with pseudo-historical conjecture they have identified as pre-Buddhist. Moreover, they have variously treated it both as incompatible with, and as combining with, Buddhism. In actual fact its relationship to Buddhism is not simple but complex, involving opposition, complementarity, linkage, and hierarchy. (1970:263)

Charles Keyes (1983) further argues that Obeyesekere's theory is inaccurate because South and Southeast Asians call upon magic and spirits to solve mundane—not karmic—problems. "Spirit houses" for local spirits are ubiquitous in Thailand, protecting homes and businesses alike. Similarly, every city has a shrine to the local guardian spirit where citizens may give offerings and ask for material wealth and well-being. In addition, festivals may be held to honor these spirits, such as the Pii Ta Khon festival in Loei Province. Amulets of certain saintly forest monks are also quite popular, even among educated urbanites. These amulets are thought be imbued with supernatural power that will make the wearer safe, wealthy, virile, or clever (Tambiah 1984). Lastly, monks are often called upon to perform ritual blessings—to sprinkle holy water, draw symbols over the door of a new house or car, or tie a white string around the wrist—as protection from malevolent spirits that bring sickness or peril.

Despite monks' involvement in the spirit cults, some Thais strive for separation. In fact, the Thai language distinguishes believing in (*cheua*) spirits (*phii*) from believing in or revering (*nap theu*) Buddhism (*sasana phut*), rather than lumping everything together as practical Buddhism. The spirit cults encompass Thai lay practices frowned upon by many reform-minded Buddhists, such as the late Buddhadasa Bhikkhu, a great spiritual leader in Thailand. Than[6] Buddhadasa further criticized the worship of Buddha images now sullied by popular ideas about their supernatural powers (an extension of the spirit cult). In his *Handbook for Mankind*, Buddhadasa cites the Buddha as saying:

> If a man could eliminate suffering by making offerings, paying homage, and praying there would be no one subject to suffering left in the world. . . . But since people are still subject to suffering while in the very act of making obeisances, paying homage, and performing rites, this is clearly not the way to gain liberation. (1956:3)

Thus, for Than Buddhadasa, Buddhism depends on reason and insight.

Returning to the issue of options available to the laity, Charles Keyes (1983) agrees with Obeyesekere that Buddhism's moral code for lay life (*sila*) is

Returning to the issue of options available to the laity, Charles Keyes (1983) agrees with Obeyesekere that Buddhism's moral code for lay life (*sila*) is vague and "humanly impossible to fulfill . . . 'to the letter'" (Obeyesekere 1968:27). However, both Keyes and Tambiah (1968) argue that this is not the only doctrinally derived option available for lay salvation. While nothing can change past karma—not magic nor spirits—an individual may balance the negative effects of past karma by improving future karma through meritorious actions. Karma is not an exclusively Buddhist concept (see note 4); nevertheless, Buddhism holds that the laws of causal dependence governing nature encompass human behavior, such that "good deeds bring good results; bad deeds bring bad results" (Payutto 1995).

Thais conceptualize karma as a relationship between *wibaaggaam*—the consequences of past evil deeds—and *bun*—merit that may be accumulated through good deeds to improve one's lot in this life or the next. As a phenomenon ordinary people experience in their everyday lives, karma may provide a stronger motivation to be "a good Buddhist" via merit-making than the elusory notion of enlightenment. Thus, making merit (*thombun*) is central to most Thais' understanding of practicing Buddhism. A typical ranking of merit-making activities in Thailand might include completely financing the construction of a temple, becoming a monk, having a son become a monk, contributing money to repair a temple, giving food daily to monks, observing every Buddhist Sabbath, and strictly observing the five precepts (Tambiah 1968:69). Most laypeople—except Asoke members—tend to rank morality and meditation low as merit-making activities because they perceive these practices as beyond their capabilities.

One Asoke monk shared with me his unsettling experience with the law of karma:

> I was traveling [to Srisa Asoke] from Bangkok, and when I got to Surin Province, there was an accident. The vehicle had a bad axle and it fell to the middle of the road. I almost didn't escape with my life. Part of my skull caved in, my molars came loose and were bleeding, the eye on this side popped out. I can't see with this eye. I was lucky [he laughs]. So I believed in *wibaaggaam*. When I was a child at home, I used to kill animals. . . . When the cutting [of the chicken's neck] was finished, the chicken was not yet dead. It would wriggle and writhe. We would grab its legs and hit it hard with a pole. Its head would break, the eyes would pop out, red blood would flow from the mouth. We did it a lot because the farmers helped each other harvest rice, so we made food following the custom of *long khaek* [feeding guest workers]. . . . I had the feeling that I had killed so much that *wibaaggaam* would come. But when? I was afraid one day I would meet with an accident, and it would surely be like this. . . . So I felt, it was urgent to make good, to sacrifice, to help others. Because I read a book, and I felt I have made karma, and I must certainly receive karma, karma will surely come. Slow or fast, this life or next, it depends. When I had this accident—Bap! It was the same image as of the chickens we killed. I thought of that. . . . Just like that, I thought, "Oh ho! This is *wibaaggaam*." We might not have a way to know [for certain that it was a result of karma]. But the

> image was the same. And so I felt that I could believe in the subject of karma. The Buddha taught that we have karma in ourselves, we have made karma, and *wibaaggaam* will come. It will come out in form: people who like killing animals, cutting life—they die. . . . They will die not as old people die but die in accidents, or they might not die but be handicapped and have pain and suffering. This is the *wibaaggaam* of people who like to kill animals, to oppress animals. . . . When the form was like this [gesturing to his own misshapen head], I thought of the teachings of the Buddha. It made me believe them.

Than Din Thaam believes that ordaining as a monk a few years before this accident may have saved his life. Thus, the urgency "to make good" to lessen future suffering caused by karma can be a force so powerful that laypeople take the leap into monkhood (or at least into a strictly disciplined group like the Asoke movement).

With the rise of the urban middle class, some Thais take a more worldly approach to Buddhism. One public example is former Bangkok governor Chamlong Srimuang (historically associated with the Asoke movement), who earned the nickname "Mr. Clean" by employing Buddhist principles in his governance. When Chamlong first met his wife, she was a devout Buddhist who adhered to the five precepts. Chamlong decided he would do the same: "I stopped smoking, drinking, and chewing gums and lozenges. We made a vow that we would not seek to be out together seeing movies or indulging in other forms of entertainment which wasted our time. In this way we helped each other and she also did very well in her studies" (McCargo 1997:79). Duncan McCargo, a political scientist who conducted a detailed study of Chamlong, points out that by curtailing activities deemed frivolous by Buddhist standards, the couple attained academic and political success.

The Dhammakaya movement is an extreme case of worldly Buddhism. Every Sunday, 50,000 laypeople are bussed in from all over Bangkok to this mammoth modern temple where they partake in highly orchestrated rituals and practice meditation on the expansive green lawn. This upwardly mobile, urban, middle-class movement sees no contradiction between striving for spiritual growth and accumulating material wealth (Mayer 1996). According to Dhammakaya, meditation helps people become more productive and efficient and thus achieve more successful lives (Taylor 1989, 1990). (In my own view, it is incredible that this group manipulates the Buddhist practice of meditation for the decidedly non-Buddhist aim of material accumulation.)

Standing in stark contrast is the Santi Asoke Buddhist Reform Movement. The Asoke movement opposes the "worldly way" followed by so many Thais, as evidenced by their rural communities stressing strict morality and cooperative, self-sufficient living. This group has been categorized along with the Dhammakaya as an urban reform movement (e.g., Jackson 1989), yet this is inaccurate since the majority of members are peasant farmers and six of the seven Asoke communities are agrarian (Heikkilä-Horn 1996b). The membership is actually quite diverse, with individuals hailing from Chinese, Central Thai, Northern, or Isan families, who grew up in rural areas, provincial towns, or

Bangkok, with educational levels ranging from none to graduate degrees and varied occupational backgrounds including engineers, street vendors, teachers, land developers, and artists (see appendix A). As for their motivations to join, political scientist Duncan McCargo says simply that the Asoke group offers to its members "a sense of belonging; an escape from economic deprivation and social disorientation" (McCargo 1997:77). Asoke communities may indeed provide a more secure livelihood than what many Thais manage on their own as well as a haven from social problems like drugs and divorce. However, the aims of Asoke movement and its members are far more complex, as will be shown in the chapters to follow.

Socially Engaged Buddhism

Another form of Buddhist practice gaining momentum in Thailand (indeed, throughout the world) is known as Socially Engaged Buddhism (SEB). While some Buddhist scholars question the legitimacy of engagement for a world-renouncing religion (Weber 1958; Schmithausen 1997), engaged Buddhists themselves claim that the "principles and even some of the techniques of an engaged Buddhism have been latent in the tradition since the time of its founder" (Eppsteiner 1988:xiii).

At a debate among monks in Sri Lanka during the first century BCE, an issue arose regarding whether or not a monk should concern himself with humanitarian service in addition to his personal salvation. Walpola Rahula (1956) relates a story brought into the discussion about the monk Cullapindatiya Tissa, who did not sympathize with a female devotee when her house burnt down. He simply came the next morning as usual to receive alms (cited in Tambiah 1970:67). Thus, the historical ideal became *gramavasi* (residing in towns and engaging in study and public activities) rather than *vanavasi* (residing in forests and engaging in meditation with no obligations to the laity). In Thailand, the established view is that monks have at least a spiritual obligation to the laity and may have social obligations as well (Somboon 1976).

Buddhadasa Bhikkhu may be regarded as the senior philosopher of engaged Buddhism in Thailand (Swearer 1989; Santikaro 1996). Than Buddhadasa did not perceive the quest for personal enlightenment as one of isolated individuals pursuing their own greatest good. Individuals do not merely live in shared environments; they are part of communities embedded in the natural order of things. Consequently, the good of individual parts is predicated on the good of the whole and vice versa (Swearer 1989). At the very least, conditions of material reality force engagement as demonstrated by Cullapindatiya Tissa's failure to collect alms from a burnt-out house. Alternately, engagement may follow from compassion that arises from true understanding about the interdependence of all things (*paticcasamuppada*). Tambiah summarizes Buddhadasa's intellectual career into a central aim: "What Buddhadasa tries forcefully to refute and deny is the fatalism, the suspension of action because of the unreality of the world, and therefore the apathy attributed to Buddhism by certain stereotype commentors" (Tambiah 1978:130). While Buddhadasa remained a thinker and not a doer, his political importance lies in the actions of individuals inspired by his ideas, such as prominent Thai social critic and activist Sulak Sivaraksa as well as Samana Bodhirak, founder and leader of the Santi Asoke Buddhist Reform Movement.

Mounting problems associated with rapid economic growth have much to do with the growth of SEB in Thailand over the last few decades. During the 1960s, Prime Minister Field Marshall Sarit initiated a program of rapid GNP (gross national product) growth through capital-intensive industrialization. In terms of nation-wide development, laissez-faire policies emphasizing efficiency and aggregate economic growth led to disappointing distribution results. Bangkok boomed, but the benefits of development did not extend to the provinces. When Thailand experienced an economic downturn compounded by the global oil crisis in the late 1970s, the World Bank and the International Monetary Fund (IMF) advised a program of structural adjustment. Geographer Chris Dixon (1996) maintains that while this plan of liberalization and deregulation may have contributed to Thailand's economic boom after 1986, it also exacerbated uneven growth both geographically and socially. Disparities in wealth and well-being exist not only between urban and rural areas, but also between the "haves" (elites) and "have-nots" in each area (Parnwell and Arghiros 1996).

The environmental impact of rapid economic development in Thailand has been devastating (Rigg 1995). Pollution manifests as the choking smog of Bangkok, the stench of overflowing garbage in Chiang Mai, and the contamination of Southern freshwater sources from increased inland shrimp farming. Aside from being polluted, resources are being depleted quickly, not through extraction alone, but through complex development-related processes. For example, deforestation in the North results from legal and illegal logging and encroachment by marginal farmers due to increased immigration and population growth, as well as the expansion of large-scale commercial agriculture (Hirsch 1996; Leungaramsri et al. 1992). The immediate environmental effects of unchecked economic growth have further consequences: deforestation triggers erosion of fertile topsoil and drought, which in turn causes surface and groundwater to dry up. Since the majority of Thais who depend on an agricultural livelihood bear the brunt of these environmental costs, ecological deterioration will cause the social divide to widen further.

Some Thais lament the change in social values that they associate with rapid economic growth. As one retired teacher observes, "The current decline in morality is a side effect of industrialization. We should go back to our old traditions and not depend so heavily on material things" (*Christian Science Monitor*, July 24, 1998). There is growing concern that Thailand's traditional culture is being replaced by a new culture centered on money and materially derived status. Although this change is most evident in Bangkok, many people in the countryside prioritize buying a TV over building materials for a house. Thus, the display of consumer goods and technology has become a symbol of social status throughout Thailand (Mills 1997). Certainly this phenomenon is common throughout the globalized world, yet it can be particularly distressing to Buddhists who view it as contrary to their central ethic of non-attachment.

Two other pressing social problems indirectly connected to economic issues are drug use and prostitution. Thai officials say 2001 was the worst for the use of methamphetamine, a form of speed called "crazy medicine" (*ya ba*). This drug is used by anyone looking for an energy boost from migrant field laborers to middle-class student club hoppers, and it is thought that five percent of the Thai population is addicted (*Christian Science Monitor*, May 29, 2002). Prostitution, though illegal in Thailand, continues to increase as poverty-stricken families sell their daughters into the sex trade and as young women become sex workers to support their families or their modern urban lifestyle. In order to raise Thailand's moral image, Prime Minister Thaksin recently cracked down on Bangkok's red-light district, closing all-night bars at 2:00 a.m. (*The Nation*, August 24, 2001).

Thus, a growing number of Thai Buddhists are motivated to action by their everyday experiences of environmental degradation, economic struggle, and change in social values. As Buddhists have done since the Buddha's time, they adapt their religious interpretations and practices to fit a changing socioeconomic and natural environment.

The work of development monks exemplifies this SEB. During the late 1970s many monks in rural villages realized that after years of living under the government's national economic development plans, villagers were worse off than before. As they searched for alternative development models based on local Buddhist tradition, economic improvement was not their only objective. They also hoped to preserve village culture and to promote communal values as an alternative to what they regarded as growing materialism, moral degradation, and the deterioration of rural institutions (Seri 1988). In 1984, Somboon (1988) conducted a study of seventy-two development monks who offered the following reasons for their activities: 1) Involvement in development activities is consistent with the Sangha's responsibility to serve society. 2) The prosperity of the religion and the Sangha depends on the prosperity of society. 3) Secular development has proceeded too rapidly and people have become excessively materialistic; as a consequence, people neglect religion.

Thai journalist Sanitsuda Ekachai writes about the experiences of one particular development monk:

> Abbot Nan Sutasilo of Samakkhii Temple used to think development meant a road and electricity for his village. He quickly found out how wrong he was. Determined to combat poverty and backwardness, he convinced reluctant villagers to give up their land to build a new road that would link their home to the city. "Development" quickly streamed in. Motorcycles started roaring into the village. TV antennas quickly followed electric poles. . . . Electric rice cookers, jeans, lipstick, shampoo, fragrant soap and other consumer goods adver-

> tised on television established themselves as an integral part of the villagers' lives. . . . And the villagers plunged deeper into debt. (Sanitsuda 1994:202-203)

When the abbot finally understood that the "real enemy" was a person's own cravings (just as the Buddha taught), he changed his approach to build "spiritual immunity" against the onslaught of consumerism.

More recently, some Thai Buddhists have focused specifically on environmental concerns. While there is an ongoing international scholarly debate as to the relationship between Buddhism and ecology, Susan Darlington (1998) contends that most studies denying a connection have not examined the conscious efforts of Buddhists to grapple with environmental problems. One example is Ajaan Pongsak, the abbot of a temple near Chiang Mai, who works with villagers to reforest and irrigate their rapidly desertifying land and runs an environmental education program and nature center for villagers, government officials, and other monks (Brown 1992). In another creative blending of Buddhism and environmentalism, Phrakhru Pitak performs "tree ordination" ceremonies now popular in protecting threatened forests. The ceremony is used symbolically to remind Thais—who will view cutting trees wrapped in saffron robes as religious demerit likened to killing a monk—that nature should be respected as much as humans (Darlington 1998, 2000).

Sadly, many forest monks have become environmentalists out of necessity, as their tradition quickly recedes with the nation's forests (Taylor 1996). While forest monks tend to have an instrumentalist perspective of nature (i.e., the forest is a conduit for Dharma), Than Buddhadasa more deeply identifies Dharma with nature. In fact, the Thai word for nature (*thammachat)* has Dharma (*thamma*) as its root. From Than Buddhadasa's standpoint, the destruction of nature is the destruction of Dharma itself (Santikaro 1996).

The Santi Asoke Buddhist Reform Movement

The Santi Asoke Buddhist Reform Movement is among these socially engaged efforts to make Buddhism more meaningful to the modern world. The Asoke movement emerged in the early 1970s when a young critical monk left the Thai monastic community to establish his own Buddhist group. Samana[7] Bodhirak denounced the Thai Sangha for its moral laxity and its social disconnect, stating: "A religious institution should help the society in solving its problems; otherwise, the existence of the religious institution becomes meaningless, which has happened to the mainstream Buddhist institutions in Thailand" (cited in Heikkilä-Horn 1996a:97). Thus, with a mission to "revive Buddhism in Thailand" (Asoke 1989:9), Samana Bodhirak and a handful of followers embarked on an experimental way of life.

Daen Asoke in Nakhon Pathom Province was the original settlement established for the purpose of practicing Dharma in a supportive community. Out of necessity, Dharma practice intermingled with building—literally from the ground up—the material aspects of this community including water wells, sanitation ditches, and dwellings. This was truly an exercise in hardship, cooperation, and becoming self-dependent. Samana Bodhirak, once a rock star and TV personality who had enjoyed an affluent lifestyle, worked up a sweat alongside his adherents; thus, the unorthodox Asoke monastic practice of *not* shaving eyebrows (to keep sweat from running into the eyes) was born. A few years later when a nearby area of land that could accommodate agriculture and the increasing Asoke population became available, Daen Asoke gave way to Pathom Asoke, now touted as the model Asoke community and school.

Currently, the national Asoke movement encompasses seven thriving communities with altogether 800 residents and several hundred boarding school students. The communities are located in Bangkok, Nakhon Pathom, and Nakhon Sawan in the central region, Nakhon Ratchasima, Srisaket, and Ubon Ratchathani in the Northeast, and Chiang Mai in the North.[8] Bangkok is the only urban center, which functions as a hub for product distribution, houses a printing press, and features a fantastic million-baht temple that serves as a bridge to outsiders (see chapter 5 for more details). The seven communities are loosely linked. While they are all subject to national Asoke operational policies, they are not micromanaged from above and have some freedom in their activities. To stay informed about—or to enact reforms of—these policies, relay ongoing activities, and discuss financial matters, community leaders meet monthly with Samana Bodhirak, his "right-hand" monk, and other esteemed leaders in the national organization. Regarding funding, communities may receive money from the central account (comprising national donations and revenue from national sales of cassette tapes and books, for example) for certain approved projects, from their own community accounts, or from grants from the government or NGOs (non-governmental organizations). On the individual level, members may move freely from one site to another, either in a permanent capacity as they seek a change of environment or to attend Asoke seminars or festivals hosted by different communities.

There are also roughly 7000 non-resident Asoke members, some of whom are considered "inactive," merely receiving cassette tapes of sermons and talks, but the majority of whom participate in local and national festivals and support the movement through lay organizations. Such affiliated organizations include the Dharma Practitioner Association, the Vegetarian Society, and a group that has taken over the work of putting out Asoke publications. In addition, non-resident members who live and work near a community may spend their days off there.

In creating the Asoke movement, Samana Bodhirak acted on Buddhadasa Bhikkhu's concerns for the fallacies of lay Buddhist practice and the escalating materialism in Thai society. The Asoke group diverges from mainstream lay Buddhist practice by rejecting the worship of Buddha images, practicing strict morality (including vegetarianism in accordance with the first precept to abstain from killing), and emphasizing everyday work as meditation. Moreover, Samana Bodhirak and Asoke intellects articulate a biting critique of capitalism—

particularly the prevalence of greed, competition, and exploitation—as the root of Thai society's problems. In their view, modern "social preferences" influenced by the global flow of Western culture and capitalism exacerbate human suffering and the ruin of nature. To counter these forces, the Asoke group proposes meritism or *bun-niyom*, Asoke's unique model development based on Buddhist and Thai values.

Two key elements of meritism, self-dependence and sacrifice, are mutually reinforcing in Asoke communities, where residents sacrifice time and energy for the good of the community, and community-wide self-dependence allows individuals to extend their sacrifice to help "outside" Thai society. While the Asoke movement has had many successes in developing individuals, communities, and (Thai) society, Asoke communities are not "utopias" as some observers are wont to report. The tensions, contradictions, and obstacles existing at the Srisa Asoke Buddhist Center include the public's drain on community resources, conflicting views among community members, the pull of modern "social preferences" for consumer goods, the overzealous pressure to remain single and childless, and the contradiction between individual release of material attachment and community-level material accumulation. These issues and others are discussed in subsequent chapters.

It should also be noted here that Samana Bodhirak and the Asoke movement have received some criticism from outside sources. Many non-Asoke Thais I know expressed their feeling that Asoke's austere way of life, though laudable, is too difficult for the average Thai and simply does not lend itself to urban living. Moreover, a number of monks fault Samana Bodhirak for his lack of knowledge and misinterpretation of the Buddhist scriptures. Bodhirak admits that at first he could not read Pali well but could translate using his own special intuition (accumulated from accomplishments in previous lives) (Asoke 1989); thus, he is further faulted for bragging about spiritual accomplishments (a no-no according to Buddhist law). In another line of criticism, a guesthouse owner in Chiang Mai protested that it would be better if Bodhirak just taught by example how to live instead of getting involved with politics. Similarly, other Thais feel that the Asoke movement's connection to former Bangkok governor Chamlong Srimuang as well as members' previous involvement with the Force of Dharma Party and campaign for Members of Parliament far exceeds the acceptable relationship between religion and politics in Thailand.

It is likely that the establishment perceived the Asoke movement's political activity as a threat. In 1989, Asoke members were charged by the Thai Sangha with impersonating monks, and a decade-long court battle ensued. They were caught on a technicality: Samana Bodhirak had been ordained for only six years before he began ordaining others—four years short of the Sangha's requirement. The Sangha's Council of Elders also ruled that some practices of Asoke monks such as not shaving eyebrows were not Buddhist. The Asoke group had a constitutional right to practice whatever religion they desired, but they could not call it Buddhism. Interestingly, many Asoke members I spoke with felt that the court case was more of a positive occurrence than a negative one since it increased white robes (symbolizing laity) back to their former brown ones (in the tradition of forest monks), and life seemed to be progressing as usual.

Conclusion

This chapter sketched the diverse forms of Thai monastic and lay Buddhist practice to provide a context for the Santi Asoke Buddhist Reform Movement. The Asoke group did not arise "out of thin air" but as a response to a particular configuration of social needs. While institutionalized Buddhism in Thailand has been slow to deal with its own internal troubles as well as problems in contemporary Thai society, alternative forms of engaged Buddhism, including the Asoke movement, have offered viable solutions.

Notes

1. See Smith 1978; Jackson 1989; Somboon 1976; Tambiah 1976 and 1978; Taylor 1996.

2. Buddhist Lent is three months during the rainy season, July through September.

3. One *rai* equals 0.4 acre.

4. Karma results from intentional thought and action. For Buddhists who have no final heavenly afterlife, karma may positively or negatively affect rebirth. Karma and reincarnation are not specifically Buddhist concepts, but were evidently religious beliefs held by indigenous peoples who inhabited what is now India at the time of the Buddha. Karma likely became part of Buddhist beliefs in India around the second or first century BCE as the various schools of Buddhism were developing (James Essen, personal communication).

5. Animism refers to the belief that spirits exist in nature, e.g., in trees, rivers, and mountains, and that humans have spirits that can exist separate from their bodies.

6. Thai monks are addressed by the honorific title, *Than.*

7. *Samana* (Pali) means a recluse or monk and is a title used by some forest monks in Thailand. The Asoke movement uses this title as an alternative to the more common title *Bhikkhu*, meaning specifically a Buddhist monk or a member of the Buddhist Order.

8. According to Heikkilä-Horn (1996b), there is also a community forming in the South, yet I heard no mention of it.

Chapter 3

Setting: Srisa Asoke Buddhist Center

The places people live, whether by choice or circumstance, can offer clues as to who those people are. The Srisa Asoke Buddhist Center is an "intentional community" where people with common principles and a common purpose gather (rather than a typical village into which people are born). As such, this place speaks volumes about its residents. This chapter introduces Srisa Asoke and the people who live there.

Isan

Srisa Asoke is located roughly fifty kilometers from the Cambodian border in Kantaralak District, Srisaket Province, Isan, the northeast region of Thailand (map 3.1). Isan is the poorest and most populous region in the country, and it shares cultural attributes with its neighbors Laos and Cambodia. The Isan language, *lao*, is a dialect of Thai very similar to the language spoken in Laos (though I have been told that people from Laos can understand Isan speakers, but not the other way around). Most Isan people are farmers, combining subsistence agriculture with cash crop cultivation such as sugar cane and cassava. Water buffalo are commonly used to plow as tractors are quite expensive and are more difficult to maintain. Like elsewhere in Thailand, Isan villages are arranged as hamlets with fields often several kilometers away. To get to these fields, farmers may walk or take bicycles, motorcycles, slow but innovative vehicles made of a large exposed engine pulling a long wooden trailer, or, for the lucky few, a pickup truck.

The land is much drier and less fertile in Isan than in other regions, which

Map 3.1 Isan: Thailand's Northeastern Region

has forced Isan farmers into labor migration and debt to survive. Deforestation is part of the reason for drought and eroded soils. Since communist insurgents spilling over from Vietnam and Laos were thought to be hiding under cover of the forests, the government offered people titles to forested land from the 1950s onward if they agreed to clear and cultivate it. New roads and communication systems were also built during this period to connect the capital with provincial towns and previously isolated areas. The clearing continued as more and more land was required to cultivate cash crops for export. Recently, the government initiated the Green Isan program to encourage recovery of natural forests with the hopes of improving climate and soil quality.

Though life is hard in Isan, aspects of Isan culture and village life ease the burden. First there is Buddhism, with the temple as a center for spiritual and material support (as well as the spirit cults for other mundane concerns). *Sanuk* or fun is something all Thais seek both while they're working and when the day is done; Isaners especially like to have fun by singing, dancing, and playing music. Unfortunately, alcohol often goes along with *sanuk*, particularly for men, and this can negatively affect social relationships and livelihood activities. Generosity of spirit or *nam jai* is another Thai personality trait that abounds in Isan. This ethic ensures that villagers help each other, from small acts of hospitality to passersby to collective efforts during harvest season. Though the Srisa Asoke Buddhist Center is not a typical Isan village, it attempts to improve on the best qualities of village life.

The Ethnographer's View

Srisa Asoke Buddhist Center is surrounded by rice fields dotted with coconut palms, banana plants, and shady trees under which farmers may be found resting on low bamboo platforms. When I arrived, hulking grey water buffalo grazed in the post-harvest stubble. Srisa Asoke lies about two kilometers down a red dirt road off the north-south highway between Srisaket's provincial capital and the district town of Kantaralak. The community is not isolated but shares the dusty road with Ban Krachaang and other villages. In the past, people living nearby avoided this unconventional village because they feared it to be communist. After thirty years, these neighbors now refuel their motorcycles at Srisa Asoke's gas station and stop off to buy cheap household items, school supplies, brown rice, seeds, and other necessities at the community Goodwill Store.

Srisa Asoke owns altogether 200 acres of fruit orchards, rice fields, vegetable plots, and crop fields, but the heart of the community—the village, temple, and school—occupies just 3.2 acres. A walk through the grounds shows a well-established operation. At the main entrance up the road from the Goodwill Store, visitors are welcomed by Srisa Asoke's museum (see fig. 3.3 at end of chapter). The museum is a graceful Thai-style building that displays murals and photographs depicting Asoke life, artifacts of ancient Mon culture, goods and handicrafts produced in the community, and an area dedicated to the life history of Pau Than Bodhirak. Upstairs is a shrine housing sacred relics where visitors may pay their respects. Just behind the museum stands the most frequently used building in the community, the Common Hall, where both secular and religious activities take place. Fifteen or twenty *kuti* (monks' sleeping huts of about five by eight feet) are tucked away in the wooded area behind the Common Hall, and a dozen slightly larger huts for *khon wat* ("temple people" who take eight precepts) line an approaching walkway. Surrounding this domain—in the community proper—are tree-lined lanes of wooden houses on stilts; facilities for cultivating mushrooms, weaving cloth, and recycling trash; organic vegetable and herb gardens in every available space; forested areas with quiet paths; and a clinic, a library, an art studio, a cremation site, a rice mill, a smithy, and much more. It is astounding that just thirty years ago, this carefully crafted settlement was a bare cemetery.

There are about eighty regular residents at Srisa Asoke including seven monks as well as 200 boarding school students. Most residents are Isan natives, born and raised there in Srisaket or nearby provinces; however, several have relocated from Bangkok, and a handful have come from faraway places such as Chiang Mai. These residents do not fit the agrarian Isan norm: in a demographic survey of the community, 57 percent of the respondents said they came from a rural area (as opposed to town) but only 19 percent identified themselves as farmers. A roughly equal percent of the population had been teachers, students, or involved with sales (shopkeepers and street vendors) before coming to Srisa Asoke. There were also various other occupational backgrounds including an engineer, a driver, an artist, and a soldier. Overall, the educational level of Srisa Asoke residents is quite high: only three respondents had less than the national required level of education, a third completed what was required at the time (fourth grade or sixth grade), several more had at least some secondary school, and a whopping 43 percent had an associate's degree or higher (including two with master's degrees). Though the demographic survey did not ask the respondent to identify ethnicity, I would classify roughly 60 percent of the residents as ethnic Lao, 20 percent as Central or Northern Thai, and 20 percent as Chinese-Thai. These differences in background are not apparent at first glance due to the Asoke "uniform": their unadorned, traditional rural dress comprising indigo-dyed Thai *mahom* farmer shirts and pants or *phathung* (wrap skirt) over bare feet.

While Srisa Asoke is not a typical Isan village, neither does it fit the stereotype of a Buddhist center. The common image of Buddhist practice is sitting still with eyes closed, monitoring the breath, but this is only one method of meditation. Asoke members practice meditation continuously through their work and social interactions. Lest one picture life at Srisa Asoke as contemplative navel gazing, consider a typical day. Residents are roused by a gong at 3:30 a.m. for chanting and sermons in the Common Hall or, one morning a week, a community meeting. Two hours later, the practitioners part company and set to their community work. At 10:00 a.m., residents and guests return to the Common

Hall for a communal meal. This meal may last until noon because it is the only meal of the day for stricter practitioners as well as a time to relax. Community work then continues throughout the afternoon and early evening with time out for personal business. At night, residents may chat with neighbors, practice sitting meditation, watch a movie, attend committee meetings, or read quietly until "lights out" at 9:00 p.m. None of these activities is mandatory, and work often takes precedence. Add the daily activities of 200 schoolchildren as well as hundreds of visitors each month, and Srisa Asoke is a veritable beehive.

Like other Asoke communities, the organization of Srisa Asoke could be called collective or cooperative. All residents volunteer for jobs that (ideally) match their interests and skills while fulfilling community needs. Though it is reasonable to assume that former farmers would farm, teachers would teach, and so on, this is not always the case. Farmers who take on new jobs become the head of the kitchen, caretaker for the elderly, and community seamstress. Moreover, many people who have never farmed seek agricultural work as the "most natural" profession. Still, most residents take responsibility for multiple tasks, including teaching the boarding school students. All this labor is non-wage, but not uncompensated. In return, residents receive spiritual guidance and support and the four necessities for a comfortable material existence (food, shelter, clothing, and medicine), as well as free education and a positive environment for their children. While a few residents maintain private houses, money, and vehicles, most give up all ownership to the collective and equally share the common resources. It is important to note that this community came together during a time when communists were killed in Thailand—especially in the Northeast—to preserve national security. Hence residents clarify that they are not communist: members are free to come and go, to choose and change their work, and to participate in decision making through democratic vote at weekly community meetings.

Ah (Aunt)[1] Payasin, a forty-three-year-old former teacher who works in Srisa Asoke's Common Hall, library, kitchen, and gardens, explains the community's organization this way:

> We eat using the central kitchen; when we listen to sermons, we use the central hall; and money—we use money from the central fund. Whenever I buy brooms or other things for the temple, I use central money. Whenever we sell things and receive money, we bring the money to the central fund. It is a system of public property that the Buddha taught, to make it central and not have things that belong to any one person. Everyone works and puts in the central part, they don't take it for their own. If it is our own, we will want to get a lot and won't want to give it to other people. But if we keep it in the central fund, we sacrifice—whoever wants it can take it, can use it. But this is for practicing Dharma. Also, it yields our defilements. When we work together, we have conflict—we have views that do not agree—so we must try to adapt our hearts. So we can reduce anger, selfishness, and have tolerance when we are different from others.

Ah Payasin's explanation indicates that the Asoke system of organization serves a larger purpose than affording convenience to members and facilitating community self-sufficiency, namely, Dharma practice.

The Asoke movement has recently created a model to describe ongoing processes of material production and social (re)production in their communities: *Bahn-Wat-Rongrien* or Home-Temple-School (see fig. 3.1). Srisa Asoke leaders explain, "These three components are melted into one entity with Buddhism as the core of faith and guidelines. . . . An ongoing society must depend on religion for rules and regulations, school for learning activities involving students, and home for bases of careers" (Asoke n.p. "Srisa Asoke"). One Srisa Asoke resident offers his impression of this model: "Monk, the symbol of religion, means foundation, direction, frame. House or adult or family means design, creative, project. Kids or school means labor, future, power, potential." Life at Srisa Asoke is clearly delineated in this way, as the major activities are religious practice, subsistence work, and the education of 200 students. Providing formal education is not actually a primary community objective and thus is not of central concern in this book. What is concerning is that the output of time, energy, and resources required to care for Srisa Asoke's steadily growing student population puts enormous strain on community development (see chapter 5).

Figure 3.1 Home-Temple-School[2]

BUDDHISM

PRINCIPLES TO PROCEED WITH LIFE
(yielding, hardworking, daring to be poor, tolerating criticism, escaping accumulation, preferring creative construction, heaven—*nirvana*)

Bahn	*Wat*	*Rongrien*
MERITISM COMMUNITY	BUDDHIST CENTER	MERITISM EDUCATION

Self-Told History

Srisa Asoke has not always been as described above. A bit of its past has already been revealed: The community began thirty years ago on a bare cemetery, and outsiders mistakenly identified its members as communist. But what happened between then and now? In the following paragraphs, residents of Srisa Asoke tell their own history through a document written collaboratively by Srisa Asoke community leaders.[3] This account of how Srisa Asoke began and developed is necessary to give the community dimensionality in time. It is also an opportunity for community members themselves to identify significant moments in their own history.

Before Becoming Srisa Asoke
The starting point was a cemetery. In Buddhist Era 2517 [1974], monks from Santi Asoke had camped out at Ban Krachaang public cemetery where corpses were cremated or buried. . . . People in the neighborhood came to the first group of monks to ask for lucky numbers in order to buy illegal lottery tickets, because they believed that some monks foresaw future events. The monks took the opportunity to teach them Buddha's Dharma, which was the opposite of what these people were looking for. The monks asked them to take five or eight precepts to reduce whatever they habitually did to harm themselves. . . . They also learned to radiate loving-kindness and to stop eating meat. Many of them became confident in themselves and gradually changed their habits.

Environmental Development
In 2519 [1976], more people from Srisaket and nearby provinces came to practice. . . . During this time people got together to plant trees and to build a simple temple and lecture hall. They also erected many *kuti*. They built more restrooms and improved walkways to accommodate walking meditation.

Being Labeled as Deviant
During 2519-2529 [1976-1986], all members of the Srisa Asoke community worked hard on their spiritual development. They took the five precepts seriously and abandoned *abayamook*. They lived strictly on a vegetarian diet. Most adults went to the temple to listen to Dharma and continued to practice at home. . . . They cut their cost of living by . . . reducing to one meal a day, wearing neither lipstick nor makeup, dressing simply like Thai farmers, and wearing no shoes. . . . They did so many things to train their minds to be free from attachments in sensual desires, anger, delusion, worldly life, and egoism. . . . Their practice seemed to go in the opposite direction from the society at large. It was therefore hard for Thai society to understand and accept a new community with its own identity. Some outsiders who were not familiar with Asoke would look at the members of Srisa Asoke as weird. Some neighbors . . . picked on the members and called them names such as crazy, deviant, and so on. These behaviors, in fact, coincide with progressive steps in Dharma.

Village of Buddha Dharma
In 2530 [1987], the number of *Yatithaam* [Relatives in Dharma] interested in practice increased in Srisaket and nearby provinces. . . . Together they founded a community on eight *rai* of land (3.2 acres) and named it "Buddha Dharma Village." . . . There were ten people in the first group of the Buddha Village. Most of them were senior citizens. They built six Thai-style houses on stilts. . . . At the end of Lent in 2530 [1987], the number of houses increased to eighteen and the population soared to forty. . . . Most of the village income came from donations by *Yatithaam*. Food supplies such as canned vegetables and dried food came from Santi Asoke, Bangkok. When there were ten people in the vil-

lage, food was not scarce. Food left over in the monks' bowls [collected during daily alms rounds] and food donated by *Yatithaam* was sufficient. But when the population increased, and those who came did not bring anything, they faced poverty. They had to live on a ration. A banana was cut into four, a kilo of mushroom was spread out to cover two days' worth of meals. No electricity was available. Water had to be fetched from a well.

Natural Agriculture, Pesticide-Free Produce
In 2530 [1987], *Yatithaam* from Bangkok bought twenty-eight *rai* of land (11.2 acres) and gave it to Srisa Asoke. The temple immediately derived a policy of self-dependence. The monks announced that they refused to eat vegetables bought from markets. This was the starting point of farming at Srisa Asoke. The community lay down many plans for growing food. . . . As members of the Buddhist Association vowed not to kill or harm animals, their farming began as naturally pesticide-free agriculture. They grew plants without adding any chemical substance just for consuming within the village, not for sale.

Eradicating Poverty among Buddhists
As a result of Dharma practice, there is no poverty among Buddhists. . . . We, Srisa Asoke, make everything our community eats and uses. Our community must first be self-reliant and then we can extend help to other people. Activities we stressed during this time were farming, planting fruit trees, gardening, growing mushrooms, planting trees, keeping the forest, making organic fertilizer, and so on. . . . We ate together and shared facilities like we were in a family. . . . In only five years we were able to depend on ourselves. People began to look up to us and come to us for advice. Many visitors who followed us were able to pay off their debts. We helped many people to be free from *abayamook* and to find new lives. During this time, more people enthusiastically joined our community and tried to prevent the downfall of society.

Education of the Community, by the Community, for the Community
In 2533 [1990], the number of students of Srisa Asoke Community increased to twenty students. The community allowed thirteen secondary school students to attend Kantaralak Public School. . . . It happened that the conduct of the secondary school students deteriorated. They created problems such as not coming home on time, becoming lazy, not finishing assignments, and wandering around aimlessly. Some retired teachers who were members of the community got together and proposed that the community manage education by itself. . . . The committee created 80 percent of the curriculum and 20 percent came from the Ministry of Education's Out-of-School Education program.

Community Business
In 2535 [1992], some small business organizations were established at Srisa Asoke. A small-scale rice mill was set up to produce only brown rice for consuming in our community. However, the surplus was sold at a low price. Other groups produced necessities such as herbal shampoo and detergents. Mushrooms were grown in the community's mushroom house. The community opened its own convenience store.

> *Community Reorganization*
> In 2540 [1997], the Srisa Asoke community began to get into its complete cycle of "close-to-perfect" self-sufficiency. . . . The community was registered under the Ministry of Internal Affairs as an official village. The head of the village was elected voluntarily. . . . By word of mouth from those who had been to Srisa Asoke, more and more people became interested in our community. We had to construct new buildings and improve space to accommodate visitors. As our work became a demand of the public, we had to take offerings from government and private organizations [see appendix B].
>
> *Current Situation [2543/2000]*
> Currently, there are 315 permanent residents in the community. . . . Visitors and workshop participants are averaged about 1,000 per month. Every member has to work fast because the community has to keep up with its standards of production, and parts of its labor are lost to services of workshops and education of the visitors. Although everybody works hard without compensation, s/he is satisfied with *bun* [merit]. Sacrificing ourselves for society and country is our pride.

I refrain from analysis or commentary here (since that would detract from Srisa Asoke members' own speech), except to say that "a banana cut into four" has become legend in this community as a symbol of how far they have come.

Community Targets

Since Srisa Asoke is an intentional community, it would be helpful to clarify what the community members *intend.* That is, what is the purpose of the community? What are its objectives? According to the self-told history, Srisa Asoke Buddhist Center came into being because the number of people interested in following the "cemetery monks" increased, and they wished to live close to the temple. This occurrence agrees with the official Asoke statement on the purpose of Asoke communities: to allow people to live close to the temple, to provide support for difficult practice, and to be a refuge for people who do not want to follow the worldly path (Asoke 1995:122). However, when I asked residents about their understanding of the community "target," I received a wide range of answers. A few corresponded to the official rhetoric; however, the majority illustrates what happens to formal group discourse when it is filtered through individual interpretations and agendas. These divergent responses may suggest the direction Srisa Asoke is heading now and in the near future.

The first few responses seem closest to the original community objective, to practice Dharma. Yai Sa, a seventy-four-year-old woman who has lived in the community for fourteen years, says simply:

> The target is to have people come and practice together, uphold the precepts, eat vegetarian, work, and sacrifice.

Ah Plekuan, a single mother and *khon wat*, describes a loftier goal:

> To build everyone to be saints. . . . People want to proceed on a path that is higher—higher and higher. This is the highest target of everybody. But emphasizing this way is very hard! [She laughs.]

Ah Jantima, who is relatively new to Asoke, alludes to the idea that there is more to Asoke Buddhism than focusing solely on oneself, yet she asserts that individual spiritual development is primary:

> As much as I understand, this community has the target to develop people. But before we develop other people, we must develop ourselves first. . . . That is the highest target of Asoke. It is a deep subject, a subject that reaches the spirit in how we will develop ourselves, and to what level. Each separate person will take how much? Will they take the five precepts, eight precepts, ten precepts, or will they rise to be a monk, an ordinand with 227 precepts? This depends on the capability of each person.

Two other women emphasize the value of group practice:

> Ah Tangbun: The target here is that everyone comes in order to uphold the precepts and live close to people who uphold the precepts—to be a group, to have good force of work, to have energy. Good people join their energy together and it is great. It is a clear form of Dharma. Doing whatever, being a big group, and getting results.

> Ah Payasin: Joining together a group of people who practice and who come to do activities together as a group so that they can create and bring about results. If we scatter out, the energy we will have to work will be small. When we join together, we use thoughts, use our brains, and work together, take care together; it makes us have a relationship.

The remaining responses extend beyond individual-level development as well as beyond the borders of the community. Mua, an Asoke university student, begins with the official line: "The principal target is practicing Dharma in this community" and then continues:

> Practicing until something arises to support the community. When we can support the community, then we discuss with the outside society, and give them knowledge and invite them to come practice. Try to let them see the value of practicing. Our principal target is to be an example for society and develop ourselves at the same time.

His is the fundamental idea for the Asoke development model, Building Individual-Community-Society, as I perceive it.

Five more community members took a national Asoke slogan, "Asoke for Humanity," as the community target. Their responses range from vague to explicit. The first four are newer residents (from one to four years):

Reun: What Pau Than said: Asoke for humanity. Everything for humanity. Because everyone comes to sacrifice.

Ah Jaenjop: The target is for humanity, to help humans, to help bring them above suffering, to be cheerful and economical.

Mae Pranee: To build the mass of humanity to be good people, to have morality, to be hardworking, frugal, and honest, to sacrifice.

Em: This community has a [saying]: "Asoke for Humanity." That means, this community's principal target is to help other communities that are still lacking knowledge—help them have a profession, including understanding of and yielding issues of sin.

A monk was able to explain in greater detail the significance of the slogan:

Than Din Thaam: They say "Asoke for Humanity," that is, for aiding and supporting the world. When we have food and shelter and we are perfect, the outside society is anxious. Anxious about what? They feel that these days there is no solution. We will take this system [meritism] to be the solution, to unite them. Then if they are unable to follow us, we will help them. Because we feel that we are family *phii nong* together. This is the target of Srisa Asoke Community. We will build the community to be abundant first. When we are abundant—it's not that we just live in this little society. We must live in the nation, with people around us. Therefore, if we live here and something happens, we cannot exist. So we have to help society.

Several other respondents indicated that the community target is to help Thai society, although they differed in specifics. Ah Ratana states:

The target is to help Thai society to be safe, to not fall to being the slave of other countries; to try to help Thai society—help them be free from suffering, help them to be able to do the Three Professions to Save the Nation [see chapter 6].

Ah Ratana was a *mae chii* (devout laywoman) for fifteen years before joining Asoke as a *khon wat*, so religious practices and principles are quite important to her. Yet this more practical and political response may be explained by Ah Ratana's attention to controversial issues in the national news such as the IMF loan to Thailand and GMOs (genetically modified organisms). Ah Ai, an English-speaking Mormon who came to learn natural farming, sees the target this way:

What they're always talking about is they want to restore the nation—to not be like America—to [not be] dominated by other nationalism. Because they say this is a cultural community. . . . So they have three parts of the community—the homes, temple, and school, right? So temple is to make people enlightened,

> and school and home—to restore the nation and keep the culture. If you see these three parts, they have their function. Very clear.

The tone of this response indicates Ah Ai's view of himself as somewhat of an outsider, not only because of religious differences, but also due to his disagreement with the notion that everything American is bad. With his master's degree in physical education, Ah Ai has made many American friends working at Bangkok fitness clubs and the Bangkok International School (see full quote in chapter 6, section 2).

Two last community members have a greater plan in mind. Ah Sompan, the assistant village leader, gave the following response:

> Our important target is to build the community to be a model and expand the good model toward other communities that need to develop quality of life—to be a model that will extend toward the district level, provincial level, national level, and so on. Because if society is to be the most peaceful and coolest of dispositions, it must be a meritism society—it must be a Buddhist society. Our Thailand may believe that we are a Buddhist country, but having looked deeply at the details, it is not so. A genuine Buddhist country must be a country like Asoke people. That being so, Thailand must expand this out, but not expand out in order to have power, merit, power from past good deeds, but for the highest peace of humankind.

Ah Oi, the village leader, also perceives the community target to be serving as an example, but she aims her concern toward the younger generation:

> The community's target is to build the culture of Asoke people, to establish a firm foundation, so the young people now and the young people who come after will have a model that is correct. That is, other villages follow the stream of culture of—education teaches this way, politics teaches this way, so we cannot grasp what kind of country Thailand is for certain. They teach many things. So Asoke people think, we ought to have a culture that gives rise to, that squeezes into and overlaps Thailand, just one community that builds a stream to see the importance of religion being the axis, na ka. This kind of education is to build people to build livelihoods—not to build people to be rulers or masters like the education that exists. This, the target of the community is like this. But it's difficult and slow.

These last few responses are worthy aims, to be sure, but they have strayed far from the original stated purpose of Dharma practice. Some of the above responses indicate a less than clear understanding of community targets, a problem that is taken up in chapter 5. Yet a number of these responses suggest that the original objectives have been accomplished and it is time to move ahead. The last two responses in particular demonstrate an ability to envision a future—a crucial quality for community leaders. Ah Oi and Ah Sompan must be forward thinking, because as the community continues to develop, the leaders must offer guidance to help members choose their direction carefully. Granted, this direction must fall within national Asoke guidelines; however, the Asoke movement recognizes that just as individuals are at different levels of development, so are their communities. Residents of Srisa Asoke thus have the power to shape goals as their community progresses. Chapter 5 looks at the process of hashing out the community direction through community meetings.

"What Is Most Important about This Community?"

To view Srisa Asoke Buddhist Center through residents' eyes, I asked twenty residents to take three Polaroid photographs within the community, of anything or anyone, that represented to them "What Is Most Important about Srisa Asoke Community?" The participants then wrote captions explaining their choices. Below are the captions organized so as to highlight both their commonalities and individuality followed by selected photographs.

"Religion" was identified as most important by over half the research participants. To represent religion Ah Tangbun, who aspires to be a saint, photographed a monk (fig. 3.2), a monk's *kuti*, and the Common Hall where she listens to Dharma. Many more of these twelve respondents felt that monks represent "an example for people to be good," "a way of life that has value and is the axis," the head of the Asoke family, and important people active in community life. Ah Oi selected the monk's *kuti*:

> It is a demonstration of the monk's contentment with little in which he discards his [worldly] life for religion. It also sets a good example of a life that should be learned. I have seen the monk's practice here, and I have gained much knowledge, that in our lives, we can be content with little.

Finally, Than Din Thaam (a monk) extolled Samana Bodhirak and Dharma teachings. This frequency of religious symbols in the responses is expected given that Srisa Asoke is a community founded on Buddhist principles for the purpose of practicing Dharma. It is more curious that "religion" did not receive a unanimous vote from all twenty participants.

Of all the places, ideas, activities, and people I as researcher observed to be important to daily life at Srisa Asoke, the museum came as an utter surprise (fig. 3.3). The museum is on the periphery of Srisa Asoke, not only geographically, but also socially, in terms of the primary activities of religious practice, subsistence work, and schooling. Three of four respondents wrote:

> It is a place to learn about Asoke people's way of life. The creation of the museum has highlighted certain symbols, namely, having Thai-ness and sharing.

> A symbol of being Thai.

> Whenever you are in this place, you feel confidence in the history that different people brought together, creating until it became a model as well as a culture

that demonstrates. . . . It genuinely shows the greatness of meritism culture of each person.

The popularity of this site is better understood when one knows that the respondents were students and former students, and that students are responsible for the upkeep of the museum and often linger there during free time to play or study.

"Vegetable garden" (fig. 3.4) also received four votes. Since Srisa Asoke residents are vegetarian and depend on the food they produce to exist, it is expected that agriculture is of great importance. The captions demonstrate the range of benefits the gardens bring. Ah Oi gave this praise:

> It is cheerful, clean, open, light, and comfortable when walking in the vegetable plots. It must be a vegetable plot without polluting substances because we should receive food that has the smallest amount of chemicals or none at all. It will make life long lasting; there is little sickness. We just walk and admire the vegetable plots and we are content. But if we look after plants ourselves, it will cause us to have even more happiness. Therefore, every house is invited to keep a vegetable plot of your own that can be praised. Other than being beautiful and cheerful, you will also eat food that it safe.

Reun, a single mother from rural Isan, identified the vegetable garden along with fertilizer and microorganisms as most important to her. No doubt, a frugal agricultural livelihood is central to life in Isan:

> I like agriculture because . . . we plant vegetables ourselves, eat them ourselves, and use them ourselves. It is economical—we don't have to buy [food]—as well as safe from polluting substances.
>
> I like organic fertilizer because you can make it yourself and use it in the household to put on the vegetable plants. You don't have to buy it from the market and waste money.
>
> I like microorganisms because . . . you don't have to buy outside substances to accelerate [the growth of] flowers and fruit. That kind makes the soil bad. . . . The best is what you make yourself and use yourself. It's quite *sabai*.

Natural agriculture is important to Srisa Asoke not only because it is economical and safe from chemical pollutants as Reun points out, but also because these practices are in line with the Buddhist ethic of self-dependence.

Another community member who chose the garden is Ah Chuan, a soft-spoken fifty-year-old man from a Chinese merchant family in Bangkok who came to Srisa Asoke recently to learn natural agriculture and practice Dharma. His garden photograph must be considered in the context of his entire response—"three activities to build community":

- Building good people to have morality and knowledge [students in morning lineup, fig. 3.6];

- Meetings for community, temple, and school;
- Creating the four necessary things [food, shelter, clothing, medicine] to use in the community [vegetable garden, fig. 3.4].

Ah Chuan identifies spiritual and material development activities as central to life at Srisa Asoke, as well as the forum for communication and decision making that allows this group of individuals to function and live together.

In addition, the forest that covers the community land is a source of pride for many members who remember planting each tree years ago when the area was a bare cemetery. Than Din Thaam gave the following detailed caption:

> Asoke people try to construct and develop the environment to give rise to abundance and wholeness, in order to bring about thriving soil, sincerity, wooded shade, soft breezes, beautiful views, richness in goodwill, energy to work, joyfulness in Dharma, [a sense of] the profoundness of karma and bad deeds, the five *khandhas* [form, feeling, perception, volitional impulses, and consciousness], doing what is natural. It is perfection, just right, support for all people together—dwelling, food, and Dharma.

Than Din Thaam shares the conviction of many Buddhists, including Buddhadasa Bhikkhu, that nature is conducive to the practice and understanding of Dharma (see chapter 2). He also expresses a common sentiment of native Isan people that the forest is a relief from the harsh sun.

For several individuals, "people" are most important in Srisa Asoke Community. Both Ah Ai and Than Din Thai (a monk) elected to represent the community's organizational model, Village-Temple-School with images of Adult (Ah Ai: house; Than Din Thai: communal meal, fig. 3.5), Monk (fig. 3.2), and Student (Ah Ai: students after swim time, fig. 3.7; Than Din Thai: students in morning lineup, fig. 3.6). Em, a university student, photographed three activities people in the community do together: weekly "morality check" for college students presided over by a monk; monks and community members eating together (fig. 3.5); and weekly community meetings observed and advised by monks. Lastly, Ah Oi took a photograph of "children having fun" (fig. 3.7) and wrote this thoughtful caption:

> Regardless of what country children are from, innocence is the adorable quality that transmits itself to the eye—smiling broadly, playing, having high-spirited fun. As such, children are cheerful flowers that all adults must water, fertilize, and beautify so they will thrive for a long time. Since all adults are the examples that children copy, how will we behave? In this way, children can become good adults. Please don't conduct your life with lack of worldly wisdom like our children must.

Next, "unity" or a sense of being a "group" or "family" is a common value in Thai society often expressed in this community. Ah Jantima chose two related images of collective production and communal sharing of the products:

- People working in the central kitchen
  Living together, working together with willingness, without force.
- People eating in the Common Hall [fig. 3.5]
  Eating a meal together as a big family.[4]

Ah Glanporn, an artist from the capital city of nearby Surin Province, photographed monks instructing students and wrote:

> We live as one family—we are *phii nong* [elder and younger siblings], we are parents. The monks are like fathers who train and instruct their children to have good hearts and thoughts.

Lastly, a student expressed a common Thai aversion to being alone:

> Coming together as a group to do whatever work will make us close, united, and not neglect each other. . . . But if one is alone, working alone, it is not fun. Because "living" means living in the world. I like being together in group line-up [fig. 3.6].

Two other participants gave delightfully abstract responses. Yai Sa has lived in Srisa Asoke for fourteen years because she found "peace" (her house), "properness" (monks, fig. 3.2), and "contentment" (Yai Sa herself). Roj, a university student, selected three inspiring images and wrote the following captions:

> Two girls husking rice the traditional way, titled "Hard Work Doesn't Ever Kill People." This work, that makes humans valuable for society world-wide and is the most genuine . . . what does it mean for oneself? The more one works, the more ability and skillfulness arises. This is the teaching of the sages giving genuine knowledge about the enormous value of a well-known animal . . . the precious animal, human.

> Young man with hoe [fig. 3.9], titled "Ambitious toward Success." Two eyes gaze toward the heavens. One brain thinks and dreams. Two hands, two feet walk toward dreams in reality. Dare to think, dare to do, dare to start, dare to change. Hold fast to ideals.

> Students prostrating before monks, titled "Be Respectful, Humble 'the Self,' Be Grateful." Know small, know large, know society, know community. Know what should be small, know what should be large. Know high, know low, know yourself, know others.

This last concept speaks to the Thai emphasis on social place and the symbiotic, hierarchical relationships (parent/child, elder/younger, boss/employee, monk/layperson) in which the superior person protects and aids the younger person who in turn owes a debt of deference and gratitude (Klausner 2000 [1981]).

A number of other individual responses fell under general categories of sites and activities. In interest of space, only two of the more creative responses are included here. One student from Chiang Mai Province took a picture of the "form-flavor-smell-sound" bathrooms (fig. 3.10) because they were designed and built by a monk he respects. He laughed as he wrote his clever caption, a Dharma practice analogy (releasing defilements) using "bathroom humor." Mootao, a twenty-four-year-old former student who serves as the community accountant, chose the place where teens and young adults go late at night to scare each other with thoughts of ghosts: the cremation site. Mootao considers the deeper significance of this place:

> Evil—actually, it does arise but it is nothing. Different people grasp at different things. They want only to get things in order to respond to desire, although they know that the things they grasp at will end. . . . Following this [Asoke] way brings about the feeling in one's heart that of all the things we build up, we can't take anything with us [after death], except the good and bad [karma].

One last point bears mentioning here. Even though a mere twelve of twenty participants explicitly identified religion as one of the most important aspects of this Dharma community, Buddhist ideas were represented in several other responses including Than Din Thaam's description of the forest, Ah Chuan's choice of activities to build morality, Roj's writing on "Hard Work," and the interpretations of the last two sites depicted above.

Conclusion

Through the ethnographer's view of Srisa Asoke Buddhist Center, the community's history as told by its leaders, a discussion of community aims, and a glimpse of Srisa Asoke through residents' eyes, emerges a multidimensional image of the community that is the setting and substance of this research. In reading other publications on the Asoke movement, one might have an impression of communities united on a few common principles such as religion and self-sufficient agriculture. This is certainly true, yet according to individuals living at Srisa Asoke, their community embodies a great deal more.

Notes

1. Most adults at Srisa Asoke are addressed as *Ah* (Aunt or Uncle) by those younger than they. The exceptions are the sixty-year-old head teacher who is addressed as *Pau* (Father) and his slightly younger wife, addressed as *Mae* (Mother). Elderly people are addressed as *Yai* (Grandmother) or *Dtha* (Grandfather). People who are the same age or younger are simply addressed by their first name.

2. Figure 3.1 was taken from a non-published document given to me by the librarian at Santi Asoke in Bangkok.

3. This thirty-five page document is titled "Srisa Asoke: Buddhist Center of Srisaket." It was translated into English by a native Thai Asoke member living in the United States and edited by a few native English speakers who have passed through, including me. Eventually it will be printed as a booklet and distributed to English-speaking visitors.

4. Ah Jantima also took a photo of a community recycling center (fig. 3.8). One of her jobs is working in the trash facility "separating trash into part that can be taken back to use anew, part that must be recycled, and part that will be discarded in the smallest amount." It is also one of the Three Professions to Save the Nation which she teaches to the elementary children in the afternoon.

Figure 3.2 Monk

Figure 3.3 Museum

Figure 3.4 Vegetable Garden

Figure 3.5 Communal Meal in Common Hall

Figure 3.6 Students in Morning Lineup

Figure 3.7 Children after Swim Time

Figure 3.8 Community Recycling Center

Figure 3.9 Young Man with Hoe "Ambition"

Figure 3.10 "Form-Flavor-Smell-Sound" Bathrooms

Chapter 4

Building the Individual

The next three chapters present ethnographic data about beliefs and practices that form Asoke's trilevel development model: building the individual, community, and (Thai) society. Like other Buddhist approaches to development (i.e., Sulak 1992; Macy 1983), the Asoke movement asserts that development must begin with the individual. Srisa Asoke residents spoke often of "building people" or "developing people" as the purpose of religion and part of their community's objective. After considering what it actually means to build people, this chapter examines four Asoke strategies for individual human development. The methods described here are ideals; while resident Asoke members generally accept these ideals and have reasonable success in living up to them, this chapter reveals periodic instances of tension and transgression.

Building People: Spiritual and Material Development

From a religious perspective, "building people" means spiritual development. In conversations I had with Asoke members comparing Buddhism with Christianity, the sentiment was the same: all religions aim to *srang khon ben khon dii* (build people to be good people), with the particularities of goodness defined in each religion's scriptures. For a Buddhist, this means following the Eightfold Path to develop morality, concentration, and wisdom. The highest ideal is the Noble One, a saint who has attained enlightenment and exhibits the Four Sublime Abodes: *metta* (loving-kindness), *karuna* (compassion), *mudita* (altruistic joy), and *upekkha* (equanimity). Admittedly, this ideal may not be met for many lifetimes. In the present lifetime, an ideal layperson behaves according to nine characteristics outlined by the Buddha:

1) easy to take care (*subhara*)
2) easy to nurture (*suposa*)
3) consuming least materials (*uppisha*)
4) satisfied with what is available (*sundhutti*)
5) polished (*sullekha*)
6) well disciplined (*thuta*)
7) not accumulative (*aparjara*)
8) respectful (*pasatika*)
9) very diligent (*viriyarumbha*). (Asoke n.p. "Srisa Asoke")

The Asoke movement has adopted these qualities and added a few more of their own. Words painted in large florescent pink letters along the crossbeam of the Common Hall remind Srisa Asoke residents of their individual objectives: be cheerful and bright, economize and have a simple life, be polite, be peaceful, have no desire, and, finally, have no attachment. Moreover, the Asoke movement stipulates five conditions for a "meritism community" that pertain to individual ideals: depend on oneself, create and construct, be hardworking and patient, do not take advantage of anyone, and intend to make sacrifices. These qualities are emphasized to varying degrees as described below.

According to Buddhism, building the individual must also involve a material aspect. The Venerable Prayudh Payutto relates the following story from the Buddhist scriptures to illustrate the relationship between spiritual and material development. One day the Buddha sensed that a poor peasant living near the city of Alavi was ready for enlightenment, so he decided to travel there to teach. The whole town gathered to hear the Buddha, but he would not begin without this particular peasant. The peasant finally arrived, exhausted and hungry after chasing a lost cow through the forest. When the Buddha saw the peasant's condition, he asked that food be given to him. Only when the peasant had eaten his fill did the Buddha begin. While listening to the discourse, the peasant entered the first stage of enlightenment. Afterward, the monks wondered why the Buddha had waited until the peasant had been fed to begin his teachings. The Buddha explained that hunger is a great source of suffering, and "when people are overwhelmed and in pain through suffering, they are incapable of understanding religious teaching" (1992:88). Thus, development of basic material needs—specifically food, shelter, clothing, and medicine—serves as the foundation for human spiritual advancement.

While monastics rely on the community for material support, laypeople must be self-dependent. Now that the community of Srisa Asoke is fairly stable and self-sufficient, basic needs are no longer a pressing concern for residents. This chapter therefore emphasizes individual spiritual development, particularly refining the precepts, enacting the Asoke slogan "Consume Little, Work Hard, and Give the Rest to Society," educating 200 boarding school students, and attending special events such as the "Intensive Human Development" training seminar.

Morality: The Precepts

When Samana Bodhirak organized his new Buddhist group in the early 1970s, he was largely motivated by his perception of moral laxity in the monkhood and laity. Morality (*sila*) is therefore a central part of Asoke identity. The principal method of morality training is following the Buddhist precepts. To live in an Asoke community, an individual is bound to uphold the five precepts for laity: 1) abstain from taking or injuring life, 2) abstain from stealing, 3) abstain from sexual misconduct (in this case, meaning adultery), 4) abstain from false and slanderous speech, and 5) abstain from using sense-altering substances. Within the temple domain, *khon wat* interpret the third precept as celibacy and add 6) abstain from body adornments, 7) abstain from taking meals after noon, 8) abstain from observing plays and dancing. Nuns and novices take two more precepts: 9) abstain from handling money, and 10) abstain from sleeping on a high bed. Monks must follow the 227 rules of the *Vinaya* code.

Precepts in Practice

Asoke people are widely known across Thailand for their strict moral practice. The first challenge aspiring followers must face is adapting to a vegan diet (no animal meat or products, such as dairy and eggs). This challenge is both mental and logistical: most Thais—including monks—eat meat or egg with every meal, and fish sauce is the most common flavoring in Thai cooking. In most restaurants, requests for a dish "without animal meat" are met with puzzled looks. Consequently, procuring healthy vegan meals with adequate protein can be troublesome. New members suffer resistance—even ridicule—from family, friends, and co-workers. Ah Peum, a long-time member, recollects, "My own friends rubbed it in. They said, 'Let's bring meat and pass in front of [Ah Peum's] house!'—they led many people too—'We'll cure her by eating it [in front of her].'" Although becoming vegetarian is one of the most difficult Asoke practices, it is viewed as the most vital because involvement in killing animals directly or indirectly is a violation of the number one precept. Residents of Srisa Asoke are so serious about this practice that I *never* overheard confessed desires for the taste of meat nor observed any Asoke members eating meat on the sly in or outside the community.

Once followers move to an Asoke community, obstacles to vegetarianism lessen. However, within this communal environment that stresses moral excellence, demands for personal development increase exponentially. In "outside" society, the five householder precepts allow a reasonably comfortable existence. The average Buddhist layperson may have a house, car, wardrobe, jewelry, and appliances for convenience or entertainment—all within moderation, of course. Yet upon entering the Asoke community, laypeople give up many of these "luxuries." The official line states that regular Asoke members (not *khon wat*) abide by five precepts; in reality, the average Asoke community member also observes the tenth precept by sleeping on a grass mat on the floor[1] as well as the sixth precept by wearing the simple Asoke uniform without makeup, jewelry, or shoes. All members also exceed the combined specifications of the third, fifth, and eighth precepts by refraining from *abayamook* (the six vices: alcohol, drugs including cigarettes, gambling, nighttime entertainment, laziness, and sexual playing). Moreover, many community members endeavor to eat just one meal a day, regardless of whether or not they are on the monastic track. Others cut out snacking between meals and reduce from three to two meals a day.

Morality is not merely an ideal dictated from above, but one shared by individuals throughout the group at every level of practice. Of the Srisa Asoke residents I interviewed, the majority (60 percent) declared morality to be the most important factor in the Asoke way of life. They do not adhere to morality out of custom, but consider the results of their practice. Residents spoke often about the practical advantages of keeping the precepts such as saving time, money, and effort in addition to the grander benefits:

> Ah Tangbun: We are drifting in the middle of the ocean—if we do not have morality to hold on to, we don't have a boat to hold on to, and we cannot escape.

> Ah Sompan: We must be able to uphold the precepts. When we can uphold the precepts, we will have mindfulness. Then we have wisdom to solve different problems. If we don't have morality, we can't go and tell or teach anybody. We have to be able to make ourselves an example.

Ah Tangbun also indicated that the value of adhering to the Buddhist moral code could and should be tested by each individual, and she spoke candidly about the negative consequences of breaking the precepts:

> The thing that is most necessary is that people must uphold the precepts and practice morality to be detailed, clean, and pure. Then everyone will receive her/his own answer. Everyone must prove for his/herself. For example, see all these ants? [We are sitting on a mat on the floor under her house. Ants are crawling all over, on the mat, on us, biting us, and crawling off in a long line off the cement floor and into the darkness.] I see them and I want to crush them. My heart has had bad thoughts already. Because I thought it, I want to crush them. But if we don't do anything, they will bite us. They came because there is vegetable oil. The children sat and ate here. Usually there are no ants. The children did not clean up; they did not want to wash the floor. If they had cleaned, there wouldn't be any. I see this and I think this is the ill effect of breaking the third precept [abstain from sexual misconduct]. Looking further, I see that having a husband and children is a burden and I must work. If I did not have children, the house would be clean, right? Ants would not come to vex us! [She laughs.] If you have children, it's like this. That is, breaking the third precept, it is *wibaaggaam*. Instead of doing something else, I have to be here with my child. This is the ill effect of breaking the precepts.

Despite the emphasis on strict morality, Srisa Asoke residents did not in my perspective seem overwhelmed or anxious. Many people practice at home for years and make week- or month-long "trial runs" living in a community before moving in permanently. Except the ban on meat, drugs, and alcohol about which the Asoke group is inflexible, there is no great pressure to follow every rule to the fullest. For example, Ah Plekuan frequently has "supplemental food" before the main meal at 10:00 a.m.—as do other *khon wat*—even though *khon wat* are supposed to limit themselves to a single meal. Moreover, allowances are made for illness and physical problems. According to my observations, sick people may eat more and sleep during the day to regain strength (otherwise thought to be a sign of laziness), and people with injured feet may wear shoes until they heal.

Pressure to Be Moral

In general, Asoke members are quite tolerant of each other's failings. At various times, residents commented that other people's actions have nothing to do with them, that everyone is on a different developmental level, and that criticizing others is one kind of defilement. Nevertheless, there is occasional criticism as is natural when humans interact so intimately. Once to my knowledge, Ah Jantima cried after someone criticized her for "snacking all day long." Another day, Ah Jantima informed me that my tailored blouse showed too much of my form and would arouse sexual desire (*gaam*) in others, causing them to break the third precept. She suggested I wear a looser shirt. She could tell me this, she said, because we are friends. I might understand why Ah Jantima reacted to criticism with tears, because I too felt like I disappointed people I respect. Ah Warn has also encountered public censure about her weakness for coffee and sweets, so she consumes them away from scrutiny in her kitchen behind the house. Such instances of peer pressure are negligible; still, there is one issue about which some community members have become overzealous.

The contentious issue is marriage and family, particularly relating to students. Ah Oi, the forty-four-year-old, unmarried village leader, relates "the problem":

> Other precepts, for the young people, there are many [problems]. The third precept—they will love, will like each other secretly, to hide and watch. They're trying to live up to—we want them to be single. But it's natural, na. We ask them to understand. So we must wait, and one day they will likely understand if they get results and do not marry and become old, and they work a great deal for society.

The ideal is to remain single so one can give everything to society without the burden of family. Yet for those who keep only five precepts—all students and regular community members—the third precept means "no adultery" and not "celibacy" (as it does for *khon wat*, novices, nuns, and monks). In general Buddhist terms, laypeople should be allowed to marry and have children. In fact, the five precepts were meant for householders with families. Nevertheless, some community members like Ah Ai suspect that the students are feeling too much pressure to live up to this local ideal:

> Like now, the college-level person, after they finish grade twelve sometimes they love somebody and want to marry or something. But they cannot, because if they do it, it seems like they're down. It seems like they stop their walking toward enlightenment because they marry. So I think, why do they think married people cannot go to enlightenment? Buddha was married! . . . But now it's like they must be embarrassed to have a girlfriend or boyfriend—even some wife who gets pregnant with her legal husband is embarrassed! . . . Even Phra Bodhirak doesn't want . . . the embarrassment to happen. He understands. Phra Bodhirak is good. But other people in the [Srisa Asoke] family set up this goal. Because it's easy for some member to have a baby born in the community after they become a member at Ratchathani Asoke and some other places. So that means we can accept it. But why we not honor [family] a little bit more? And make them get out of this concern and worry.

Ah Ai's bias is that the Mormon church strongly emphasizes family. Regardless, Ah Ai is a teacher who truly cares for the students and listens closely to their concerns. How this pressure may negatively affect the community is considered in chapter 5.

"Morality Check"

The formal Asoke method of evaluating progress in morality development is quite relaxed. Every Sunday night at 7:00 p.m., Srisa Asoke residents gather into three groups of students, young people (eighteen to twenty-nine years old), and adults (over thirty years old) for "morality check." A monk leads each group confession by explaining the precepts one by one and inviting those who have violated each precept to raise their hands and to describe, if they wish, what they did. The monk then offers guidance to the erring practitioner. Occasionally, members are not sure whether a certain act violates a precept, so this is their opportunity to ask the "authority." These evenings are not solemn but matter-of-fact and punctuated with laughter. Thus, this group confession is more for the purpose of self-reflection and learning from each other's mistakes than social sanction.

In a typical adult session at the Common Hall, twenty-nine people were present but only five people raised their hands to a violation. An old woman's admission that she killed a mosquito is met with kind head nods. Another elderly woman uncertain if something she said would be considered lying is reassured when the monk tells her she had good rather than slanderous intent. Ah Plekuan's joking self-deprecation about forgetting to ask before she borrows things elicits lighthearted teasing. The other two individuals who raised hands did not volunteer information about their violations. When the monk begins to talk about the sixth precept, my next-door neighbor Ah Glanporn speaks up. "It's after 8:00 p.m. It would be better to go to bed." Another woman agrees that the old people need to sleep. The monk accepts this request, so we *graap* (prostrate ourselves) to the monk in respect and part company for the night.

I also observed fifteen young people during morality check at the community's natural-medicine factory. This evening there are not enough monks available, so one young man leads the evaluation. To begin, they *graap* toward the picture of Samana Bodhirak on the wall that would "oversee" their morality check in absence of a live monk. Left on their own, the young people proceed quickly through the precepts. The leader asks, "Who violated the first precept? The normal things like killing mosquitoes?" Everyone raises a hand. "More serious things?" Everyone is still. A few people acknowledge "normal" violations of the second and fourth precepts such as telling someone you are busy when you are not or borrowing things without asking. No one responds to the third and fifth precept. On the sixth precept, two female university students reluctantly raise their hands when the session leader reaches "talcum powder" in the list of "bodily adornments." These women argue that using powder is not in violation of the sixth precept because it is necessary for comfort in this hot, sticky climate. The leader calmly replies that talcum powder is a luxury and a waste of money. He suggests to his peers that if they gradually stop using powder, they will discover that they no longer need it. At this point, the group decides to stop since none of them keeps more than five precepts. When Ah Wichai looks in on the young people and finds them finished so soon, he sits down and gives them a Dharma lesson.

The students' morality check runs much the same way, except for one evening when a student is punished for violating a precept (see below).

"Consume Little, Work Hard, and Give the Rest to Society"

The second strategy for individual development is living by the Asoke slogan "Consume Little, Work Hard, and Give the Rest to Society" in order to practice non-attachment and concentration. This slogan is not empty rhetoric but is enacted daily by Srisa Asoke residents. The ideas embodied in the slogan are expressed by Ah Kaenfa, the administrative leader of Srisa Asoke:

> We have a principal philosophy that we here must eat little, use little, and work much. The leftovers support society. This is sacrificing to society—the part that is left over. We do not accumulate. Accumulation is sin. Therefore, we stipulate that we will come to be poor people in the view of people in the other world. The other world is the system of capitalism, which must have much money, much property. . . . We will be people who do not have property. But we will be people who are hardworking and industrious, who have knowledge, effi-

> ciency, capability. We will have great diligence but we will not accumulate—we will spread it out to other people. . . . Everything we have here, we have in order to help other people. . . . We don't believe it's ours. We come to live together, not hoping to find the material way. That is, we come to help each other to reduce desires that cover the hearts of humans. The less desire you have, the more hardworking you are. . . . But the things that arise from our needs fall to humanity. We don't organize this to be ours. We are not possessive.

This section looks separately at each of the slogan's three components to determine how these practices build the individual.

Consume Little

The Buddha was born Sidartha Gotama, a prince who enjoyed all the trappings of his royal position. On a walk outside the palace one day, Sidartha encountered an old man, a sick man, a dead man, and a holy man. These four meetings profoundly affected the young prince. He took them as signs that life is impermanent—that he himself would die someday—and that being the case, all his riches were meaningless. Sidartha renounced his worldly life including his wife and child and set out to find out the truth about suffering and happiness. At first, he followed the ways of holy men he met in the forest, but he soon found their severe self-deprivation to be another form of suffering. The Buddha thus charted his own path to end suffering, the Eightfold Path, and called it the Middle Way of neither extreme luxury nor extreme asceticism.

Asoke members value *mak noi*, "to be content with little," but caution, "Use enough; don't use little to the level that one is lacking—not a shortage" (Ah Oi) because "the Buddha taught to support life by a proper amount, not to be too needy and not too luxurious, but just right to be able to have happiness" (Ah Jaenjop). How much is enough must be found by each individual. For example, a single meal in a day is simply not enough for some people like Ah Chuan, a slight fifty-two-year old man. On the third or fourth day of eating only one meal, Ah Chuan feels quite weak and lacks energy for agricultural work. Though he would like to meet the Asoke ideal, the work is more important to him, so he eats more to support his labor.

A second idea members stress in combination with *mak noi* is *sandood*, "to be satisfied with what one has." The Buddha's second Noble Truth states that desire—in this case, wanting more than one already possesses—is the cause of suffering. Alternately, "Being content with what one has is important because if [what you have is] enough, you are richer, suddenly richer" (Ah Wichai). Perhaps this is why half the Buddha's characteristics for an ideal layperson relate to minimizing consumption. Whether or not people actually *feel* satisfied is more difficult to ascertain than actual consumption practices. At least a few people expressed their desire for more, either in conversations with me or through their actions: my twenty-three-year-old housemate Raud would like to make a million baht in her lifetime, own a 4 X 4 truck, and fly in an airplane; Ah Jantima hopes to have her own house in the community; and Ah Glanporn likes to buy sweet, juicy Chiang Mai oranges from the market in town. The fact that others besides Ah Glanporn also seek outside market goods creates problems for community self-sufficiency (see chapter 5).

In the Asoke movement, reducing consumption relates directly to an individual's morality. As stated previously, Asoke members uphold precepts by not consuming meat (first precept); using alcohol and drugs including cigarettes, gambling, or seeking nighttime entertainment (*abayamook*; third, fifth, and eighth precepts); or using cosmetics, perfume, jewelry, the latest clothing fashions (sixth precept), and furniture (tenth precept). Furthermore, reducing consumption targets the root defilement greed and its external manifestation, luxury:

> Ah Payasin: It makes us be thrifty people, using only things that are necessary, not luxuries. And then it makes us not greedy, to want to get other peoples' things, to bring many things to ourselves. It empties greed, na ka. It allows us to sacrifice—we have much, so we give it away to people who are poor or who need it.
>
> Em: Before I had to have clothes to sleep in, clothes for going out, athletic clothes; I had to wear shoes that were for sports or playing; I had socks, hats, jeans and many other pants, na ha. But when I turned to having few clothes, a very few, I knew that we can decrease luxury. It is not necessary to wear all those kinds of clothing. Just wear this kind of clothing [pointing to his own faded but neat peach cotton Thai-style shirt and black farmer pants]. We can exist.

Perhaps equally significant for the average Thai with financial troubles, reducing consumption decreases suffering in economic matters. Mae Pranee tells the story of how following Asoke advice helped her family out of debt:

> Most of us go astray, na, by using more than the income we receive. It causes suffering—being in debt. The Buddha said being in debt is the suffering of the world. Being in debt is the most suffering. If we use little—have little, use little—use what is enough for ourselves—it will give rise to happiness. . . . At that time [when we first started to learn about Asoke], the children were many and the monthly salary was small. We had much debt. We built a new house. We were in debt to the bank. The money was not enough. So we came to consult the monks. The monks said, "You have to stop up the leaky hole," meaning, don't spend money on luxuries. "However much clothing you have now, use it all first and then buy [more]. Don't buy cosmetics—they're not necessary. There are four necessary things: shelter, medicine, clothing, and food. These are the four things. A fifth thing, you don't need to be interested. Plug the leaky hole. Then look for additional [money]." We thought, eh? What will we look for? We came back to ask the monks again, and they said, "Sell soy milk!" We started to sell soy milk. The first day we sold seventy baht. We felt very shy because we were teachers. We were government officials. So we felt

> shy. We sold little by little, and our income increased and increased. . . . So we took [the income] and used it for our debt. On the outside, we saved money—in fifteen days we collected 3000 baht. We built up our own position because Asoke taught us.

Although Mae Pranee, Pau Paithun, and their family were finally doing well financially, they abandoned their material life on the outside and moved to Srisa Asoke.

Ah Jaenjop also speaks of the strain to support higher consumption levels:

> If we have little and only use little, we will not be anxious. We don't have to borrow money. . . . We do not increase debt. Then, even if we don't borrow, but we have ten baht and want to get big things and use a lot, we must increase our labor. If we only work during the day, we have to work more at night. It wastes time to get happiness. The body must sleep appropriately and work appropriately. When we don't have rest, the body must use too much energy, and instead of getting happiness we get suffering. Too much luxury will bring about suffering, either through debt or being very tired.

Americans with mountains of debt from credit cards, mortgages, and car payments may well relate to Ah Jaenjop's sentiment. Without these economic worries, Asoke members can focus better on their spiritual development.

The question remains, do Srisa Asoke residents really "consume little"? The benefit to living in individual homes is a certain amount of privacy to consume what one wishes. However, a look inside these homes reveals a spartan existence compared to the average American and even rural Thai household. Most homes have no furniture, except residences of old people who have trouble getting up from the floor.[2] Noticeably absent are electrical appliances of every kind including the most common: televisions, radios, refrigerators, and hot-water pots. Bedrooms are simply furnished with a reading lamp, mat, blanket, pillow, mosquito net, and metal cabinet for storing clothes and books. Bathroom accoutrements are similarly sparse: toilet, faucet on the wall, water bucket and scoop, mirror, a few containers of soap and toothpaste, and possibly a showerhead. Some but not all households have cooking implements. There are a few houses containing many more possessions, such as the homes of Ah Warn, who had no idea what to bring to live up-country (although her husband forbid her to bring the microwave), and Ah Ai, whose family likes to play instruments and watch videos. Both individuals are middle-class Bangkokians and neither feels fully integrated into the community.

One example of Srisa Asoke residents *not* consuming little is the amount of food they eat at the main communal meal. As carts of food pass between our two rows, men facing women, we heap our plates with brown rice, beans, nuts, seeds, tofu, colorful vegetables and dark leafy greens, fruit, soy milk, herbal teas, and cookies occasionally donated by outsiders. Rather, I fill one plate while other residents fill two or three. Almost every day, someone would ask in surprise when I finished eating long before everyone else, "You're full already?" I was astounded by how much Srisa Asoke residents could eat in a single sitting. It seems that Asoke members do not actually consume less by eating only one meal as opposed to three; they just consume it all at once. Many women even brought baskets and recycled jars to fill with food for an evening meal at home. Nevertheless, it does not appear that Srisa Asoke residents are eating too much since only one person is overweight and many residents need extra calories to fuel their physical labor.

Work Hard

The Thai word *gnan* is often translated into English as "work," but it can mean any of life's activities: livelihood activities, festivals (such as temple fairs, weddings, and funerals), or simply "things to do." Now that wage-based labor has spread throughout Thailand, the phrase "to do *gnan*" (*tomgnan*) is commonly limited to work that earns money or affords a living. However, as one Srisa Asoke resident indicates, Asoke has not forgotten the original meaning of *gnan*: "From the time we wake up until we go to sleep, it is all work, any kind of work, even work of the heart, that is work just the same, to build our spirit" (Ah Jaenjop). Aspects of work considered here are material needs, meditation, duty, and diligence.

In concrete terms, Srisa Asoke residents must work hard to provide for their material needs. Members collectively produce the things they use regularly: food, clothing, fertilizers, detergents, and medicines. They also build their own homes and devise their own laborsaving machines. To support at least 80 adults and 200 students (in addition to feeding hundreds of visitors a month), residents are busy from before dawn until after dark. Work can take precedence over other activities, including the communal meal. Although Srisa Asoke is not entirely self-sufficient,[3] members endeavor to depend on themselves as one condition for a meritism community. In their written history, Srisa Asoke leaders state, "Because meritism emphasizes self-reliance, the community depends upon activities or work bases that are responsible to the needs of the community." Table 4.1 lists and classifies livelihood activities at Srisa Asoke. The group has taken a fundamentally Buddhist concept—to depend on oneself rather than on any external force for spiritual salvation—and extended it to the worldly realm.

For the Asoke movement, work also serves as the primary method of *samãdhi*—achieving concentration through meditation. This approach shows the influence of Buddhadasa Bhikkhu, who was in turn influenced by Zen Buddhists. Than Buddhadasa explains the concept simply: "Dhamma sweeps the heart while the broom sweeps the ground."[4] Through daily activities, each individual strives to develop general awareness, a calm mind, concentration on tasks and interactions, and control of feelings such as anger, jealousy, aversion, and pleasure. Below, several Srisa Asoke residents describe how they practice *samãdhi* through work and why they believe it is the proper method:

Table 4.1. Examples of Work Bases

Activities	Work Base	Income
Preparing food for members	Kitchen	no
Agriculture	Farm, Orchard	no
Construction	Services	no
Making herbal medicine	House of Good Medicine	yes
Scientific testing for lives	Services	no
Sewing clothes	Sewing Shop	yes
Making rice chips, mushroom grit	Food Transformation	yes
Making soybean paste and soy sauce	Food Transformation	yes
Making tofu	Tofu House	no
Milling brown rice	Mill	yes
Gasoline	Gasoline Pumps	yes
Growing seedlings	Greenhouse	yes
Maintaining library	Library	no
Mixing organic fertilizer	Clean Fertilizer	yes
Trash management	Trash Science	yes
Growing mushrooms	Mushroom House	yes
Making bamboo wares	Weaving House	yes
Taking care of sick villagers	*Arokaya* (No Illness)	no
Making cleansing agents	Herbal Shampoo	yes
Selling basic goods	Goodwill Store	yes
Selling community produce	Pesticide-Free Store	yes
Artwork, painting	Fine Art	no
Growing vegetables, herbs	Garden of Merit	no
Picking produce	Picking	no
Woodwork	Carpenter's Shop	no
Steno	Central Office	no
Maintenance	Maintenance	no
Taking care of museum	Ancestors	no
Tending herbal garden	Herbal Garden	no
Supplying firewood	Firewood Yard	no
Boxing merchandise	Boxing	no
Taking care of Common Hall	Common Hall	no
Taking care of tools	Equipment Shop	no
Growing bean sprouts	Life Power	no
Auto maintenance	Mechanics Shop	no
Weaving cloth	Weavers Shop	yes
Greeting visitors, guiding tours	Public Relations	no
Keeping accounts	Accounting	no
Making microorganic solution	Microorganic Lab	no
Making cutting tools	Blacksmith	no
Managing accommodations	Welfare Unit	no

Ah Peum: My *samãdhi* is in every level. Working I also have meditation. According to Buddhism, according to Asoke people, we must have concentration the whole time, na ka. . . . Not separating meditation, going to sit and close the eyes, apart. That's not right. Even working, even talking with you, I must have concentration. This is—*samãdhi* is like this.

Ah Siriwarn: Elsewhere they do sitting meditation with closed eyes. [At a temple in Bangkok] they say, "Sit and close your eyes, na? And you'll see the light of Dharma, you'll achieve the Dharma, you'll see. . . . " But we didn't see. I discussed it with my husband: "Did you see?" "No, I didn't see—did you see?" "No, I didn't see." See what? . . . I don't know, but I know I fell asleep! [We laugh]. . . . The word *samãdhi* means to concentrate on whatever, any one thing. Sitting meditation is concentrating on oneself: Concentrate, think to the heart, think to the stomach, or whatever. Here, concentration is the same. When we work, we concentrate on the work, such that we will have full benefit. If we do anything absentmindedly, it is detrimental, it's not good, and it's dangerous. A knife cuts the hand, a machine eats a finger, like this, accidents like this, na. So concentration in working is very important. For here, *samãdhi* means to do work.

Ah Jaenjop: When we work, our heart is with our work. Like [this morning] when I was sitting soaked in water pulling weeds. My heart was not somewhere else. Then we look at our thoughts. It is similar to looking into a glass. We see the glass itself, and then we see the water in the glass. We can see if the water is swirling, and when it stops. We can see if it's different colors—green or red—or if it is clear. If we can develop mindfulness, it brings about knowledge and understanding. The heart sends the body to stay. That is *samãdhi*. While we are working, we have awareness, wisdom, and knowledge of the work we do.

Mua: My *samãdhi* is, I don't sit and close my eyes. I try to have mindfulness [*sati*] in working because if we have mindfulness we will have concentration, right? Sometimes when we are working, we are angry about our work, but if we release our disposition and let the anger follow—that is, following our disposition of anger can ruin our work. To help this work, I will try to control my mood. Sometimes we do things wrong, so I will try to be able to hold back my angry disposition to be still, to be peaceful. Think anew, then find a new way to solve.

Ah Plekuan: *Samãdhi* here means knowing oneself. But it is difficult. Meditation that I've done before was sitting with closed eyes. But when I came here, while we walk, while we talk, while we work with our hands, we must have concentration the whole time. Because when we don't have concentration, we will make a mistake. For example, when we talk, if we don't have concentration, we . . . are not careful about what we say. . . . Then there is the area of seeing, watching videos, watching each thing. They say the six gates [senses]—this is where desire arises. For example, ears hear a sound, a good sound, and you will like it. Right? Then you hear a sound that is not good at all—*Wah!* You don't like it! What do you do? You must have concentration in listening, seeing. When your mouth eats, do you have concentration? When the nose smells something bad—*Wai!* You don't like it! How will you make your heart?

> Therefore, concentration is an important thing, na ka. We must have concentration to prepare ourselves. If we do sitting meditation, it's not stable. We will give in to ourselves. Everything—walking, like that—if we have concentration, we have perfect awareness. When we work, we will have few accidents. This is *samãdhi* here.

Of course, it is difficult to tell if people are actually practicing meditation while they work, as it is largely an internal process. The Asoke members say that the outward signs of good *samãdhi* are harmonious human relations and high-quality products of work. While I cannot fault their work for being shoddy and I heard few serious quarrels, it is not clear whether the latter is due to good *samãdhi* or Thai cultural norms. Thais commonly *krengjai*; that is, they act in consideration of others, are reluctant to impose, and, by implication, avoid conflict. Furthermore, with so much work to support the community and help Thai society, it is easier to imagine people hurrying to the next task than taking time to examine every thought and action. Although monks do roam the community to observe residents while they work, ensuring that they do not make mistakes relating to the precepts, *samãdhi* may be something that occurs on a sporadic rather than continuous basis.

Duty is a third significant aspect of work. Asoke members often spoke of taking responsibility (*rap phit chaup*) not only for their own spiritual development, but also for anything that needed to be done. By upholding their duty to the community, members simultaneously act in accordance with Dharma. Santikaro Bhikkhu, a disciple of Buddhadasa Bhikkhu, describes duty at his master's forest temple: "At Suan Mokkh, any necessary work is considered a duty, and duty is one meaning of Dhamma. Doing duties is practicing Dhamma. . . . Our hearts are defiled by selfishness, so we clean them by unselfish work. The value is in the working, in serving unselfishly."[5] In speaking of duty, Santikaro Bhikkhu emphasizes work that is done in service without ego. This idea reappears in the next section. Some Asoke members also expressed a grander duty to fulfill the human potential, to think and create as only humans can do. Using one's talents and skillful means (*kusala*) fulfills another condition for a meritism community: to create and construct.

Lastly, not just "work" but *hard* work is important as a Buddhist virtue. Diligence is included in the Buddha's nine ideal lay characteristics as well as Asoke's conditions for a meritism community. The opposite of diligence is laziness, and Asoke members' favorite example of this defilement is sleeping late in the morning. Keep in mind that 6:00 a.m. is considered late at Srisa Asoke, as most residents are already working at that hour. Those who are physically able are encouraged to rise at 3:30 a.m. for sermons or community meetings at the Common Hall. Residents gave the following responses to the question, "Why is waking up at 3:30 a.m. important?"

> Ah Ratana: It makes us practice getting up, to be hardworking people. It's good self-training.

Ah Payasin: Waking up early in the morning allows one to have more time to work. It is polishing ourselves so we are not lazy and attached to sleeping. Sleepiness is one kind of defilement, na ka.

Ah Plekuan: It's important because it trains us to wake up and take responsibility. Before, I used to sleep a lot during the day. These days, sometimes in the winter, I don't want to get up. But Pau Than says when you are born a human, one who is precious has a life that is awake, accepts responsibility, is able to see, to listen to whatever—more than those who are still sleeping.

Than Din Thaam: You have lots of time to do work [He laughs]. . . . And you can train yourself to be a hardworking person. . . . When you are diligent, you are able to do much work, and then working increases morality. By sharing and helping, [morality] follows. . . . If we are still selfish, it is sin, taking advantage of other people. Therefore, it is something that makes us increase morality. . . . Diligence has strict morality, right? It doesn't accumulate anything. It gives to others. It has a life like this. It is an example. . . . When they see it, they follow in practice. Then we will have a society with people like this, more and more. We won't waste the world's resources. There will only be creating. It is peaceful and cool, livable, right?

Interestingly, Than Din Thaam expands the idea of diligence to associate working hard with working for others and with creating, not accumulating. He ends by suggesting an image of an ideal society: "What if all people in the world were as hardworking as Asoke people?"

While waking up early is valued highly, it is not a strict requirement like the prohibition of meat and sense-altering substances. Attendance at early morning activities ranged from a handful of old ladies[6] to the entire student population at *tom wat chao* (religious service), and between forty and sixty residents including monks at the more popular weekly community meetings. Elderly and sick people are not expected to attend early-morning activities. Some young and healthy Asoke members such as Ah Kaenfa and Ah Sompan may excuse themselves from getting up every morning because they stay up late some nights working. Others like Em admit that their tendency to sleep in is a weakness they are trying to overcome. I personally found the early-morning loudspeaker ruckus of cuckoo chimes, upbeat music, time announcements, taped sermons, and live chanting and sermons—all beginning at 3:15 a.m.—to be an effective cure for laziness.

Give the Rest to Society

During interviews, several people corrected my question, "How important is it to have little, use little?" as Ah Kaenfa did:

We shouldn't say "have little, use little"—we should say "have much, but use little," na krap. Because [if we] say "have little, use little," sometimes they will

> be mixed up. Because having little, using little means not doing anything at all, and then you have little. If you say, "Have much, but use little so there is left-over to give others," this is better, na krap.

The ethic of consuming little in combination with diligence has the potential to build great wealth for Asoke followers. However, rather than amassing the products of their labor, members keep only what they need and use the surplus "For Humanity" (another Asoke slogan mentioned in chapter 3's section on targets).

Some scholars such as Peter Jackson and Gananath Obeyesekere have drawn parallels between contemporary Buddhist Reform movements and Protestantism during the Industrial Revolution in Europe. Jackson notes:

> Many religious reformists emphasize a this-worldly asceticism and contentment with a frugal lifestyle. However, this asceticism and frugality is not associated with inactivity but is linked with calls to productive and fruitful activity in the world. . . . Such emphases on work and frugality can be regarded as providing a justification for the accumulation of wealth that is required for capitalist investment by middle-class entrepreneurs. (1989:50-51)

With a seemingly superficial understanding of Buddhadasa Bhikkhu and the Asoke movement, Jackson includes them both in this category of Thai urban middle-class reform movements. Jackson rightly identifies frugality and fruitful work as key characteristics; however, both Than Buddhadasa and the Asoke movement are decidedly anti-materialist.[7]

There are at least three Buddhist reasons for giving away surplus. First, "accumulation is a sin" as noted by Ah Kaenfa (quoted above), and according to the Buddha's ideal characteristics for laypeople, monks are not the only ones who should be "non-accumulative." Therefore, to accumulate capital, even for investment purposes, goes against the Buddha's teachings. A second and related reason to give away surplus is that Buddhists aim for non-attachment not only to material things but also to feelings of possessiveness. Sikkhamat Chinda, the nun who runs the Santi Asoke school in Bangkok, relates physical and mental non-attachment to the rather esoteric Buddhist concept of emptiness:

> The ending is a zero, 0, is emptiness, you see, or everything just comes to emptiness—less and less and less to the top. [She is drawing the zero as she speaks]. . . . When we're all gone [dead] we have nothing. So don't misunderstand that this all belongs to me, this mine—no.

Mootao expressed this same idea in relation to the cremation site (chapter 3): essentially, when we die we cannot take along anything we have gathered up in our lifetime, so in a sense it is not really ours. There is no point, then, to grasp things or feelings of ownership. The third reason for giving away surplus is, in the words of Sikkhamat Chinda, "Giving is the heart of Buddhism, giving without taking—but in reality, they just compromise to give more and take less." In sum, the act of giving is training in selflessness or non-self (*anatta*)—a central pillar of Buddhism.

Sacrifice is thus a key element of the Asoke Buddhist way of life. Giving to make merit, the currency of spiritual wealth, is a common practice for Thai Buddhists, but while most Thais give offerings to temples, Asoke Buddhists reverse the flow to benefit the wider community of monastics, ordinary people (Asoke and non-Asoke alike), and the environment they live in. Ah Payasin explains this approach to merit making:

> Merit means sacrifice. We make sacrifice; for example, I make rice for them [community members], or boil beans or plant vegetables or whatever. We have sacrificed if we do not act against our hearts but do it with pleasure in what we do for them. Because people have other duties and they don't have time to do this, we do it for them, and they go do other work. They don't have time to make rice, but they have rice to eat.

The Asoke movement's organizational model, meritism (*bun-niyom*, "to prefer merit"), operates on this notion of sacrificing to make merit.

Meritism stands in opposition to capitalism (*thun-niyom*, "to prefer capital"), which, according to Asoke view, functions by taking advantage of others to accumulate capital. The conditions for a meritism community stipulate *both* intending to make sacrifice and not taking advantage of others. The following representation of capitalism and meritism comes from an interview with Samana Bodhirak, published in an Asoke magazine in 1988 ("15 Minutes with Pau Than" in *Saan Asoke*, January 2531):

> The current of capitalism is strong and swift. Therefore, it is necessary to initiate *bun-niyom* to confirm that the value of humans is found in "sacrificing" not "taking advantage"
>
> *Niyom* translates as to admire, to approve of, or to prefer. Then to *niyom* "*bun*" is to *niyom* things that are meritorious and not *niyom* things that are sinful, exploitative, selfish, gathering in, not sacrificing.
>
> These days, there are only people who take advantage of society as much as possible, and then hoard until they turn into a big capitalist—a great wealthy person, creating a gap between classes of people.
>
> Rich people then pile up, staying only with rich people. The section of people who are very poor, who are the floor level of society—the majority of society—turn out to be the people who are squeezed ever more. They are attracted by capitalism in such a way that it creates a bad situation that cannot be resolved.
>
> Each separate person is a slave to capitalism, having the view that one must be energetic in building this system for one's own sake, creating the way to help oneself . . . so that one receives income and advantage, more than others, without end.

> But capitalism only deceives.
>
> Capitalism......is the doctrine that vies, gathers in, accumulates. Whose ever hand, man or woman, takes until it's rich, able to fully overflow the sky, causes suffering and sin directly for that person and suffering all around society.
>
> Meritism......is the doctrine that sees truth and genuine wisdom: that making sacrifice, creating, being generous, and aiding others is value directly for the person and value all around society, until the heart is truly full.

Samana Bodhirak's commentary puts a fundamental Buddhist idea into modern terms: The worldly path (capitalism) is founded on delusion that happiness can be reached through material accumulation. There can be no end to this accumulation and, thus, no end to *samsãra* (the cycle of rebirth) and the suffering it holds. The way of Dharma (meritism) is founded on the Noble Truth that suffering is the result of this same desire. Following the way of Dharma brings about enlightenment, *nirvana*, liberation from *samsãra,* and the end of suffering.

Srisa Asoke residents first sacrifice to their community to achieve a stable level of subsistence. Thai society or humanity may then benefit directly from Srisa Asoke's material leftovers: surplus produce, detergents, fertilizer, clothing, medicine, and dry goods are sold for a price no more than 15 percent higher than production cost at Srisa Asoke's public Goodwill Store or at the national Noble Market held in neighboring Ubon Ratchathani Province on New Year's Day. Thai society also benefits from knowledge Asoke members pass on through free publications, free elementary and secondary education, and free trainings about Buddhist morality and the Three Professions to Save the Nation (natural agriculture, waste management, and organic-fertilizer production). Asoke members serve Thai society further with cheap vegetarian restaurants, free vegetarian food giveaways in honor of the king's birthday, and, perhaps in the future, with a prime minister who receives no salary. These ways of giving to Thai society are detailed in chapter 6.

Asoke Elementary and Secondary Education

The Asoke group further fosters individual development in children with its own system of elementary and secondary education. What started out as "Sunday school" for members' children has grown into a formal program recognized by Thailand's Ministry of Education as "out-of-school education" (what Americans might call "homeschooling"). Presently, there are just over 200 students in the first through twelfth grades at Srisa Asoke. Classes are held five days a week, Friday through Tuesday. Teachers are residents or volunteers from town who come to Srisa Asoke on their days off.

Motivations for Asoke Education

As the number of school-age children in the community grew, several trained teachers at Srisa Asoke proposed that the community manage education by itself. Srisa Asoke residents were motivated to establish their own system of education by behavior problems (identified in the self-told history, chapter 3) in addition to several other reasons:

> - The existing education system of the Ministry of Education did not meet the needs of the community.
> - The existing education system "stole" children who were the developmental power from a community, especially those who were bright. . . .
> - The system taught children to be skillless, "big head but small hands." (Asoke n.p. "Srisa Asoke")

These rationales were part of the education committee's original proposal.

Before joining Asoke, Ah Kaenfa was an unmarried engineer who spent his income on expensive designer clothes and alcohol. He explains that Srisa Asoke's educational system intends to provide children with an alternative way of life:

> The crucial point is we want the children to have a choice in the way of proceeding with life in society, because children are born and have social preferences that crowd in on them. They've never seen anything outside or above that. Social preferences from childhood are that they must study [books] a lot, na krap, and earn lots of money, look for many different things to be their own wealth. This social preference is taught by the old system of education. So we thought, eh, we ought to organize teaching that allows these children to know some new things, that is, let them know a new way of sustaining life. In place of aiming for studying, working, finding easy work, and making lots of money or getting money without working, we change the social preference to the view that the truth of humans, na, we were born in order to come and work, work and sacrifice for society, giving to friends. In place of working, looking for many things to be one's own, and storing them away in a cabinet, these things are not precious to humans. What is good and beautiful about humans is being able to work, being able to help oneself, not being a burden on society, and being able to help society. This is what [Asoke] education wants to bring about.

Many parents bring (or send) their children to school at Srisa Asoke because they worry about the negative influences their children encounter in Thailand's public schools. They hope the environment at Srisa Asoke will help their children to be "good." Here are two examples:

> Ah Plekuan: We have a daughter and she had to separate [from us] to go to school because we had to stay here to watch the store, right? . . . And we were anxious about whether or not our daughter would arrive at school, na, and what kind of friends she had. Did she have friends that invited her to go outside of school, take "crazy medicine," watch TV, [do] anything indecent? These are

the worries of a mother. But here [at Srisa Asoke], they said they had village, temple, and school together, and we practice Dharma. . . . I like going to the temple. But outside temples . . . only take adults—not children. I thought . . . there must be [a place] with a school for my daughter to attend as well. Then I encountered this place.

Ah Jaenjop: Because I have a son, I thought the outside society, I can't depend on it. I was afraid my son would receive an environment or education in social preferences . . . that were not good to follow. Because I saw many young people who in the evening were not willing to help their parents at home. They would look for a football game when evening came. Instead of helping to fetch water and make rice, they would play football. And when I would see them and tell them [that they should help their parents], they did not believe me. We are adults, but they do not listen. I thought, I don't want my child to be like that.

Curriculum

In response to these needs, the education committee at Srisa Asoke created a model school later copied by other Asoke communities. Twenty percent of the curriculum came from the Ministry of Education (including the ministry's "out-of-school education" exams so that the students' level of schooling would be recognized by the state). The rest of the curriculum was designed by the committee, approved by monks, and voted on in community meetings. Asoke education emphasizes *sindaen*, "outstanding morality," *benngan*, "ability in work," and *chanwichaa*, "mastery in subjects," in descending order of importance.

Morality is the most important aspect of Asoke education, comprising 40 percent of the curriculum. Ah Oi and Ah Payasin expound on why morality is essential:

Ah Oi: I think the target of education is not just to have [students] only be able to read. We emphasize moral principles the most, because we in this era are really lacking in moral principles. If moral principles do not follow the teaching of academic subjects, it is the same as not having a rudder, and there will be no clear aim. Kids of this era don't really have aims that you'd notice.

Ah Payasin: About the academic subjects, they think it is enough to be able to read. But morality, if we were not in the temple but in a house outside, there would be no one to teach us, no one to train us to make us understand. . . . [The students here] will be good people, diligent. . . . They will be responsible for themselves. At whatever time they must research and they must learn, they will be responsible for learning. They will do their homework, reports, like that. They will be able to do good [things]. But if the children here do not have morality, nothing will be good. They will be lazy, not willing, not really working, not really learning. So morality must be the most important.

For training in morality, students practice the five precepts as adult community members do, attend special sermons and classes taught by monks as well as weekly morality checks, and adhere to many rules designed to help students keep the precepts, such as "no meetings between boys and girls after dark."

When students violate a precept, the repercussions depend on the gravity of the offense. They may get a warning or a punishment such as losing bicycle privileges. Repeat offenders may be asked to leave. During my stay at Srisa Asoke, one instance of a fifteen-year-old boy and girl meeting after dark was handled with a public spanking before the regular morality check. All students, the monks, and many community members were present, and Ah Peum delivered the punishment. Before she did, however, she spoke to the group of students, explaining the violation and the adults' concern for the children's safety and well-being. Than Yutt (a monk) added that this violation has to do with ignorance, which must be cured with a spanking. Ah Peum also told the children that only the female offender was there to receive punishment because the boy left the community on his own accord—he was not asked to leave. As the girl and Ah Peum stood before the students, Ah Peum said, "We don't want to spank anyone, but I do it with love, not anger, as a mother must spank her daughter when she does something wrong." Then Ah Peum gave the girl three solid whacks with a strip of bamboo on her behind over her thick cotton skirt. The girl did not wince or cry. After, Ah Peum and the girl kneeled on the ground, put their hands together in a *wai*, and then hugged each other, and it was finished.

The next day, Than Yutt asked if I understood about the spanking and wanted to know what I thought. I said something non-committal about it not being my place as an anthropologist to judge. Still, he insisted. I maintained that it depends, if someone believes an action—spanking or something else—will bring the best result, then s/he should pursue it. I also commented that it did not seem to be a "big issue" because the punishment was given in a loving way. There was no harsh criticism and the students did not appear apprehensive or scared. It did not even seem like the spanking hurt much. In fact, I wondered to myself whether such a punishment would be an effective deterrent.

On another occasion, I witnessed the teaching of morality and sacrifice in a second-grade class. I was chatting with the head teacher Pau Paithun while two of his students worked on a drawing project. When the boy and girl finished their pictures, they rushed up to show Pau Paithun, pushing each other to be first. Pau Paithun made them go back to the table and reapproach him. After the third time, each child was still subtly vying to be first, so Pau Paithun asked, "Who will sacrifice and let the other go first?" He indicated to the boy that he should be the one to sacrifice, and the boy reluctantly agreed. Pau Paithun told me that the boy is "fierce like a dog barking," always hitting his friends and competing. The girl handed Pau Paithun her picture of a man, woman, and child next to a house in a tree. She said the meaning was a family going home to their house in the forest. Pau Paithun gave her twenty out of twenty points. The boy had drawn two people shooting each other and a helicopter dropping bombs. Pau Paithun told the boy that drawing people killing each other was not good and gave him twelve out of twenty points for poor subject matter. In this way, the boy also learned a lesson in the first precept.

Vocation is the second component of Asoke curriculum, making up 35 percent. A common complaint about public education in Thailand is that when students finish school, they are unable to do anything practical. Book learning does not amount to useful skills, and mandatory school attendance prevents children from learning how to operate the family farm or business. Conversely, hands-on work experience prepares Asoke students to support themselves as adults. Following are two of countless praises for this aspect of Asoke education:

> Ah Ratana: I agree with this kind of learning. It can make the children able to work, able to plant vegetables, eat and cook, depend on themselves. I agree that this way will make Thailand progress if we do like this a lot, na ka.

> Mae Pranee: I think it directly establishes the life of humans. Right? We study in order to use the subjects to sustain our own lives. The children here study and then are able to work. Whether it is their own work or working with other people, they will have efficiency and quality. The children here can leave and work by themselves—they can do their own activities. [They can do] everything, na ka. Selling, marketing, agriculture. . . . They can do it themselves because they practice, because they learn by doing. . . . They learn, and then they have to practice until they can [do it]. Then they pass.

Students work at least two hours a day, five days a week at their assigned work bases. Students are free to select any type of work that interests them, such as mushroom cultivation, building construction, or natural-medicine production. Each term, students submit their top three job choices, and the coordinators try to accommodate them based on availability and past performance. Student workers are supervised by adults who give weekly evaluations. If a student receives more than a few negative evaluations (e.g., tardy, lazy, or careless), that student may be placed in a different work base until his/her evaluations improve.

A few residents like Ah Ai worry that the children work too much and do not have time to just be children. However, I have often observed "kids being kids" when they are supposed to be working: a teenage girl sleeping in the shampoo making area, three twelve-year-old girls reading to each other instead of preparing bean sprouts, and a group of little boys jumping repeatedly in a pile of rice straw, neglecting their gardening duties. The problem of insufficient supervision is taken up in the next chapter. The point here is that the vocational aspect of Srisa Asoke's education is not meant to force children to work, but to teach livelihood skills to those who are willing to learn.

The third component, academic subjects required by the Thai government, covers the remaining 25 percent of the curriculum. Asoke students learn English, Thai, math, and science just like every other student in Thailand. However, Asoke educators contrive to apply these subjects to daily life. Science classes take place not in indoor labs but in vegetable gardens where students may examine living plants and animals, observe the weather, and learn about all that pertains to agriculture. English class may also be held in the gardens so students may acquire and practice vocabulary in a meaningful context. Two more comămunity members give their impressions of how Asoke applies academic knowledge:

> Ah Jaenjop: It's not right that reading books is education and working is working. . . . The children are practicing the academic subjects they see here. I think doing this point is very good.

> Ah Peum: I think the education helps humans to be able to think, to be able to solve problems. Because in education all over, there is only learning by reciting aloud. . . . Reciting is memorizing what other people have written. . . . But people don't yet understand. They think learning like that is correct. Studying in the classroom—it's *sabai*—who wouldn't like it? Sitting and reading, sitting and taking notes. But truly doing it, as you [JE] are doing, it's not so easy—to have true thought and ability. I think education should be actually doing.

From what I have observed at a distance and during English classes that I helped teach, the idea of instruction in a "living lab" is a good one, except there seems to be much more difficulty controlling younger students when they are not confined to a desk.

Most Srisa Asoke residents praised Asoke's system of education; however, Ah Siriwarn and her husband Ah Wichai voiced concern about the limited emphasis on academic or outside knowledge. They are worried that their ten-year-old son Chim will fall behind his "outside" friends in English, and they fear that without access to outside knowledge and technology like computers, the children will have less chance for higher education and fewer career choices. Ah Siriwarn points out that people from urban and rural backgrounds may have different livelihood goals:

> They do not want people who have professions other than the Three Professions to Save the Nation, huh? . . . In order to study engineering, you have to have knowledge as the base. To study medicine, you have to have knowledge in those areas—I don't know what they are, but you have to study heavily, right? It's not right to have them only be people who dig the soil or people who carry things, or people who mix fertilizer, or people who separate trash. . . . If they want [professions in other areas], they have to accumulate [knowledge] from now, na ka, so they are not [overburdened] in the future. . . . But if they only want dirt diggers, it does not matter.

Training in Thai Culture

In addition to morality, work, and academics, students at Srisa Asoke also learn how to be proper according to Thai cultural standards. At regular training seminars for outsiders, participants are told, "We are a cultural village—if our culture is not good, the children will see it and take it in." "Good" culture involves being *riap roy* (proper and orderly) by dressing neatly in Thai-style clothing, following mealtime etiquette such as sitting while drinking and not stepping over food, showing respect for others—especially elders—by greeting them with a *wai*, and keeping one's personal area tidy. A fitting example of students learning to be *riap roy* is morning *kao taeow* (lineup), which is done in schools across Thailand each day before classes begin. At Srisa Asoke, students get into straight lines according to height and stand tall and still. Their hair and clothing must be neat. During this time, students sing Thai and Asoke anthems and receive instructions for the day.

While sitting together on a bench watching *kao taeow*, Ah Ai (a teacher and a parent) tells me his major concern about education at Srisa Asoke:

> They train the kids to follow the leader too much. They not follow themselves. They have a lot of timetables set up by the community. Have to wake up, you have to do this, you have to learn at 9:00 a.m., but they have few things they can make decisions by themselves. . . . So now they do what the leader tells them to do. So when they grow up, when they go out, the leader may be IMF, or the leader may be a bad politician, but they have to follow because they learn to follow. There is a man, Mr. Paithun (the head teacher), said before you let them think, let them do by themselves, you have to train them to do good first. But I said, what you have to do is train them to be masters in thinking and doing by themselves.

Ah Ai explains his preference for *self*-discipline over externally imposed discipline with a rhetorical question: "If the discipline comes from this face, this body [he points to himself], what happens when this face and body are gone?" I say I am confused, because I thought Buddhism taught people not to believe blindly but test and prove for themselves. In response, Ah Ai waves his hand at the students in formation and says, "This is not Buddhist; this is Thai."

Raw Phaw Maw: "Intensive Human Development"

Training seminars are the final method of individual development examined in this chapter. This section details a weekend "camping trip" hosted by Srisa Asoke in early January at *Rai* 39, a piece of land owned by Srisa Asoke covered with fruit orchards, vegetable plots, and crop fields. My first inkling that this was no ordinary camping trip came the week before while sorting trash with Ah Jantima and Ah Tangbun. Ah Jantima mentioned that she planned to go with the group to *Rai* 39 and welcomed me to come along. Ah Tangbun argued that this was not a weekend for "fun" but for "practicing hardship." Later, I overheard my neighbors saying that the weekend was supposed to be training for *khon wat*, but the *khon wat* were weak and did not want to go. Ah Glanporn said she might "escape" to her sister's house to avoid people who might try to cajole her into going. Being the curious researcher, these threats of difficulty intrigued me. Clearly, I could not miss this key event.

Friday: Opening Activities

Everyone participating in the "camping trip" rallied at the Common Hall at 2:00 p.m. on Friday. In attendance were about thirty-five laypeople from Srisa Asoke (many of whom lived in town) and ten laypeople from Sima Asoke (Nakhon Ratchasima Province) aged between thirty and fifty years (with the exception of a few energetic seniors). Two shouting, whistle-blowing leaders informed us that we were on the way to "build a new society." We were participating the first annual *Raw Phaw Maw* (*Rangrot Phatana Manutsayachat*), a training seminar for "intensive human development." Our level of enthusiasm was rather low until the leaders, Ah Wichai and Ah Kamen, commanded us to behave like fifteen-year-olds and play a game.

Following instructions, we quickly jumped up, scurried into three lines of men and three lines of women, rearranged ourselves according to height, stretched out arms for even spacing, and dropped to the floor again, laughing and yelling all the while. The leaders then told us we had one minute to decide how long it would take to count ourselves and how we would do it. We settled on 30 seconds, counting from the outside woman and continuing up and down our lines. We began, each barking out the next number as our turn came. There was much confusion, and the group far exceeded our allotted thirty seconds. We tried once more and were just barely successful. The leaders asked us if we could do better, so we voted on a new time limit and tried again, first twenty-five seconds, then twenty-two seconds. . . . At nineteen seconds, the vote was close between those who were satisfied and those who sought improvement. We took stock after each round, and anyone who tripped up was cheerfully admonished to take responsibility and try harder. We counted off one last time, and much to our great surprise, we did manage to improve, counting forty-three people in fifteen seconds. Triumph was visible on every face. There was no debriefing about the purpose of this game; however in my assessment, it was an excellent exercise in cooperation as well as a confidence builder. The activity demonstrated that when one doubts his/her ability, it is possible to try a little harder and succeed.

After this game, we split into five groups, played another icebreaker, and prepared to start our adventure. I was on the "red team" along with three Srisa Asoke residents (a twenty-year-old man named Dthun who we voted as our leader, Ah Tangbun, and Ah Japjai—both women around forty-years-old), a tiny, quiet thirty-year-old woman from nearby Kanthalak nicknamed Lek ("Little"), another man, Ah Somchai, who teaches in Kanthalak, and one woman from Sima Asoke. On our way to *Rai* 39, we had to "scavenge" for our evening meal. Colored flags along the way marked each group's supplies and a clue for the next flag. As we walked and scouted for our red flags, we built our solidarity by naming our group *Palang Ruam* (Cooperative Force) and making up a slogan to chant throughout the weekend: *Choygan khit! Choygan thom! Mii chiiwit chiiwaa!* (Help each other think! Help each other act! Be lively!). The yellow team led by Ah Plekuan made the six-mile hike more bearable with a cheerful call and response as they walked in time:

> Ah Plekuan: Are you hungry? Rest: We're not hungry!
> Ah Plekuan: Are you tired? Rest: We're not tired!

Unfortunately, our team missed two flags and had to backtrack. We were indeed tired and hungry, but when our leader Dthun imitated Ah Plekuan's call to encourage us, we mustered some enthusiasm to respond.

As we neared our campsite, we encountered the "guard" who protected the "city." Each team had to meet with the guard and play a game to learn the "city's" rules. We were the last team to reach this point (not only because we had to go back for missed flags, but also because we let a group with older people go ahead of us). Time was running short, so we skipped the game. Still, the guard made us wear blindfolds for the remainder of the trip to keep the "city's" location a secret. The group leaders retained their power of sight in order to direct us across banked fields, over planks, down steep embankments, and through an irrigation ditch calf high in mud and water. We walked single file at this point and held onto each other so no one would fall and get soaked. When the leaders warned us of leeches, a few women shrieked in horror. I was more concerned about schistosomiasis. I had taken off my shoes and socks to wade through the muck, so I chose to walk barefoot until they dried. As my feet are more tender than those of Asoke members who never wear shoes, I was considerably slower than the rest. Dthun kindly hung back and walked with me as I picked my way painfully through the shorn corn and rice fields.

Finally, we approached the "city gate," but our journey was not yet over. An old lady checked our dinner supplies, and upon finding that we did not have salt (apparently, we missed that flag too), she would not let us through. We would have to bargain with her for passage, so we sat down in the growing darkness to decide what to give her. Dthun exhibited good leadership by trying to elicit everyone's opinion. I suspect this was meant to be an exercise in group problem solving; however, only Ah Japjai (who seems manic) and Ah Somchai took interest in the debate. The rest of us said, "I don't know," either because we were too tired to care or were deferring to others in typical Thai *krengjai* fashion. At last, the old woman took everything we had but the rice and cooking pot in exchange for a packet of salt. A pickup truck then delivered us the rest of the way. Since we (and two other groups) were two hours later than expected, the coordinators had driven back to fetch food from the kitchen; thankfully we did not have to cook dinner as planned. My team members seemed to regain some life after food, water, and rest, whereas I did not. After dinner, I pitched my tent and passed out.

Saturday Morning: Sermon, Work, and Weaknesses

The rest of the weekend's activities seemed like a holiday after Friday's journey. Saturday began as a typical day in Srisa Asoke with a gong at 3:30 a.m., followed by chanting and a sermon. The subject of the sermon was building a new society. This weekend, explained the abbot of Srisa Asoke, we would live like Daen Asoke (the first Asoke community). We should focus on hardship. In jest, he asked how many people missed cars the day before during the trek to camp. There was laughter, head nods, and several hands raised. Than Yutt praised Ah Plekuan's group for singing to encourage each other. "This is Dharma practice," he said. "One should feel *nam jai* (goodwill) to help each other in difficulty." Than Din Thai questioned the group, "Why live in a society like this?" Participants responded variously: to be good people, to build meritism, to develop ourselves, to be like friends, to solve problems, and so on. After the sermon, Ah Plekuan led us in calisthenics to get our blood circulating after three hours of sitting on the cold ground. Some of the exercises were movements representing Buddhist and Asoke virtues like cleanliness, cheerfulness, and diligence.

At 7:00 a.m., we went to work. Each group was assigned a different task: cutting vines off fruit trees, clearing an overgrown area for cultivation, weeding baby green onion and cilantro plants, and constructing a Common Hall. During this time, two members from each group prepared the morning meal (Ah Japjai and Ah Tangbun were our cooks). My group and one other were responsible for clearing the overgrown area. We first used a hoe to chop large plants and long vines and drag them into big piles. Lek said it was a shame to waste so much morning glory. The "weeds" we were removing were the wild version of a green vegetable commonly sold in markets. Lek gathered up a big pile, intending to take it to the cooks. Dthun was also collecting the roots of another "weed" we dug up, remarking that it is delicious in fried rice. I agreed with my co-workers that we should not waste edible plants, and together we carried our soon-to-be lunch to the kitchen.

After two hours of work, we met in the new Common Hall (a fabric roof stretched over wooden posts to provide shade) for an activity in self-reflection. The training coordinators asked everyone to write their weaknesses on a piece of paper. Ah Wichai and Ah Kamen collected these and then redistributed several to each group. We were to pick the most common problems and try to find solutions. Our leaders declared, "Eight heads are better than one!" To overcome the weakness "anger," our group suggested

- Try to think of good things about the person;
- Be patient and the anger will pass; and
- See that the problem is in ourselves and not just the other person.

Ah Warn's group chose "I don't have courage" from their assortment of weaknesses and proposed

- Dare to get hurt;
- Dare to lose face; and
- Give yourself willpower and confidence.

Another group responded to "I don't say what is in my heart and mind" with "We are Dharma practitioners and we must speak straight and true." When every group had had a turn to speak, the monks gave a quick summary and deemed the exercise valuable because opening up in this way allows us see that our friends have the same problems.

Saturday Afternoon: Skits and Rice

After lunch and a bit of free time, everyone reassembled back at the make-shift Common Hall for skits. Although the skits were supposed to be about weaknesses from the morning activity, most skits reenacted events from the day before. Skits about the opening counting activity, the "city guard," and the blindfolded trust walk provided much hilarity. Our skit dealt with "anger": Ah Japjai, the woman from Sima Asoke, and I pretended to be visiting Srisa Asoke for the first time. We saw people "arguing" about how to best prepare a vegetable plot. "This is not what we saw on TV!" we exclaimed. "The community seemed so peaceful!" (Srisa Asoke has been the subject of a few TV news stories.) The Srisa Asoke residents tried to explain that they were not arguing, but we visitors did not believe them. To help us understand, the residents took us to a monk who said, "We encourage people to 'dare to speak' and 'speak straight' in accordance with the second precept. But this is not anger." (Than Din Thai played the monk and improvised these lines.) After we visitors had been enlightened, we left "Srisa Asoke" smiling and nodding to show we were pleased with our experience. After each skit, random audience members offered praise and "experts" (one of whom was Chim, Ah Wichai's ten-year-old son) analyzed the skit and gave a score. Our skit was rated the best!

For the rest of the afternoon, groups took turns threshing and winnowing rice the "traditional way." These days, this process is all done by machine, even at Srisa Asoke. Since there were only two sets of equipment, we rotated one group at a time. When not processing rice, groups worked on projects such as building a seedling nursery or spreading hay around fruit trees and tomato plants. My group continued the morning's work of clearing weeds, breaking up soil, and building long raised beds. The sun blazed on us while we worked. Every head was covered with a hat or head wrap, and every face dripped with sweat. Ah Somchai expressed relief when our turn came to process rice in the shade.

At the Common Hall, we met Ah Sompan who was facilitating this activity. Ah Sompan instructed us to take a partner to share the equipment and then described how to thresh rice by pounding it in a large mortar with a pestle long enough to use while standing. It is necessary to use a fair amount of force, so my arms quickly began to ache. My partner Ah Somchai had greater success due to his greater upper-body strength. When all the husks were cracked, we transferred the rice to disk-shaped winnowing baskets. We shook and bounced the rice in these baskets to separate the lighter husks from the grain. Our team member from Sima Asoke was especially good, and when she saw Ah Somchai and me struggling, she tried to teach us her technique. The last step was to sit on the ground and pick out any remaining husks. We would be eating this rice the next day, so we tried to be thorough (the rough husks are hard to digest). As we worked, Ah Sompan and I chatted about the different ethnic groups in Thailand and America and how they got along. Afterward, Ah Sompan told me in English that this was an activity for "human interaction." Working together as a team, though not actually necessary to the process, indeed involves more human interaction than a solitary operator flicking switches on a threshing machine.

At 5:00 p.m. we were free for an hour to bathe and eat before the evening sermon. After an exhausting day that began at 3:30 a.m., I was the first in bed and sound asleep by 7:00 p.m.

Sunday: Food, Self-Dependence, and Departure

We were roused again on Sunday by a gong at 3:30 a.m. After chanting Pali prayers, the monks spoke briefly about food:

> "Food is number one in the world" [an Asoke slogan]. It is about life; it is about health; it is about community perfection. But we are not yet successful.

The abbot introduced Ajaan (Teacher) Udom, an expert on natural farming who has frequently advised Asoke communities and individuals. Ajaan Udom spoke about the benefits of chemical-free agriculture and explained his basic methods following Fukuoka (1978, 1985), originator of the modern natural-farming movement in Japan. Ajaan Udom then answered endless questions posed by his enthusiastic audience. For example, Ah Jantima asked why it is that a certain woman puts "microorganisms" on her crops every day, but they do not grow. The *aajan* answered that it is too much and the soil is too hot. Microorganisms should only be applied every ten to twenty days. Another woman from Sima Asoke said that her grandmother says it is not good to plant all year round because the soil "needs a break." The aajan responded, "Don't believe it!" He explained that planting legumes is better than planting nothing because they add nitrogen to the soil. Many other individuals asked Ajaan Udom's advice on how to solve their particular problems.

The questions went on for so long that there was no time for exercise. We went right to work clearing weeds and preparing vegetable beds as we had done the day before. At 10:00 a.m. we ate together, cleaned up, and were free again until noon. Sunday afternoon's activity centered on self-dependence: *Dthua Rao*

Ben Thii Pheung. It turned out to be an exciting brainstorming session on community problems and possible solutions. This activity is discussed in chapter 5.

The seminar finished around 3:00 p.m. A few people stayed on at *Rai* 39 to work more in the fields. I opted to catch a ride back to Srisa Asoke along with several others in Ah Wichai's pickup truck. Ah Wichai and I chatted on the way back in a mix of English and Thai. He told me that he came to Srisa Asoke for many reasons, but mainly "to help train the new generation." We discussed the benefits of this particular training, and I commented that having this sort of "practice run" gives people confidence to start new Asoke communities as membership grows. As we parted, I applauded Ah Wichai on his first effort to organize and lead a training seminar. *Rangrot Phatana Manutsayachat*, "Intensive Human Development," had definitely lived up to its name.

Conclusion

In summary, Asoke members have a wide variety of methods to promote individual development. The foremost concern is increasing morality by following the precepts. Second, residents develop through daily activities encompassed in the slogan "Consume Little, Work Hard, and Give the Rest to Society." Asoke members "consume little"—or rather, consume enough to sustain life comfortably without excess—in order to practice morality and to lessen economic distress. While people "work hard" to provide for their material existence, they also practice Dharma through *samādhi*, duty, and diligence. In giving, members train themselves in non-accumulation, non-attachment, and non-self (*anatta*). Third, education at Srisa Asoke develops the younger generation by giving them a strong foundation in morality, vocation, the application of academic subjects, and Thai culture. Lastly, special training seminars such as the "Intensive Human Development" weekend challenge members outside their daily practice. As is to be expected, these methods are not perfect, and not everyone agrees with them. These activities—including both their positive and negative aspects—have significant implications for building community, the subject of chapter 5.

Notes

1. Sleeping on just a grass mat is actually the norm in poorer households. People with a bit more money may sleep on a three-inch mattress on top of the grass mat. Western-style raised "beds" are more expensive and, thus, less common.

2. It is Thai custom to sit on the floor, even to eat. Chairs and tables were introduced around the turn of the last century in an effort to modernize Thailand with Western culture.

3. The community is not entirely self-contained as some goods come from outside the community. For example, tofu is not made on-site but distributed from Sima Asoke in Nakhon Ratchasima Province, a portion of rice comes from outside farmers who are contracted for organic cultivation, and certain items such as pots, water tanks, cooking oil, hoes, pencils and paper, and lightbulbs are purchased from the market in town. Money used to pay for market goods (as well as electricity, phone, and drinking-water bills) passes into the community as income from the Goodwill Store and as donations from non-resident members. The community has also received grants of money and materials from external organizations for various construction and agriculture projects (see appendix C).

4. http://www.suanmokkh.org/archive/skb/garden1b.htm, 2002.

5. http://www.suanmokkh.org/archive/skb/garden1b.htm, 2002.

6. At temples throughout Thailand, "old ladies" is the largest demographic group. They take the responsibility of making merit for their whole family.

7. Moreover, the majority of Asoke members come from rural areas, not urban.

Chapter 5

Building Community

This is a story not just about a community but a community making itself. In describing their "economics for community" model, Herman Daly and John Cobb Jr. state that the term community "suggests people are bound up with one another, sharing, despite differences, a common identity" (1989:170). In the national Asoke community, individuals with diverse backgrounds do indeed share a distinct identity as members of the Asoke group of Dharma practitioners. Regarding "community development" within specific geographical confines, Daly and Cobb explain:

> Community development as applied to village development in general involves taking the village rather than the individual or the nation as the unit of development. One then asks how the village can better meet its needs. The villagers themselves make the decision and thus determine their own fate. The result usually involves increasing their productive capacities. They may increase their water supply by introducing a pump, or their food production by replacing wooden ploughs with metal ones. Whatever the decision, the community is usually made more productive in doing what it wants to do as a community. Its community character and its productive capabilities are strengthened together. (1989:165)

As Daly and Cobb suggest, building community involves not only developing the community's material aspects that support its members but also deciding as a group the particular goals and methods of development as well as creating a sense of unity through shared responsibility for the community.

The first objective in this chapter is to identify the ways in which individual development—especially personal efforts in non-attachment and work—fosters development at the community level. Second, while Srisa Asoke has had a fair amount of success in its development, conflicting views, too few adults, and incomplete self-dependence hinder its progress. This chapter examines these obstacles to community building as well as proposed and attempted solutions.

From Individual to Community

From the start, Srisa Asoke residents have made conscious effort to develop their community. Followers of the first Asoke monks who camped out in the Ban Krachaang cemetery labored to make their existence more comfortable by digging wells, planting trees, and building homes. As the community's population grew, residents combined their creative energies to meet increasing needs for food, places to cook, store, and meet, and a more sophisticated sewage system. Certainly, this community could have been built in the absence of Buddhist principles, but the characteristics of the community would likely be quite different. Srisa Asoke is an intentional community established for the purpose of Dharma practice; thus, individual Dharma practice has shaped the course and quality of community development at Srisa Asoke.

Non-attachment

Non-attachment is a central Buddhist aim that partly concerns the stuff people use, accumulate, and throw away. The Asoke group encourages its members to practice non-attachment by consuming little (the proper amount) and by using publicly owned resources (rather than accumulating personal property). The main objective of limiting personal consumption and accumulation is individual spiritual development; however, non-attachment at the individual level benefits community development in several ways.

First, non-attachment conserves community resources. As mentioned in the last chapter, reducing consumption in accordance with the precepts (e.g., not eating meat, not adorning oneself, and not sleeping on a high bed) saves resources by reducing material needs. Moreover, using resources communally rather than privately furthers conservation. For example, electricity is saved when everyone watches television together in the Common Hall instead of each at home on multiple sets. The water shortage on Children's Day, January 11, 2001, also exhibited how communal use conserves resources. Children's Day is a Thai national holiday celebrated at Srisa Asoke with fun activities for the children, including a special dinner hosted by several homes in the community. The students typically eat a simple dinner together at the central kitchen, so this "home-cooked meal" was a treat. This evening, the adults took great pleasure in "nurturing the children," who traveled from house to house sampling noodles at Mae Pranee's house, papaya salad next door, and sweet squash cakes across the lane. After dinner, I discovered that the water pressure was not strong enough for a shower, so I bathed Thai-style by dousing myself with bowls of cold water.

As I refilled the bathroom water bucket (also used to "flush" the toilet), the water flowing out of the faucet slowed to a trickle and then stopped altogether. By late afternoon the next day, the water still was not running. I asked my housemate Raud what caused the water stoppage. She answered, "Sometimes the power goes out, and sometimes people use too much water and the pump cannot keep up." Last night, she surmised, the many people who made dinner for the children used large quantities of water to cook and clean up. The pump was still struggling to replenish the community's water supply. This situation suggested to me that cooking communally might indeed conserve water.

Although "saving the environment" is not a primary Asoke concern, some members do articulate the larger ramifications of consumption practices:

> Ah Oi: Society now aims for consumerism. Correct? So if each person has only consumerism, and there is no section opposing, no section yielding, the world's resources will all flow away. We must use little.

Asoke's practice of "consuming little" promotes a more environmentally "sustainable" development than other forms of development that have no such ethic to limit resource use. However, I observed at least one instance in which Srisa Asoke residents do not conserve resources as well as they might. Although members say that only eating once a day reduces the amount of cooking fuel used, they still use raw wood for their cooking fires, which burns much faster than charcoal. If Asoke members had the expertise, they could first transform the wood into charcoal and conserve woodfuel.[1]

It should be noted that in the Asoke movement, limiting personal accumulation does not necessarily limit public accumulation. The most startling example of public accumulation is the fantastic million-baht Asoke temple in Bangkok. This four-level, spiral-shaped temple has a thirty-foot artificial waterfall up the center with authentic-looking cement trees as support posts and exquisite black Burmese rock (imported at a high price) scattered around the ground level, fine artwork in a different genre (traditional Thai, abstract, and gold leaf surreal designs) on each ascending level, and a gleaming marble floor on the uppermost level where only monks are allowed to walk. When I first arrived at the Asoke center in Bangkok, I viewed this extravagant use of materials as a contradiction to Asoke rhetoric. I asked one Srisa Asoke resident I met in Bangkok what she thought about using so much money and materials to make this temple. Mootao's response was simple: "Where will all the people sleep? We must have space for all the people who come to Santi Asoke for special festivals." I also asked Sikkhamat Chinda her opinion. She waved her hand in dismissal, stating that she does not use the temple. The temple is not for her or regular Asoke people, but for outsiders—it is a bridge to the outside world. Sikkhamat Chinda explained that in order to make a connection with more people who perhaps do not have as much wisdom as the first wave of Asoke followers, it is necessary to compromise. The Asoke movement therefore builds a beautiful temple as expected by average Thai Buddhists to entice more people to come.

The materiality of Srisa Asoke was equally troublesome at first. Several aspects clashed with my mind's image of minimizing consumption and accumulation: the well-equipped, modern office with air-conditioning, computers, digital camera, fax machine, and cordless telephone, plus three new buildings under construction—a huge kitchen to replace the original modest one, an elegant guest and meeting facility, and a new natural-medicine factory to accommodate growing demand. It was not only the expanding construction that bothered me, but the materials used. Like the temple in Bangkok, the materials used for the guest and meeting facility struck me as excessive: molded, tinted tiles covered cement walls on the lower level and high-quality wood molding and paneling covered the fine wood structure upstairs. An Australian passing through Srisa Asoke commented, "This waste of materials is not Buddhist." At the time, I thought to myself that the use of materials may not be Buddhist, but such attention to an attractive appearance is certainly Thai.

I have since found ways to reconcile the material accumulation at Srisa Asoke. The community's administrative leader, Ah Kaenfa, stressed to me that residents do not think of the things at Srisa Asoke (including the buildings and technology) as theirs; rather, they create and care for these things in order to facilitate the transfer of knowledge to others (see the full quote in chapter 4). Regarding modern technology, Ah Kaenfa clarified that the Asoke movement is not opposed to technology *per se*, only the negative or destructive uses of technology. He gave the example of nuclear energy that may kill people or provide clean energy. Ah Kaenfa insisted that there is no problem with technology as long as it is used for good purposes, and Srisa Asoke uses their technology to communicate with a wider range of people.

Based on these notions, I reasoned that while development within Asoke communities may appear the same as development everywhere else, it is not. The difference is the *intent* of development. Conventional development aims for material accumulation in order to increase comfort and pleasure and facilitate further accumulation. In contrast, Asoke development means to facilitate the spread of Buddhist knowledge and practice, which ultimately results in non-attachment to the material world.

The second way non-attachment supports community development is by saving time and energy. A number of residents told me that having few possessions means that less effort must be expended in order to acquire and care for them. In the last chapter, Ah Jaenjop mentioned that by reducing consumption, the body is not exhausted by laboring overtime to satisfy one's desires. Em, still reflecting on all the clothing he once had, points out that having few possessions decreases the amount of time needed to care for them: "We don't have to waste time having to wash, iron, put away [clothes]. We don't have to suffer because time is lost." A female student also points to the Asoke uniform as a way to save time:

> Regarding clothing, here we wear a suit that is neat and easy. You don't have to adorn yourself so much. Shoes—you don't have to wear them. . . . It's not like

> outside [the community] where you have to make a fuss over dressing. It wastes time unnecessarily.

Time and energy not spent on one's own possessions may be used for adequate rest and leisure; more often the case, this time and energy is applied to other work needed by the community and thus promotes the common good.

Third, non-attachment aids community development by reducing problems with waste disposal. Americans produce such an enormous amount of garbage—150 million tons a year—that it cannot be contained in the United States and must be shipped to other countries that will accept it. Cities in Thailand with trash collection service have similar problems with disposal, though on a smaller scale. A few years ago, Chiang Mai (the largest city in the North) ran out of landfill space. Garbage piled up on the city streets for months, causing an infestation of rats and an unbearable stench. In rural areas where there is no "curbside" trash pickup, people reuse what they can and burn the rest. Burning trash is not a desirable option since smoke from burning plastic and styrofoam pollutes the air, depletes the ozone layer, and is harmful to one's health.

Conversely, Srisa Asoke minimizes its waste by reducing consumption. I learned from Ah Tangbun and Ah Jantima while we sorted trash together that "consuming little" also means reducing waste through the "Four Rs": reuse, repair, recycle, and reject. We took the time to separate trash into piles of like objects because the majority—dry paper, plastic bottles, glass, and metal scraps—could be sold to the recycling center in town. The rest would be dealt with in other ways. Ah Tangbun complained when students threw out notebooks that still had clean paper in them, and she would set these aside to be used again. Both women picked out clothing that needed only washing and minor mending for themselves, their children, or poor neighbors in their old village. On this subject, Ah Jantima says:

> Having little, using little is very important because if we have a lot, it can be a waste, na ka. Like clothing, we shouldn't have more than three sets. Keeping them is difficult. They are hiding places for insects, for mice, . . . or even mold because we don't shake out the clothes that we don't wear everyday. . . . Whatever we have we should use, and if we have a lot, we can split up and give to many people. . . . There's still a lot of waste. When I work collecting trash, I collect [clothing] for people who extremely need it and must use it. I collect what they discard in order to give to people who require it.

Other items that found their way into the garbage such as electrical parts, twine, cups, pens, and plastic bags were left in boxes at the community recycling center for future use. The little that was left would be taken to the town dump or burned (except batteries, which were kept in a box so as not to pollute the ground). In this way, Srisa Asoke residents have incorporated a Western environmental concept (the Four Rs) into their Buddhist practice of non-attachment.

The fourth benefit to community development results from the compilation of the other three. Because non-attachment conserves resources, saves time and energy that can be put to other uses, and reduces problems of waste disposal, it increases the community's capacity for self-dependence. It is quite clear that reducing consumption in accordance with the precepts, optimizing resources through the "4 Rs" and communal use, and dedicating time and energy to productive work instead of caring for personal belongings translates into an enhanced ability to meet minimized material needs.

Work

Productive activity fosters community development in a very obvious, practical way: providing food, shelter, clothing, medicine, and other material needs. However, as detailed in the last chapter, there is much more to "work" at Srisa Asoke than the mere production of goods. Striving to be self-dependent (a condition of a meritism community), doing one's duty (Dharma), increasing concentration, and cultivating diligence affect the kind and quality of the work individuals do, and, consequently, the nature of their community's development.

Reun, an Isan farmer and mother, is quite concerned with self-dependence. In Reun's view, the three most important things in the community are natural agriculture, organic fertilizer, and microorganisms (water steeped with fruit peels and sugar used to accelerate plant growth). The captions she wrote next to her photographs are as follows:

> I like agriculture because . . . we plant vegetables ourselves, eat them ourselves, and use them ourselves. It is economical—we don't have to buy [food]—as well as safe from polluting substances.
>
> I like organic fertilizer because you can make it yourself and use it in the household to put on the vegetable plants. You don't have to buy it from the market and waste money.
>
> I like microorganisms because . . . you don't have to buy outside substances to accelerate [the growth of] flowers and fruit. That kind makes the soil bad. . . . The best is what you make yourself and use yourself. It's quite *sabai*.

Each caption speaks to the benefits of producing things for oneself rather than buying from the market. Self-dependence in food production through natural agriculture, organic fertilizer, and home-brewed microorganisms keeps one safe from harmful chemicals, and it is economical as well.

When an individual can produce more than s/he needs, individual self-dependence supports the community. Ah Jaenjop, who works in Srisa Asoke's natural rice and crop fields, informed me that with his labor alone, he can manage a plot of land that will feed ten people. This is especially helpful for old or sick people who are unable to support themselves adequately. Seventy-two-year-old Yai Sa says, "Because we exist within our central fund, I can eat." Moreover, while there are limits to what a single individual can do alone, individuals' working collectively to harvest rice or put out a forest fire (as I observed one day) enables community-level self-dependence through their mutual support.

Similarly, individuals' doing their duty—that is, using their talents, developing skillful means (*kusala*), creating and constructing—benefits the entire community as can be seen in the following examples. Ah Jaenjop, formerly a street vendor, had to develop proficiency in agriculture in order to surpass self-dependence and feed others. Ah Plekuan became adept in answering phones, greeting guests, and providing information by working in a stationery store she and her husband used to own, and although Ah Plekuan would rather work in the garden, there is no one as qualified as she to manage public relations for Srisa Asoke. I also shared my particular talent that was lacking in the community so students and adults could better communicate with English-speaking visitors. Finally, as mentioned in the previous chapter, Ah Payasin's cooking skill frees residents to use their talents in other areas without going hungry.

It is possible to have expert knowledge and ability for a particular task yet still do poor work. Sikkhamat Chinda asserts that "the tool must be good in order to get a good result of work." The tool Sikkhamat Chinda refers to is the person, and concentration makes this tool good. According to Mae Pranee, concentration means "we don't think about anything that is worrisome, so . . . the result of the work is good." With concentration, people work carefully with fewer mistakes and accidents, they work efficiently because they are not distracted, and (ideally) they can work together harmoniously by measuring thoughts, feelings, speech, and action. In theory, as their concentration improves, so does the quality of their work and social interactions. The lush gardens, well-built structures, and relatively congenial relations between residents at Srisa Asoke are signs that the "tools" there are good. Thus, Asoke's emphasis on *samãdhi* in work or "open-eye" meditation can promote sound community development.

The last aspect of work emphasized by Asoke is diligence. With regard to community development, diligence means more work can be accomplished in a certain amount of time. Srisa Asoke residents practice diligence by waking up at 3:30 in the morning and, in this way, have "more time to work." Although Em confessed to being a late riser, he calculates the value of waking up early this way:

> Many people don't really see the advantage of waking up early in the morning. People all over wake up at 5:00 or 6:00 a.m., right? I don't wake up at 3:00 a.m. If I woke up at 3:00 a.m. for seven days, in one day I would have advantage over them—two hours, right? Then multiply seven times two, and I would have advantage over them fourteen hours a week, na ha. Then I have much more time than they to do work in the time I wake up.

Asoke members also tend to keep moving throughout the day. There is a general rule at Srisa Asoke that one should not lie down during the day except to recover from illness, whereas in "outside" Thai society, people may be found sleeping in the most unlikely places at any hour of the day. One day while I was riding a bus from Srisa Asoke to Ubon Ratchathani Province, I caught a glimpse from my window of three generations of women sprawled out on a bamboo platform in the shade. My reaction of distaste to this "unsightly display of laziness" indicates the degree to which I had internalized the Asoke work ethic. This ethic of diligence means that members of Srisa Asoke community can be quite productive and more easily meet their development goals. Alternately, a community full of lazy people could not be self-dependent as Srisa Asoke aspires to be and would likely starve without external assistance.

Non-material Qualities of Community Development

Thus far, I have talked only about how individual advances in Buddhist practice affects material aspects of community development. Yet individual efforts in Dharma practice also have a profound effect on less tangible elements of community development. In previous chapters, I mentioned that some Srisa Asoke residents came looking for a positive living environment for themselves and their children. Similarly, American citizens often consider quality of life issues when moving to a new town. Crime rate is regarded as a strong indicator of livability. Theft, violence, drug use, and prostitution detract from the quality of life where these crimes occur because they trespass on one's safety and peace of mind.

Living in accordance with the Buddhist precepts largely prevents this sort of "wrong action." While speaking about the problems experienced in Srisa Asoke, Than Din Thaam mentioned a few problems residents do *not* face:

> We don't have problems of addictive drugs. Theft, we still have a little, but it's not a big issue. Mostly people take things without permission—they should tell them first.

Ah Ratana takes a step further to stress a causal relationship:

> If there are no addictive things—no alcohol, no cigarettes, no playing cards, and so on, it makes society or the community content. Then there is no stealing.

In general, Asoke members seem to find their communities much safer than "outside" society where people follow the "worldly way." In fact, many Asoke members I met during the New Year's Festival at Ratchathani Asoke expressed concern for my safety when they learned I was staying alone in a hotel. In their unanimous opinion, "many people on the outside are bad" or "scary." In contrast, by following the Way of Dharma to develop morality (as well as concentration and wisdom), Asoke community members cultivate an atmosphere of *Santi Asoke*, "Peace without Sorrow."

Moreover, as individuals progress in their ability to yield defilements, they increase their ability to sacrifice. That is, life is less about grasping to selfish desires and feelings and more about giving to others. This affects the quality of relationships among community members. Almost everyone at Srisa Asoke identified their communal living as being a family or *phii nong*—a relationship that implies responsibility to each other. Ah Plekuan describes this relationship:

> Everyone here, na, we came and we live as *phii nong* [older/younger siblings]. We have sacrifice. . . . Going to any house, we can eat if we are hungry—we can eat at this house, eat at that house. . . . There's generosity and hospitality together, to depend on in old age, to depend on in pain, and to depend on in death.[2]

This familial relationship reflects a common Thai practice of addressing others by kinship terms appropriate to age relation and treating them as one might treat one's own mother, older brother, younger sister, and so on. Typical Thai rural villages may come together as a single unit during special festivals or harvest time when shared labor is required, but individual families generally keep to their separate households for day-to-day interaction. The community of Srisa Asoke is indeed noteworthy as a 300-member family that eats, works, worships, and plays together on a regular basis. Being able to depend on one's neighbors for companionship and aid in this way brings peace of mind that further enhances the quality of a place.

Obstacles to Community Development

Collectively organizing the lives of 300 people is a complicated and challenging undertaking. Many Srisa Asoke residents stressed to me that their community is not yet perfect—Srisa Asoke is not a "utopia" as some reports label it. While the community is "on the way," it still has problems to overcome. Minor troubles ranged from everyday difficulties in "living with people" or "ordinary problems about working," "the same as people outside have" to issues of individual/collective development such as these:

> Ah Kaenfa: Problems . . . not very bad ones. For example, problems relating to yielding one's own defilements. What should we do gradually to be content with little, content with what we have—this is a problem, na krap. . . . Most problems are nothing.

> Mua: At this time, there are many kinds of problems. Not setting oneself to—regarding practicing Dharma—actually, we are not very good at anything. . . . For example, regarding education—we aren't yet putting ourselves fully into it. . . . That is, we don't yet have a curriculum that is certain relating to new education. People don't yet believe in it much. But now, people are . . . beginning to accept it. We have only just let it be better. This is an example in education.

> In many matters, there are still defects. We have to develop little by little. Whether it's activities that we do or—there are details, but they are not things that cannot be solved.

In general, Srisa Asoke residents were not overly concerned about such problems as they could be resolved through practice. Conversely, residents commonly expressed concern for larger dilemmas that require more serious attention: differing views, too few adults, and incomplete self-dependence. The remainder of this section explores these obstacles to community development.

Differing Views

Srisa Asoke community is a heterogeneous mix of individuals: single, married, divorced, and widowed men and women aged eighteen to eighty-four, with and without children, from Chinese, Central Thai, Northern, or Isan families, who grew up in rural areas, provincial towns, or Bangkok, with educational levels ranging from none to graduate degrees and occupational backgrounds covering the entire spectrum (see appendix A). There is even a Mormon and at least one former Christian residing at Srisa Asoke. These individuals joined the Asoke movement from one to twenty-five years ago and have various personal agendas including becoming a *khon wat* or a monk, bringing a child to school, learning methods of natural farming, helping Thai society, or living peacefully. Thus, it would be suspect if these community members did *not* have differing viewpoints. Here, three residents—a monk, a university student, and the former village head—talk about how diverse backgrounds bring differing views and levels of morality into the community:

> Than Din Thaam: So many [problems]! The problems arise when many people come and have many views. Morality is different; it is not equal. Views are different. Then each person comes from a different terrain, from different families. Some people come from perfect families that don't have any problems. But some families are not perfect and are still lacking, but they come here in order to train themselves.

> Em: Problems here are . . . the people in this community—their views are not yet in line. And the perfection of individuals who live here is not yet evenly good. Such that we must practice together. It's not yet good, so we still have different problems, no matter if they concern the children, students, or adults.

> Ah Peum: Problems in adapting ways of thought—that there is difference in thought. Some people come from many regions, many groups that have many thoughts far apart from each other. Adapting thought to enter the religious way is difficult.

These folks seem to indicate that uniformity is better than difference. A variety of perspectives can certainly bring creative new ideas into the community, yet they may also steer the community off its course. Indeed, numerous residents worried that so many differing opinions keep the community from mastering its goals. There are even divergent views as to what those goals actually are, as discussed in chapter 3. These views include

- The target is to have people come and practice together, uphold the precepts, eat vegetarian, work, and sacrifice;
- To build everyone to be saints;
- The target is for humanity, to help humans, to help bring them above suffering, to be cheerful and economical;
- The target is to help Thai society to be safe, to not fall to being the slave of other countries; and
- Our important target is to build the community to be a model and expand the good model toward other communities that need to develop quality of life.

Srisa Asoke's original primary objective was to allow people to practice Dharma close to a temple in a supportive community. As the movement evolved, individual development remained the foremost aim, while community development and helping Thai society became increasingly important. According to the Asoke movement's trajectory, each step should be achieved before proceeding to the next, and religion must stand as the axis of all three. In this light, residents who articulate the community target as helping humanity *without* referring to individual development are neglecting an integral component of Asoke development.

When I asked Ah Wichai if he thought the way of life at Srisa Asoke was in line with Asoke views, he answered, "The model is direct, but the thoughts of people—some direct and some not." He explained this disjuncture as the neglect of individual spiritual development:

> Someone—here they have the mix. Someone, they have the "green world" thinking come here. Someone to help the nation come here. Someone they believe about religion come here. Like that—they mix together. So if you don't understand about religion, the Buddhist thought, of course, you have some problem. Because it's deeper than you understand. If you just want to help the nation, you catch [are attached to] the nation. . . . The answer is you must find yourself and help yourself first. If you can help yourself, then you have more power to help others. What you help? The nation? The world? The Greenpeace? Everything—you can do it, but not *only* to help the Greenpeace, to help the students, to help the nation . . . no.

Ah Wichai's point is that the *problem* is not so much that people have conflicting opinions or draw out different aspects of Srisa Asoke's objectives, but that "they don't understand enough about Buddhism." Conversely, if Srisa Asoke residents developed a solid foundation in Buddhism, their efforts in any objective would be more effective.

In examining this problem more deeply, there can be seen at least two reasons for lower levels of spiritual development. On the one hand, many new students and adults enter the community at lower levels than veteran members and have varying degrees of difficulty "adapting thought to enter the religious way" (Ah Peum). For example, although Reun is a *khon wat,* when asked what is most important about Srisa Asoke Buddhist Center, she turns to what she knows best—agriculture. Reun told me she has some difficulty understanding Buddhist concepts expressed in the sermons, so she has to read about them at night. Ah Jaenjop makes a valuable point: This should not be considered a problem because "it's like schools that teach children—the children who have newly entered, they can't write yet or read. They look like problems but they are not problems because they have come to learn."

On the other hand, community members and students may lack depth in their Buddhist knowledge because they are too busy with work. Although few members actually complained of being overburdened, I heard almost daily about how much work there was to do. The problem of "much work" reappears in the next two subsections; here, Em points out how work may infringe on learning Dharma:

> I feel, my personal thoughts, na ha, in the teen level, they haven't gotten as much Dharma as they should. They still aim for work—most of them. The problem is that there is a little too much work to do. So it causes the receiving of Dharma to decrease.

For adults, children, and teens alike, the relative emphasis of work to Dharma may bring about variations in people's understanding of Buddhism and community goals. Several adult residents including Mootao, Raud, Ah Kaenfa, Ah Sompan, and Ah Komwai confessed that they sometimes do not go to activities at the Common Hall because they have too much work or because they are too tired from working late the night before. When I asked Mootao how often she goes to the Common Hall, she responded:

> Mostly, I don't ever go because sometimes . . . I have my regular work [accounting] and I can't catch up. This work must be up to date, to the present, like affairs that have passed, I have to write a lot. Really, I know that I am lacking with regard to doing the temple activities. I think about it. But sometimes I don't do [my work] on time! There's a lot of work—many subjects. So I never go.

To their credit, even if these adults cannot go to morning religious services, they do at least try to stay informed of community goings-on by attending community meetings.

Once community members agree upon community goals, they must still decide *how* to accomplish them. For instance, say the community agreed that members must concentrate for a while on individual development because the gap in understanding of Buddhism was a critical issue. There would surely be heated debates as to the best way for newcomers to "catchup" with more seasoned residents. Although Ah Tangbun upholds only five precepts, she pushes for stricter morality for everyone:

> We must have a clear target here. The target of Asoke, that Pau Than Bodhirak has us follow, is to eat one meal a day—the five precepts is like on the way, we oblige them. But if any society has many eight precept [followers], that society will have peace and happiness.

Ah Plekuan who upholds eight precepts disagrees:

> What I don't like is that people are not yet wide open to people who are new. They're not yet obliging to them. . . . New people "you must be able to eat only one meal! You must be able to eat vegetarian!" You "must do" many things. This way, it seems hard to do. We must sympathize with them. They lived on the outside, and they have experience with *sabai*. We should have some levels for them, so they can yield little by little, step by step. Because in traveling toward the peak, it's a hardship for them if we have them fly right to the top. We must have stairs for them to climb.

Ah Wichai might agree with the idea of levels, but he does not feel that particular practices are as important as the thought behind them. His opinion of Asoke practices (e.g., eating one meal a day, waking up early, and being vegetarian) is that "everything is the instrument; yeah, it's just something we use to train ourselves." Focusing on the practices themselves may prevent one from seeing their meaning, so he advocates more emphasis on larger concepts such as *metta* (loving-kindness).

This is a small sample of the disagreements waged daily at Srisa Asoke. To document even half of them would be a voluminous tangent. More important than the specific issues in contention is the method residents use to reconcile differences of opinion and build their community, described in section 3 of this chapter.

Lacking Adults

Another pressing concern is the paucity of adults able to run community operations. Officially registered adult members of Srisa Asoke number 124, yet during my stay, I counted only half that many on an average day. It seems that many non-resident members live and work in town and only come to Srisa Asoke on weekends or for special events. Other members living farther away built houses in Srisa Asoke intending to live there permanently in the future. I rarely (if ever) saw these absentee owners, including the woman who built the house where I stayed. It is reasonable to assume that a community of fewer people requires less effort to sustain it. Sixty adults (minus a dozen elderly folk and seven monks whose activities are limited) might well have been sufficient for daily community operations if they did not also have to watch over 200 students and "save" Thai society.

Srisa Asoke's elementary and secondary school has grown tenfold from its original twenty pupils in 1990. Since this is a boarding school, Asoke adults are responsible not only for class time but also for ensuring that the students eat, bathe, do their chores properly, go to bed and get up at a reasonable hour, and do not get into too much mischief in their free time. A few mothers and fewer fathers who accompanied their children share the caretaking burdens. Ah Jantima is one of the more engaged mothers who actively pursues her own spiritual development while farming, instructing the elementary students in their afternoon garden-watering or fertilizer-making duties, and watching the children in the evening if needed. Despite her efforts, Ah Jantima feels that supervision is inadequate:

> We can't watch over all the children because there are few adults. There are more children than adults. . . . If the adults don't watch over all of them, there will be negative outcomes for the children and the community.

One "negative outcome" of inadequate supervision I observed had to do with a ten-year-old boy, Mick, and three of his friends who had been stealing from Ah Warn's locked storeroom. One afternoon while Ah Warn took a student into town to see a dentist, Mick crawled over the bathroom wall into the storeroom and stole a package of noodles and a battery-operated toothbrush (still in its package) as the other three boys stood guard. When Ah Warn returned home, she noticed things were missing. She had complained previously about these boys stealing, as had others, but nothing had yet been done to stop them. Ah Warn could no longer endure it, so she approached the head teacher, Pau Paithun, hoping he would take action. Instead, Pau Paithun rebuked Ah Warn for having things the boys would want to steal. "It's your own fault" was not a satisfactory response for Ah Warn, so she decided to take the matter to the monks. Unfortunately, the monks were all away that day at a special event. Ah Warn was impatient for resolution, so she consulted her teacher-friend Ah Ai, who gave her the go-ahead to punish the little burglars. The next afternoon, Ah Warn called the boys to her and elicited a confession by asking where they hid the toothbrush. She gave Mick a choice of a spanking or sweeping the road, and Mick chose a spanking.

Ah Warn's independent handling of the situation caused an uproar in the community between those who supported her, those who criticized, and those who tried to mediate. The head teacher faulted Ah Warn because, according to the "rules," adults are not supposed to punish the children. This is the teachers' responsibility. Conversely, Ah Warn felt her actions were just because there was simply no one around to help her. The conflict between the adults was resolved through a community meeting described in section 3; however, the dilemma of inadequate supervision could not be solved so quickly.

The problem is not just a matter of too few adult warm bodies to supervise the students. Srisa Asoke lacks people who have a knack for teaching and relating with children. Ah Plekuan describes the "teacher type" she feels is needed:

> There are not enough people—adults—ones who will take responsibility for the children. . . . There aren't many teachers who are able to take the burden. There are the old people, and then [others] who don't yet have enough of the teacher spirit. So now we are lacking people who are true teachers, who will love the children, take responsibility for the children. Their mothers come, but they don't yet understand as much as they should. They are lacking depth.

Only thirteen of thirty-seven respondents to a demographic survey (see appendix A) identified themselves as teachers, and most of these individuals perform multiple jobs in the community. After adding monks involved with moral instruction and a few non-resident Asoke residents who teach on the weekends, the teaching power is still insufficient for 200 full-time students.

Ah Komwai, a long-time Asoke member with one son, also identified a problem in having too few adults, not only because "sometimes the supervision and watching over is not complete" but also because

> There is much work, but we don't have many adults. We only have many children and the work that children do is not quite the same as what adults do. There are many mistakes and things lost.

Again the matter of work arises. Ah Chuan concurred that "mostly there is a lot of work, but we are lacking in good people that will come and help in the work." Ah Sompan, the assistant village leader who confessed to "work overload" also hopes for more adults to help with community functions:

> The most important problem is that now we have few people. We have few adults and many students. . . . We need people who will be able to be workers here, from the level of organizers to receivers of guests. That's my own principal want—we really need it! (He laughs.)

I cannot help but wonder if the problem of "not enough people to work" stems from a different problem: The community has simply created too much work for itself. This subject is addressed in the next subsection.

There might *not* be too few adults in the community if more students stayed on after they finished their schooling. True, Asoke education is meant to better prepare students for adult life, whether they choose to live in or outside the Asoke community. For example, Mua finished school at Srisa Asoke two years ago, but he will remain until he is stronger in his heart/mind to handle the pressures outside and better in his occupational skill. Mua will then set himself up outside the Asoke community where he may be able to reach more people:

> I thought I would like to study about fertilizer since these days we use only chemical things, that the more they are used, the worse it gets. There's no one

> to tell [the chemical users], there's no one to help change this. There's also no one who dares to change. But now they're starting to become interested. I think it is a good opportunity.

Mua's plan suggests that his education at Srisa Asoke was successful.

However, there might be other reasons students leave besides putting their learning to good use. One day while I helped my twenty-three-year-old housemate translate herbal-tea labels into English, Raud told me she was feeling sad because she was the only one left in the community from her graduating class. When I asked how many more of the twenty university students currently residing at Srisa Asoke intended to leave, Raud guessed that some would likely leave. She explained, "Some want money, but they teach not to have money here; some want to get married, but they teach not to get married here." (Raud herself is not thinking about marriage at this time because she likes freedom, but she would like a 4 X 4 truck.) It is possible that in the effort to control youthful physical and material desires, Srisa Asoke has succeeded only in driving away individuals who would not only add to the community's adult labor supply, but also make fine leaders.

Incomplete Self-dependence

A central problem at Srisa Asoke is that the community is not self-dependent in the provisioning of material needs, particularly food. Since the community should be self-dependent before extending itself to help the outside society, this is a major flaw in their implementation of the Asoke development model. The most common explanations for failure to be self-sufficient in food production are "not enough time" and "not enough people doing agricultural work." Based on my observations and impressions gathered from Srisa Asoke residents, the community lacks time and laborers for its own food production partly because members are occupied with other outwardly oriented activities.

Ah Komwai, the manager of the rice mill, is concerned that community members put too much time and effort into making things to sell to the public. Asoke members nation-wide make and market products that are healthy and environmentally safe as a service to Thai society. These goods are sold at community stores like Srisa Asoke's Goodwill Store, the yearly Noble Market, and "Asoke-friendly" shops throughout Thailand. Primary products include herbal shampoos, conditioners, detergents, and medicine (in the form of teas and capsules), brown rice, dried mushrooms, tofu, and beans. Secondary products also provide Thai society with natural, healthy alternatives: citronella candles (to replace toxic mosquito coils), Thai-style cotton clothing, kitchen utensils and bowls made from coconut wood, a wide array of vegetarian snacks, and so on. Since one condition of a meritism community is to create and construct, Asoke members are constantly developing new products. For example, Ah Warn does not yet have a specific job in the community, so she is thinking of making small natural loofah sponges to sell at Srisa Asoke's Goodwill Store.

In addition to quality, Asoke members must also attend to marketing so these goods will appeal to the average Thai consumer. Asoke shampoo comes in stylish plastic bottles purchased from a supplier in Bangkok. Herbal tea is packaged in neat "Ziploc" plastic bags with a label showing a picture of the herb, indications, and directions for use. Each product is packaged (mostly in plastic) with equal care for its attractiveness. This attention to appearance is decidedly Thai, but it may also be considered Buddhist since the "body of Dharma" is beautiful, neat, and of good quality. Students especially spend time learning modern marketing techniques from Kwang, an Asoke member who works at the Lemon Farm organic shop in Bangkok. It should be noted that aside from labor expended on marketing products, the plastic packaging is not in agreement with the Asoke ethic to "consume little" since it creates waste problems, an issue related to self-sufficiency.

As the mill manager, Ah Komwai deals with processing and marketing, as well as distribution. He says he often has to drive the finished rice product to customers in Bangkok or other provinces. Due to this aspect of the job, he is sometimes too tired to get up for the 3:30 a.m. sermon. Ah Komwai volunteered for his present job because there was no one else to do it; however, like Ah Plekuan, Ah Sompan, and others, he would much prefer to do agricultural work. He shared these feelings with me:

> I have the feeling that the Asoke community these days, we emphasize the material way, selling, such that it makes us not have time to do other things or to work following what we ourselves love like agriculture, planting vegetables, what is natural. Life would have more peace and happiness. But if we do this point, we wouldn't be able to help the outside much.

Ah Komwai sees that a compromise has been made in order to help outside society with Asoke products, but he seems to indicate that it is a compromise leading away from peace and happiness, not toward it.

Aside from making and marketing goods, residents are also quite busy with hundreds of visitors who come to Srisa Asoke each month. Visitors include interested individuals who wander in; small groups of government officials, Red Cross workers, or foreign clergy who come for an afternoon tour; and groups of 50 to 300 university students, teachers, or villagers who attend three-day training seminars about the Asoke way of life. Taking care of visitors takes residents away from work that keeps the community functioning, not only while the visitors are present, but also in the time it takes to plan the training events. Trainings for outsiders are described in greater detail in the next chapter, "Building (Thai) Society." Here, Ah Jantima offers her view on the trainings:

> I think these trainings are too much for, too heavy for Asoke people because those who are the axis are not many. . . . I feel the different media of communication that come to Asoke—like the television, the report of *Lan Ban Lan*

> *Muang* or other reports that come here—are transmitted widely. [Outsiders] see that this village is a very strange village. It's worth seeing and studying. So many people come, and it's hard for us to refuse them, because each person wants to study, to see how true or false. Then we do as much as we can, to our full ability.

It is understandable that an Asoke community would not want to turn away people who wish to learn about their ways, particularly since the movement's main objective is to spread the Buddha's teachings. However, by spreading themselves too thin, Srisa Asoke members impede their ability to make their community an example for others to follow.

A secondary reason for Srisa Asoke's incomplete self-dependence is that people are still buying things from external markets. They may do so for convenience as my neighbor Ah Glanporn frequently does. Ah Glanporn loves to cook and to take care of people with healthy food. A few times a week she drives her truck into town to pick up fruits and vegetables from the market. Using a blender and other kitchen utensils she brought from home, Ah Glanporn mixes up "V-8" drinks to share with me, passersby, and anyone who was not feeling well and needed a vitamin boost. One day, Ah Glanporn bought a load of the sweetest and juiciest Chiang Mai oranges and squeezed them by hand. She gave the juice to several monks who had caught cold to help speed their recovery. Another exceptionally chilly winter morning, Ah Glanporn cooked a breakfast cereal of barley and squash from the market on a gas stove she brought from home. Anyone who walked by was invited to sit and eat, and even Ah Plekuan (who is only supposed to have one meal a day) succumbed to the comfort of having something warm in her stomach. It is hard to fault Ah Glanporn for relying on outside markets rather than what is available in the community since she does so with the best intentions to care for others. Nevertheless, by conducting her individual activities in this way, Glanporn detracts from the community-wide goal of self-dependence.

Others may seek consumer goods from outside the community due to certain attachments they have. The talcum powder issue raised at the young people's morality check is one example. Ah Ratana revealed another example of attachment to "store-bought" goods:

> Here, they produce *seeiu* themselves, right? *Seeiu* is called "sauce" in English, right? It's white, made from soybeans. But people here, most, or some people, buy *seeiu* on the outside to eat here. The outside, na, they put in substances to prevent spoiling and a powdery substance to enhance flavor, na. . . . MSG—monosodium glutamate. . . . But what we make ourselves here, it doesn't have [preservatives or MSG]. But some people like to buy it on the outside. *JE: Why do you think some people buy* seeiu *on the outside?* Because *seeiu* on the outside is delicious. They're addicted to delicious flavor. Because it has MSG.

Thus, according to Ah Ratana, buying things from outside markets may be considered a defilement. Community members who eat a second meal in the evening may eat at the central kitchen with the children (as I often did) or bring containers to the midday meal to fill with leftovers. If they prefer to make something fresh at home, they may collect vegetables and purchase any "Asoke-approved" processed food products (such as cooking oil, tofu, and soy sauce) at Srisa Asoke's Goodwill Store. These are all acceptable approaches to food consumption according to Asoke principles. Conversely, residents who shop at conventional markets because they seek pleasure from a particular taste compromise the community's goals by their self-serving actions. In both examples of the talcum powder and the sauce, privileging self-interests over community interests hinders the community's self-dependence.

Solutions

Srisa Asoke residents have by no means figured out how to solve all their problems, but they are fully committed to trying. This section describes Asoke's well-established method of reconciling differing views—meetings—as well as Srisa Asoke's newest efforts to be self-sufficient in food production.

Meetings

Sikkhamat Chinda said it well: "Meeting, meeting. Everything has to come to meeting." Within the Asoke movement, there are daily formal and informal meetings of every kind: national, regional, community, committee, and subcommittee, as well as ad hoc groups of concerned individuals. The meeting is the forum through which Asoke members set goals, resolve conflicts, and make decisions.

It may be helpful to have a closer look at the actual meeting process. Every Wednesday morning at 4:00 a.m., between forty and sixty residents of Srisa Asoke gather at the Common Hall for their community meeting. This attendance is considerably higher than for sermons or study on other mornings. The meetings are conducted in such an orderly, business-like manner, I would not be surprised if they actually followed Robert's *Rules of Order*. As village leader, Ah Oi directs the meeting. Ah Plekuan takes notes and later types the minutes. Attendees are each given a copy of the last meeting's minutes as well as an agenda for that day's meeting. Following standard procedure, corrections are made to the minutes from the previous meeting, and a motion is passed to accept them. Ah Oi then leads the meeting through old business, giving the floor to different individuals who report on various topics. Next, several items of new business (listed in the agenda) are discussed and motions are made, seconded, and voted on. A motion must receive two-thirds majority vote in order to pass. Toward the end of the meeting, there is time for members to bring up other new business that was not included in the printed agenda. The subject matter of one community meeting is described in chapter 7, in a day with Ah Jantima.

Because there are so many individual agendas and perceptions of community targets, meetings are crucial to ensure that the community's conduct is in line with the national Asoke movement's views and objectives. When I asked residents if practice at Srisa Asoke was in line with national Asoke thought, most answered in the affirmative. Ah Payasin explains why:

> They are in line because there are monks and Pau Than, who is the head of the big group. The administrators of each place must go to meetings to preserve the policies. The monks must go to meetings. When there are policies from Pau Than meeting with the higher levels, each place preserves the policies. We take the policies and do them and see how far we can do them, and we report, when we have done it, it is like this and like that, and is it correct? If it is not correct, it will be adapted.

That is not to say that there is no questioning of national Asoke policies. Ah Oi suggests that negative feedback does flow upward to higher levels of the movement:

> Sometimes we feel constricted by what we don't like in the Asoke view. But when we deliberate we are likely to see—Ah! Sometimes Asoke is like turning a frame upside down. We turn it one way and another. It's like thoughts are not with the evidence. The thoughts of Asoke people. Asoke people, if we criticize them, the big Asoke circle, they are the pillar already. They must be the pillar. We must take our thoughts, the minority, to meet them. That's correct, right? So we can live *sabai sabai*. But there are some times when we hold on to our thoughts as correct. So we think, Asoke does not do it correctly, does not do it—they are not with the evidence. There has been some criticism. This answer is not very clear, na.

On the contrary, Ah Oi's answer is quite clear. While many individual dislikes ought to be stifled or adapted for the good of the whole community, some instances of conflicting views point to a disconnect between theory and practice. Samana Bodhirak and other senior monks may after thirty years be considered the authority on all things Asoke, but a Buddhist knows that nothing is permanent. Asoke policies must be tested and retested to assure suitability to the changing times. Moreover, regarding Samana Bodhirak's intellectual imaginings, Sikkhamat Chinda says, "Sometimes Pau Than says something, but if people cannot really do [it], they have to stop that idea." That is, Asoke communities may reject new ideas from above that simply are not feasible in practice. During my stay in the community, I did not observe an instance of Srisa Asoke members dropping an old policy or rejecting a new one. Regardless, meetings are the forum through which individuals and communities may fit themselves to the Asoke image, and the Asoke image may adapt itself to lived experience.

For Srisa Asoke, the weekly community meeting has a tremendous unifying capacity. Ah Chuan arrived at Srisa Asoke just shortly before I did, yet he could see clearly the value of these regular community meetings:

> We must have frequent meetings because these meetings will help us to have the same target, the same target and the same method. When we have these meetings, we discuss a great deal with each other. Sometimes there are differences, so we come to talk. But this conversation is not to overcome each other. It's not to overcome each other but to find the best method, the most economical, that will allow our work to succeed, na krap. Then we come to a decision. When we have come to a decision about what, how we are going to act, everyone will acknowledge and follow that resolution, such that everyone will have a single target. Then when someone has something that is unhappy, or has been offended, we talk about it in the meeting. "It's like this, and like this." Talking together in this manner makes us able to have the opportunity to understand each other more—being one face, a single heart together. I think meetings are important and are what allows us to join together, na krap.

The conflict over Ah Warn punishing the boys who stole from her was resolved at a community meeting. Ah Warn and Pau Paithun (the head teacher) both had an opportunity to present their sides of the story. Pau Paithun declared that he advised well, but Ah Warn did not follow. To Ah Warn, he said, "This spanking is too much. How would you feel if it was your son Chim?" Ah Warn countered that she could not sleep that night because the monks and community leaders were absent, and she did not know what to do. When the two central figures of this conflict finished speaking, members and monks offered their views on who was at fault. Ah Wichai, Ah Warn's own husband, stated that Ah Warn's action was wrong because she is not really a community member. Ah Plekuan responded quickly in her friend's defense: "You can't say she's not a community member! We are all family!" Ah Peum then offered her diplomatic assessment of the situation. She did not criticize Ah Warn directly, but suggested that adults need to be a bit more patient. She then put blame on the community in general, as other people should have helped Ah Warn so she did not have to punish the boy alone. They could have helped her to think of alternative punishments, such as hard work. At this point, the monks added their observations: One agreed, "There should be clear advice," which was lacking; another preached, "If you practice the Eightfold Path, you can prepare yourself" to make the right decisions; and a third warned, "Everyone has a chance to be wrong—today it is this person and tomorrow that person."

In the end, the community decided that 1) everyone was in the wrong, and 2) right or wrong, it happened. Residents must now think about what they could do to make their community stronger. This meeting was instrumental in bringing to the floor the serious subject of guidance for children. The thieving boys and other problems involving students were signs to community members that the children were lacking in morality. To rectify the problem, it was decided that the students needed to spend more time with monks and adults who would serve as examples. In place of Wednesday "movie night," the students would meet in the Common Hall for conversation or special activities with adults (including monks) such as life history interviews.[3] Furthermore, it was voted at this meeting that Srisa Asoke's school would accept no more students the following year.

Srisa Asoke's system for goal setting, decision making, and conflict resolution is not perfect. While everyone has the right to contribute opinions, vote on matters concerning the community, and formally submit ideas for new development projects, activities, regulations, and so on, there are some people like soft-spoken Ah Komwai who do not feel their voices are heard. Ah Komwai makes this criticism of the meeting process:

> I feel that adults who have the power or are able to lead the way have not yet really listened to the thoughts of the little people as much as they should. They use the system of whatever they think, they would like it to be like that. It is not yet wide open. It is still the characteristic. But in meetings, actually they submit proposals but, actually, sometimes, they have the leaders meet together, so we are not able to oppose, or maybe we don't speak well, or—I would like the technique of submitting proposals to be better.

This flaw, though not unique to Srisa Asoke, could be a significant problem. However, it is not for me to judge whether this is merely a case of strong leaders being carried away by their enthusiasm or a real issue of power disparity. I can only urge Ah Komwai to express his criticism and work to reform the process so that everyone has equal opportunity to be heard.

Taking Charge of Food Production

During this research, Srisa Asoke residents developed a comprehensive plan to increase food production. The impetus was an activity at the "Intensive Human Development" seminar called *Dthua Rao Ben Thii Pheung* or "Self-dependence." For this exercise, participants broke up into three groups (minus members of Sima Asoke who had already left) to identify problems in the community relating to self-dependence and to brainstorm solutions. Our group identified several problems including 1) "there are not enough people to do agricultural work," 2) "the farming methods are too difficult," and 3) "people do not yet see the danger of chemicals and still buy things from the market." Individuals in our group then made suggestions that would obviously solve the problem, but were not specific enough as to how to do so. For example, to solve the problem of "not enough people," the community should "increase the ability of each person" and "find more people." To solve the problem of "difficult methods," the community should allow residents to farm in whatever way is easiest for them (which they do anyway). Regarding buying food at the market, Ah Oi and Ah Cheun, the female *khon wat* with one arm, argued heatedly to the exclusion of everyone else, such that we never agreed upon a solution.

After an hour, we reassembled so that each small group could present its findings to each other. Group three led by Ah Jing Jing actually took the initiative to create a concrete plan for increasing agricultural production that dealt with issues of land, time, labor, and supervision. The excitement that arose in the crowd indicated that this was a promising plan. Right then, we voted on the details of this plan: how many new plots, what size and where, whether we should work as a group or individually, how many people should be on the new farming committee, and who should take what role. Three individuals who wished to lead the committee gave a "campaign speech" and an "election" followed. Ah Jing Jing was voted in as chair of the farming committee, and the other two candidates as his assistants. It was agreed that the participants of *Raw Phaw Maw* would be responsible for organizing, overseeing, and evaluating this project in addition to contributing labor. The efficiency with which this plan was decided upon was inspiring. The plan was approved at the next community-wide meeting and immediately put into action.

The goal of this new plan was to produce 5000 kilos of food by the Pleuksek festival in April when 2000 practitioners would descend upon Srisa Asoke. I was dumbfounded by this staggering amount. Though this goal turned out to be overly ambitious, I applauded their motivation to tackle not only self-dependence for day-to-day community operations where they had previously been lacking, but also to strive to feed their guests. Perhaps in this case, the process of striving to achieve goals is more important than the outcome.

Conclusion

In Asoke's tripartite model, each level is made possible by the previous one, such that individual development—especially personal efforts in non-attachment and work—contributes to development at the community level. This development is material as well as non-material, including aspects such as safety as well as identity as a family and as a group of Dharma practitioners distinct from "outside" society. Through meetings, this community of diverse individuals works to generate new ideas, mediate conflicts, agree on common goals, find solutions to problems, and determine the specifics of how residents will conduct their lives as a community.

Members of Srisa Asoke have made promising headway with obstacles to their community's development, yet they still face problems associated with too few adults and too much work. Since they cannot (and would not) force students to stay after they graduate, the community must find other ways to accomplish its work. Asoke members may transfer from other communities, new members may join, or Srisa Asoke may decrease the amount of work it attempts. A few residents such as Ah Jantima and Ah Komwai suggest that the community may be expending too much time and energy on activities to help outside society when it should be focusing on individual- and community-level development.

These issues have not yet elicited the full focus of Srisa Asoke's members, but when they do, solutions will surely follow.

Notes

1. I observed this practice elsewhere in Thailand during my service as a Peace Corps community forestry extension agent.

2. Even in death, they are a family. One resident told me that it is not necessary for an Asoke member to return to her/his place of birth to die. The community will act as blood relatives by holding the customary cremation service. In early January, I had the honor of witnessing a funeral for one Asoke member arranged by the residents of Ratchathani Asoke that was attended by a mix of the man's consanguine and Asoke families.

3. Students still have "movie night" on Saturday.

Chapter 6

Building (Thai) Society

The final stage of the Asoke development model is "Building (Thai) Society." Although Buddhism is traditionally viewed as an individualistic religion with no social ethic (e.g., Weber 1958), the activities of engaged Buddhists like the Asoke movement indicate otherwise. A simple way to reconcile traditional Buddhist thought with social engagement is that sacrificing to others beyond the community offers Asoke members additional opportunities to make spiritual merit. Yet King and Queen actually perceive a philosophical change in contemporary engaged Buddhist movements:

> The most distinctive shift in thinking in Socially Engaged Buddhism is from a transmundane (*lokuttara*) to a mundane (*lokiya*) definition of liberation. Accompanying this shift is a de-emphasis on the stages of transmundane liberation (for example, the Theravada stages of stream-enterer, once-returner, non-returner, and arahant, or the Mahayana stages of the bodhisattva path), and a new focus on the causes, varieties, and remedies of worldly suffering and oppression. (1996:11)

In other words, to relieve human suffering, engaged Buddhists are more apt to strive toward diminishing tangible causes of suffering here and now than to renounce the world they live in. The new emphasis still targets internal factors that affect individual suffering and salvation (i.e., greed, anger, and delusion), yet it adds attention to equally significant external factors that touch all humanity.

In their self-told history, Srisa Asoke leaders answer the question, "Where are we going?" with a pragmatic approach to liberating Thai society:

> We are walking forward to rescue the society at large. [The year] 2541 [1998] was the beginning of the economic crisis. Most people in Thailand suffered, but Srisa Asoke and other communities in the Asoke network were not affected.

> Because we did not choose to live under the crisis, we did not have to escape or walk against it. Instead, we saw ways we could help fellow citizens. We had to sacrifice ourselves to increase our potential to help the society. . . .
>
> Although many activities in Srisa Asoke are not ready for the public, we have to open our gate wide for more outsiders to inspect because of a poem written by Samana Bodhirak on one New Year's Day. All Asoke [communities] take it implicitly as a policy.
>
> *Unite your generosity*
> *To be refuges of society;*
> *Build your own Merit Ship*
> *To rescue human lives.*
>
> At the present time [2543/2000], there are 315 permanent residents at Srisa Asoke. . . . Every member has to work fast because the community has to keep up with its standards of production, and parts of its labor are lost to services of workshops and education of visitors. Although everybody works hard without compensation, s/he is satisfied with merit. Sacrificing ourselves for society and country is our pride.

Thus, the Asoke group aspires to aid Thai society with the alleviation of pressing economic difficulties in addition to spiritual development. The recent economic crisis indeed brought hardship to urban and rural people alike. Yet poverty was pervasive even before the crisis, especially in Bangkok slums and areas of Isan where, according to Mootao (Srisa Asoke resident and Isan native), "families are so poor, children eat off the hard, cracked ground." To a lesser degree, the Asoke movement is also concerned with cultural preservation and political reform. The bulk of this chapter describes particular activities through which the Asoke movement and Srisa Asoke help "outside" Thai society with spiritual, material, cultural, and political matters. The final section then considers what makes "an ideal society," both in formal Asoke rhetoric and in the imaginations of average Srisa Asoke residents.

Spiritual and Material Aid

As discussed in the chapters on "Building the Individual" and "Building Community," material and spiritual development are mutually supportive. Sufficiency in the four basic necessities—food, shelter, clothing, and medicine—meets the minimum material requirements for Dharma practice; Dharma practice in turn promotes certain qualities that facilitate material development. For example, Ah Sompan describes how following Buddhist practice may support Thailand's economy:

> We can greatly help reduce expenses in Thailand. That's regarding the economy. How do we help so much? We don't drink alcohol, we don't smoke ciga-

rettes, and we don't gamble, na. This helps us have time, labor [power], mindfulness and wisdom, good health. This reduces the expenses of the nation and increases the income of the nation.

The connection between spiritual and material endeavors may in this way be regarded as concrete and practical.

On a deeper level, the relationship between spiritual and material development has to do with proceeding with life along the worldly path or the Eightfold Path. Before he became a monk, Samana Bodhirak was a popular TV personality and songwriter (known as "Rak" (Love) Rakpong) who enjoyed all the accoutrements of his success: a grand house, expensive cars, and an indulgent bachelor lifestyle. Despite his fame and monetary wealth, Rak felt his life was without value, "like water flowing away" (Asoke "30 Years of Work" 2000). His career was at its height when his attention turned to Buddhism. After two years of devout practice as a lay Buddhist, he resigned from his job and ordained at a temple in Bangkok. By changing his life in accordance with the Eightfold Path and by encouraging others to do the same, Samana Bodhirak and the Asoke movement have crafted an alternative material reality that reflects their Buddhist values.

The remainder of this section details five types of outwardly oriented programs implemented by the Asoke movement to promote spiritual and material development in their country: publications, vegetarian-food giveaways and cheap vegetarian restaurants, meritism markets, free public trainings in meritism, and the Three Professions to Save the Nation.

Publications

For a quarter century, the Asoke movement has sought to reach people outside its close circle of practicing members by putting Asoke views and pursuits into print.[1] The Santi Dharma Foundation (a lay organization) now handles the logistics of publishing three monthly magazines for the Asoke movement. *Saan Asoke* (*The Essence of Asoke*) has been informing Asoke members and interested outsiders on Asoke happenings for twenty-five years. In addition to regular columns including "15 Minutes with Pau Than," "Impressed with Dharma," and "Letters from *Yatithaam*," *Saan Asoke* features articles on special occasions such as Buddhist Lent or a festival celebrating Pau Than Bodhirak's thirty years of work, summary reports of Asoke nation-wide and community events, and thoughtful essays on various topics like "The Culture of Thai Music." The second periodical, *Rao Khit Arai* (*What Do We Think?*), began just five years ago as a forum for social commentary. Regular columns include an opening letter

Figure 6.1 Asoke Magazine Cover: *Rao Khit Arai*

from former Bangkok governor and Asoke member Chamlong Srimuang, letters from readers, "Political Thoughts in Buddhism," and "The Vegetarian Kitchen." Lead articles in *Rao Khit Arai* take a more critical or analytical tone than those in *Saan Asoke* as evidenced by the titles "Thais! How Long Will You Be Slaves?" or "The Benefit or Value of People," and, more pointedly, by the cover illustrations accompanying these articles (fig. 6.1). The last monthly publication is *Dauk Yaa* (*Grass*), a magazine of essays, games, and cartoons designed to convey Asoke ideas to children.

Although Srisa Asoke is not directly involved with publishing, several residents first learned about the Asoke movement through its publications, and many residents now read them regularly. At least two Srisa Asoke residents identified "distributing books to the public free of charge" as one way the Asoke group helps Thai society:

> Than Din Thaam: We propagate the essence [of this way of life] in the form of books; we print books and give them away. This is helping society. We give away books: *Saan Asoke*, *Dauk Yaa*, and other books. We don't charge money. We send them to members all over, or whoever wants them; whoever comes to see us, we give them books.

> Ah Jantima: The large Asoke group helps Thai society by producing books—different media of transmitting messages, books, tapes—for ones who are interested, who will listen and practice following the way of genuine Buddhism. Having practiced, benefits will arise in themselves, their family, and their community where they dwell.

My tall, unsolicited stack of Asoke magazines and booklets are proof that Asoke communities do indeed give their publications away to visitors. In addition, at a natural-agriculture training event that Srisa Asoke hosted in town, participants were each given a current copy of *Saan Asoke*. Recipients seemed somewhere between indifferent and pleased about this free gift. It is likely that many would look through it—even individuals not already sympathetic to Asoke—since reading Dharma books produces merit for the reader.

Than Din Thaam's caption for "Asoke Dharma Books" in the "What Is Most Important about Srisa Asoke Community?" photo activity clarifies the Asoke movement's objectives for circulating publications:

> The philosophy of Asoke people . . . [is that] we will print Dharma books for the world, with these objectives:
>
> - To increase the force of Dharma for readers;
> - To recall, review, summarize the state of Dharma and activities that have been done;
> - To be the compass directing the practice in continuing steps; and
> - To benefit young people [who] can depend on it as information in studying Dharma practice and "Asoke" methods of proceeding with *gnan* [work, life activities] that are one line in the weaving of religion.

These four objectives are actually printed inside the front cover of *Saan Asoke*; however, Than Din Thaam adds one more in his own words:

- To promote consciousness and wisdom, and to bring about the realization of the value of the dharmic foundation of religion, in areas that will be used to solve problems in life and society.

Asoke publications are therefore instrumental in cultivating "right understanding"[2] about the causes and cures of suffering.

Vegetarianism

Since the Asoke movement views vegetarianism as the most vital practice in upholding the precepts, members would be remiss if they did not urge others to stop eating meat. Thais are already familiar with the Buddhist ethic not to kill or harm animals. To make merit, Thais regularly feed stray dogs in the streets and may release caged birds bought from temple vendors. With some thought, they can surely transfer this concept to the food they eat. Than Din Thaam speaks to the importance of helping Thai society in this manner:

> They call [vegetarianism] the number one qualification of Asoke people. We let people become acquainted with vegetarian food—food that is pure regarding morality. It is not necessary to go oppress the lives of animals. So we have them practice upholding the precepts too. . . . Eating vegetarian food is good for the health, mentally and physically.

The Asoke movement "acquaints" outsiders with vegan food by running several inexpensive restaurants and offering free meals once a year.

Chamlong Srimuang and his wife Sirilak (who heads the Vegetarian Society) established the first Asoke vegetarian restaurant years ago next to the enormous Chatuchak weekend market in Bangkok. Now, there are Asoke restaurants in some provincial capitals near Asoke communities. These restaurants are open from 7:00 a.m. until 2:00 p.m. and are staffed by volunteer workers. The restaurants I visited in Bangkok and Chiang Mai look like any other cafeteria-style restaurant in Thailand, except that the walls are colorfully decorated with Asoke slogans and posters illustrating the Asoke way of life rather than calendar pictures of naked women. At lunchtime, these restaurants are absolutely packed with Asoke members, office workers, shop owners, street vendors, and the occasional tourist. The non-vegetarian patrons I spoke with said they come because the food is cheap and delicious. Many commented that the tofu used to make common Thai dishes tastes "normal"—"just like meat."

In addition to running these restaurants, the Asoke movement also offers free vegetarian food to the public every December 5th to honor the king on his birthday. In the year 2000, Asoke members gave away food in seventy-three locations around Thailand to commemorate the king's seventy-third year. Ah

Tangbun describes this event:

> On December 5th we have Vegetarian Merit Factories all over Thailand. We have done this the whole time, starting from when Asoke was established, for thirty years, and we have done it continuously, every year. Groups all over Thailand make food and take it to make merit. We do this for society; that is, on that day, let people eat vegetarian food, one day, all over the country. Suppose everybody did it one day, they wouldn't kill animals, right? They receive food to eat. This is our sacrifice.

On December 5th, 2000, while I assisted Asoke friends in distributing food at the Force of Merit Shop in Bangkok, I discovered that this activity is not an exclusively Asoke affair. Countless other groups pay tribute to the king in similar ways, though not with vegetarian food. For example, when I stepped off the bus into the stifling rush hour smog, I was especially thankful for a cup of water handed to me by a member of the nearby Vishnu temple. At Sanam Luang (a park next to the Grand Palace), hundreds of people shuffled through endless lines to get a free meal hosted by a Chinese organization. There was also a tent full of busy barbers giving free haircuts, as well as a table of lonely Red Cross workers offering free blood pressure checks. Although Asoke people do not have a monopoly on sacrifice, participating in this national event allows them to introduce others to a healthy "Buddhist" diet while demonstrating their solidarity with fellow Thai citizens.

Meritism Markets

The Asoke movement also sacrifices to outside society through daily community markets like Srisa Asoke's Goodwill Store and the annual Noble Market held during the national Asoke New Year's Festival. The main purpose of these markets is to provide the Thai public with low-cost, useful goods. However, they also serve as vehicles to convey the concept of meritism.

The Goodwill Store (*Ran Namjai*) faces the dirt road that fronts Srisa Asoke, easily accessible to passersby. The store stocks durable household goods, school supplies, mechanical and building materials, seeds, cooking staples like brown rice and oil, toiletries, snacks, and more. Not only is this shop a convenient place for Srisa Asoke residents and nearby villagers to buy common and necessary items; it is also the cheapest. Asoke shops have a policy to charge no more than 15 percent over original production or purchase cost. Price tags on each item show both the original cost and the sale price so that customers may know for themselves the amount of markup. The Goodwill Store accomplishes two objectives for Srisa Asoke: It provides a service to neighbors and generates non-exploitative income to fund other community projects.

The Noble Market (*Talad Ariya*) is held annually for three days over New Year's on a large expanse of undeveloped land at Ratchathani Asoke (Ubon

Ratchathani Province). The fair-like atmosphere and discount prices attract thousands of serious shoppers and fun seekers alike. Most market goers are poor Isan farmers dressed in T-shirts over faded *phathung* or polyester pants and rubber thongs, but there are also wealthier women made up in department store outfits and faux-leather shoes, as well as teens in jeans. Booths on either side of canopied walkways are piled with all sorts of goods: basic household items (e.g., woks, plastic buckets and washtubs, sticky-rice steamers, brooms, mats, field hats, laundry soap, and cooking oil), handicrafts, bicycles, eyeglasses, herbal medicine, snacks, produce, and so on. There is quite a clamor as sellers hawk their wares—some with the aid of microphones—shouting "Sugarcane! Five baht a bunch!"[3] and "Hurry before they are gone!" Eager customers stand in long lines for the best deals. When they tire, shoppers squat in the shade to wait for friends or wander over to the "food court" where each plate of vegetarian food costs a single baht. They may then rest on the lawn and enjoy a variety show performed on a stage by Asoke members. This entertainment area also features a giant, fifteen-foot puppet with poles attached to its arms and mouth so children may operate it.

I participated in this event as a "window-shopper" as well as a seller. On the first day, I helped a group of Asoke friends from Bangkok sell watermelon. They had bought enough grapefruit-sized melons to fill a pickup truck at the nearby market and were now selling them for one baht a piece.[4] Shoppers drawn by this incredibly low price crowded around our table, and we had to ask them repeatedly to queue up. When they reached the front, many individuals were disappointed to learn that they could buy only one melon and that they could not pick and choose the best. We patiently explained that everyone must have equal chance to buy a melon, and that the melons were all good—they did not have to be beautiful. The next day, I helped Kwang and students from Srisa Asoke sell durian-flavored banana chips for five baht a bag. (These snacks are ordinarily sold for 12.5 baht at the organic shop in Bangkok where Kwang works.) Kwang employed an effective marketing tactic by positioning one or two students in front of our booth with a plate of banana chips for shoppers to taste. Our sales increased markedly when I held the plate since more people came to marvel at the tall *farang* who could speak Thai. I felt vaguely uncomfortable this day selling such an unnecessary item since the Asoke movement frowns on snacking as a form of luxury. I also became increasingly aware that the way some Asoke sellers urged people to buy their goods seemed to reproduce the "modern social preference" for consumerism, which the Asoke movement strives to counter.

What makes the Noble Market "noble" is that goods are sold for *less* then the original purchase cost. The Asoke group reckons that lower prices, even taking a financial loss, result in higher "noble profit" or merit. For example, if a pencil costing ten baht is sold for twelve baht, the seller does not gain, but loses merit equivalent to two baht. However, if the same ten-baht pencil is sold for eight baht, the seller earns two baht "noble profit." Asoke members do not actually calculate merit in this fashion, but it is a frequent explanation of how the meritism concept works in trade. Ah Tangbun relates how much money Srisa Asoke "lost" at this national event:

> For example, the organization that went to sell things for the Goodwill Store, they lost 200,000 baht. Being short 200,000 means they sold [goods] and received money, and that money was lacking 200,000 from the whole investment. That—that's losing money. We worked in many areas: for example, soybean sauce lost money, shampoo lost money—usually they sell for twenty-five [baht] a bottle, right? So they sell it for ten [baht] a bottle. Also vegetables from the chemical-free agriculture, clothes, it all lost money.

According to this computation, Asoke members clearly make spiritual merit through their sacrifice at the Noble Market.

Besides providing the Thai public with inexpensive everyday items, this market also allows Asoke members to introduce the basics of their way of life to outsiders. Ah Tangbun explains how the Noble Market helps Thai society on a spiritual level:

> It has people come see that it really exists; there are people like this. Then those organizations have sermons, shows—each person, each place. It is practice, showing to let people see what we do together. This is one way we help society.

Ah Tangbun refers to the Noble Market itself as well as the variety shows of music and comedy, a palatable way Asoke members inform the public about their way of life. Many bargain shoppers come to the Noble Market knowing nothing about the Asoke movement, but they leave with at least an inkling that an alternative lifestyle exists.

Trainings for Outsiders

The Asoke group seeks further to improve material and spiritual aspects of Thai society through trainings for outsiders in the Asoke way of life. In the old days when the Asoke group was small, Asoke monks and lay members walked together to universities and government offices across Thailand to teach about Dharma and the Asoke movement, following the wandering tradition of forest monks. As they became more involved with agriculture, schooling, and other community-development activities (and as travel became more hazardous due to less forest cover and more traffic), Asoke members no longer ventured out as they once did. Now, instead of Asoke going to the people, the people come to Asoke.

According to Srisa Asoke's tabulations, this community alone sees 1000 visitors each month.[5] These visitors may come for an afternoon tour or they may camp out for a four-day training seminar, free of charge. To announce each longer training sessions, a banner is hung in the Common Hall:

Foundational Training No. 26
"People Build the Nation" at Srisa Asoke
January 14-17, 2544 [2001]
Clean-Hardworking-Thrifty-Making Sacrifice-Grateful

The title is part of an Asoke slogan: "Dharma Builds People; People Build the Nation." During these "People Build the Nation" seminars, separate groups of 30 to 300 people (e.g., students, government workers, teachers, villagers, or members of the regional chemical-free agriculture group) listen to talks, observe Asoke life, and take part in daily activities at Srisa Asoke. When I asked Ah Payasin about problems in her community, she expressed concern for people *outside* the community. She then proceeded to list the particulars of what Asoke teaches people through their trainings:

> The problem is how can we help people more than this? At present, we are helping, but there are still people outside our community who are anxious. . . . They must work hard to get a little money, and the price of things is expensive. So they are anxious. They do not know that using and paying for luxuries makes them anxious. We help them by having them come train in Dharma. We teach them to be economical, to stop *abayamook*—don't drink alcohol, don't smoke, don't gamble—and practice eating vegetarian food. Vegetables are cheaper than meat. And then don't eat food that doesn't have benefit, food that looks good, that they sell in the supermarket, na ka. . . . We tell them so they understand not to buy luxury items. And then yield the things they use in adorning themselves. Have fewer clothes, you don't have to have many. Cosmetics, you don't have to use them; they are not necessary. . . . They will have a salary, but they will not be anxious. And then no one will take "crazy medicine" [*ya ba*, methamphetamines], addictive drugs—they will see the danger of addictive things. . . . Let them practice planting vegetables to eat themselves. . . . Then they will be economical with their expenses; that is, they don't have to buy vegetables from the outside because they have their own vegetables.

In sum, these seminars aim to teach people specific knowledge and skills in the area of Buddhist morality and occupation. Even if training participants are not inspired to become members and live at Srisa Asoke, they can improve their lives on the outside by adapting the Asoke example.

The "People Build the Nation" seminars all follow the same basic model, with slight variations in activities and leaders to target specific groups of participants. During the course of my stay, the content of these trainings did change some as organizers incorporated parts of the successful "Intensive Human Development" seminar. The long training weekend typically starts around noon on Friday. After signing in, the attendees gather in the Common Hall for two hours of icebreakers and introductions to Asoke. The introduction is led by both monks and laypeople and includes a brief history of the movement and Srisa

Asoke Buddhist Center, a description of Srisa Asoke's organizational model (Village-Temple-School), and an explanation of basic Asoke culture such as following the five or eight precepts, vegetarianism, dress, self-dependence, and sacrifice. From 2:15 p.m. to 4:15 p.m., the participants are led in small groups on a tour of community, through living areas, work facilities, gardens, and the museum. In each area, the Asoke tour guide explains Asoke beliefs and practices and answers individual questions. The participants then break until 5:00 p.m., when they gather again at the Common Hall for dinner. The meal is followed by an evening program of talks by lay and monastic members and/or a performance of traditional Thai music and dance. "Lights out" is officially 9:00 p.m., but many participants stay up chatting.

On Saturday, the trainees rise at 3:30 a.m. (regretting going to sleep so late) with the rest of the community for morning chanting and sermons. They learn how to *graap* properly before monks, and they can follow the Pali chanting with a pamphlet printed in Thai. Afterward, small groups spend the morning learning and practicing livelihood skills such as cultivating mushrooms, composting, gardening, and processing soy. Trainees return to the Common Hall for the communal meal, during which they learn Asoke mealtime etiquette—not to eat until everyone is served and the meal reflection has been recited in unison. The rest of Saturday and Sunday pass with more talks, work, and leisure (e.g., watching a movie Saturday night); the participants then return home early Monday morning.

Srisa Asoke residents sacrifice large amounts of time, energy, and resources to perform these trainings with no guarantee of a successful outcome. It was difficult to gauge participants' reactions. I believe they were reticent to give their opinions to me due to either the *krengjai* ethic or shyness about speaking with a foreigner. The responses I did receive were benign: Getting up early is hard; the work is hard; the food is good; it is a good way of life. When I asked Pau Paithun after a training he led if there was an evaluation process whereby participants could give feedback as to what was and was not helpful about the training, he indicated there was not. (I suggested this might be a good idea.) In any event, by allowing people to see Asoke life in action and to practice it for themselves (rather than merely reading about it or hearing about it at other Asoke events), the Asoke group hopes that these trainings will have a greater impact on the lifestyles of the Thai populace. While these trainings may impart knowledge and skills with tremendous value in both the practical and the spiritual realm, the trainings can help Thai society only so far as the participants are willing to take what they learn and apply it to their lives.

Three Professions to Save the Nation

The Asoke movement's newest approach to facilitating Thailand's spiritual and material development is the Three Professions to Save the Nation, namely, natural agriculture, waste management, and clean (chemical-free) fertilizer production. At Srisa Asoke, "natural agriculture" currently signifies no chemicals. This practice meets two of four qualifications (no chemical pesticides or fertilizers) laid down by Masanobu Fukuoka (1978, 1985), founder of the Japanese modern natural-farming movement. The other two qualifications, no plowing and no weeding, are under experimentation in Srisa Asoke's rice and vegetable fields and fruit orchards. In terms of waste management, Srisa Asoke residents not only separate trash to "recycle-reuse-repair-reject"; they also make organic fertilizer from biodegradable food and farming waste. This transformed waste is returned to the land to form a connected circuit: from agriculture, to food, to waste, and back to agriculture.[6]

These Three Professions form the foundation of Srisa Asoke's self-dependence, and they are extended to neighboring farmers as well. Ah Ratana relates how the Asoke group helps Thai society with the Three Professions:

> We help by suggesting to them, "Farmers, na? Do like this, na? Until you are safe." Like that. "You must plant rice, without using chemicals. Don't use insecticide; don't use herbicide." Asoke people are the ones who suggest, the ones who tell the farmers to help in this objective.

More specifically, the Asoke group "suggests" the Three Professions to outside society by demonstrating the Three Professions to visitors and trainees at Srisa Asoke, leading training sessions at farmers' homes in surrounding villages (when invited), and participating in regional activities of the (non-Asoke) Chemical-Free Agriculture Group. During my stay, it was Srisa Asoke's turn to host a Chemical-Free Agriculture Group meeting in Kanthalak for members and other interested local farmers. At this meeting (organized by Mootao, Ah Kaenfa, Ah Sompan, and Ah Peum), members sold produce at a roadside stand, Asoke monks gave a sermon, a local government official extolled the merits of Asoke and chemical-free agriculture, farmers shared their successes and failures of their chemical-free approach, and group leaders spoke at length about financial matters and mismanagement of funds. An Asoke-style lunch was also part of the day.

Samana Bodhirak instigated the "Three Professions to Save the Nation" because Thailand's land and climate are better suited for agriculture than industry and because "Food is number one in the world" (Asoke n.p. "Three Professions to Save the Nation"). In an edition of *Saan Asoke* featuring the Three Professions, Samana Bodhirak talks about the significance of this program, stressing responsibility and pride (Asoke 1992 "15 Minutes with Pau Than"):

> I emphasize "save the nation" because in agriculture, we grow food, rice, vegetables, and fruit that is truly the food of the nation, of the world. But these days it does not save the nation because people have a bent way of thinking—they have values that do not favor doing agriculture, cultivating crops or rice. They think it is low-class work, that it oppresses them. They look down upon it with contempt. And the prices are not high so [agricultural work] becomes a force of circumstances.

> Here, we meritist people, we understand the way of merit correctly. Thus we must pick up the duty of farmers in order to grow rice and sell it cheaply or, if possible, give it away free. We must take responsibility by correcting the nation's economy according to the principles of the Buddha that allow us to know the world, not misunderstand the world. We will make our own economy, and we can live with the world without being inferior, without taking second place, even though we have an agricultural profession or grow rice, vegetables, or even the occupation of sorting trash and making fertilizer.
>
> If we do this much, take this much responsibility, I am confident that we will prove that this is the basis or axis for life. We can feel proud that we are helping to save the nation—we don't save the nation by fighting, killing, struggling, and competing for the Kingdom. Not at all. But we aid in living safely together in a constructive way, by sincerely making a sacrifice. You must know the importance of genuine life.

After reading such documents discussing the Three Professions, I sought the impressions of Srisa Asoke residents who practice the Three Professions on a daily basis. Many individuals like Mua were able to iterate the model:

> It will help Thailand well because Thailand is an agricultural country. Then, agriculture must have fertilizer also—it is the basis. These two professions must be a pair. Then garbage is also related. Take garbage to make fertilizer, take the fertilizer to use in agriculture, when agriculture is finished, it makes garbage. Garbage circles back here—a circle of use. The garbage in the world—there is a lot. If we didn't have this profession, the garbage would overflow with no one to manage it. . . . [The Three Professions] produces food to feed the world, and then also helps pick up the trash in the world because most people produce trash—especially America [he laughs]. It helps to solve these problems well.

Other residents emphasized the benefits of avoiding chemicals that the "modern" farming industry advocates:

> Ah Tangbun: For example, the first profession is chemical free agriculture. . . . The soil is not polluted, and the air is not polluted; there is no pollution. This is important, na. It's like we are a big Bodhi tree [the tree under which the Buddha achieved enlightenment]. It spreads out coolness to cover the world, to help animals of all kinds who live under the tree.
>
> Ah Warn: Now, on the outside, they all use a great deal of chemicals. Actually, my mother who lives in Kanchanaburi still has a garden that tends to have [chemicals]. She grows very beautiful vegetables, but she herself does not eat them. If she eats them, she is afraid she will die. I ask her, "If you sell them, other people don't have to eat them, huh?" [said with sarcasm]. One more thing: these days, she says her eyes are starting to have problems, so she went to see a doctor. The doctor said she sprays too much chemicals and the chemicals get in her eyes. . . . After she was better, she did it again! She didn't think it was a problem because she got better. So she continued to do it.

> But the way of natural agriculture, she does not see the true results, that she doesn't have to use chemicals and she can do it. I asked her but she doesn't want to do it. She doesn't want to invest much capital. Using these chemicals, I asked her—you have to buy fertilizer, buy insecticide—How much do you use? I asked her then for three months, how much can you sell, how much money do you make? If she's lucky, no matter about her health, na, how many thousands of baht does she get a month? But if it happens that she must see a doctor, the money is not enough and she has to borrow. These days, everyone has debt. Why do they have debt? They say, "I am sick." Why are you sick? "My body is not strong; I am old." They say this and never think it's because they use chemicals. *Oiy*! They do it in all households, in all districts, and they don't see what's the matter! They say they do not want to change; they don't listen! They say, "The less I do it, the worse the product is, and then there is no one to buy. If I don't do it, my family will die, so I must do it." But if natural agriculture arises, and is able to be an example, if the farmers take it and do it as an example, they will have money left over and they will not create social problems. Their descendants will return [i.e., come home from jobs in Bangkok] and do it because they can have a monthly income. It is important.

According to these accounts, the Three Professions are indeed helpful to Thai society. Yet I wondered if the Asoke movement was straying from their central mission to "revive Buddhism in Thailand." To determine how the Three Professions and Buddhism relate, I first spoke with Sikkhamat Chinda. She affirmed that Buddhism and agriculture are closely linked for the following reasons: 1) Buddhism supports life and agriculture supports life; 2) the mind and body go together, and we promote both for a complete life; and 3) Asoke does not use what is harmful to life. Of course, Sikkhamat Chinda is a nun and can be expected to give an articulate answer. For a more realistic picture of how regular members view the relationship between the Three Professions and Buddhism, I asked Srisa Asoke residents. Their responses also confirm a connection:

> Mae Pranee: Most people can depend on themselves, na ka, with the Three Professions. Buddhism is a religion [that teaches] to depend on oneself: *adtahi adtanonatho* (Pali), which means *"dthua rao ben thii pheung"* (self-dependence). Therefore, the "Three Professions to Save the Nation" means that everyone should depend on her/himself first.

> Ah Jaenjop: It is related to Buddhism because it is a way of proceeding in life that doesn't make us break the precepts. For example, about garbage: Buddhism emphasizes cleanliness. [The Three Professions] is a way of creating cleanliness. . . . Take one kind of garbage to make fertilizer, and in making fertilizer it cures the soil. We don't use chemicals. Chemicals destroy the soil and it is hard, and insecticide destroys animals. In this subject, Buddhism is directly related to Three Professions to Save the Nation. . . . It helps us proceed with a life that has morality, clean morality, and to promote a life that practices Dharma.

Ah Chuan: The Three Professions to Save the Nation . . . is related in my thoughts, na krap. It is related to Buddhism because it is "right livelihood" (*samaachiwa*). The Three Professions, aside from being occupations that are honest, help us develop ourselves in the area relating to the Eightfold Path, that is, a path that goes toward *nirvana*, na krap.

Ah Payasin: It is related because we are able to help the world. We do not let our world have pollution, and we help economize energy. . . . It economizes money also. While we are doing the Three Professions to Save the Nation, if we can depend on ourselves—we plant vegetables to eat, so we don't have to buy them—we can eat vegetables without harmful substances, without insecticide. If we have a lot, we can give it away to other people or sell at a cheap price so that they can eat vegetables without harmful substances. . . . If we help them, have *metta* (loving-kindness) for them. . . . It is helping nature, helping the world that is related to Buddhism. That is, Buddhism is doing for humanity.

Clearly, the Asoke movement promotes sound material development in Thailand with the Three Professions, as these occupations are more suitable for Thailand's land and climate than industry, provide food for the nation, solve problems of overflowing garbage, do not create pollution, improve people's health, economize, and enable self-dependence. The Three Professions are certainly appropriate for impoverished Isan farmers. On a broader level, the concept resonates with national protests against the $17.2 billion IMF bailout loan (in the aftermath of the 1997 economic crisis) that called for (national) self-reliance instead of reliance on foreigners. Equally important for this group of Dharma practitioners, the Three Professions also foster spiritual development among Thais by promoting the Buddhist ideal of a "right livelihood" that upholds the precepts and helps the world.

Cultural Preservation

In addition to these outreach programs, some Srisa Asoke residents see themselves as preserving Thai culture. There is concern within the Asoke movement as well as among many other Thais that Thailand's "traditional" culture is being replaced by a new culture centered on money and materially derived status (e.g., *Bangkok Post* July 27, 1997). Sulak Sivaraksa, a prominent Thai social critic, turned his attention to globalization after the economic crisis (*Bangkok Post*, September 21, 1997):

> Indeed globalization is a new demonic religion. It uses the media to create a sense of lack. Hence we are driven to earn more in order to acquire more yet we can never reach a point of contentment. Since globalization is under the control of the big corporations, the media is used to direct us blindly toward the monoculture of more and more technology, of the McWorld of fast food, junk food and the cola and jeans syndrome.

Globalization has certainly affected Bangkok, which looks like any other large cosmopolitan city boasting the usual emblems of "modernity": McDonalds, metal and glass shopping malls, and traffic jams. When Srisa Asoke residents looked at a photograph of Siam Shopping Center on the ever congested Sukhumvit Road in Bangkok, they described a society full of selfish (*hen kaeh dthua*) people who compete with each other (*khad yaeng kan*) and remarked that living on the outside makes one feel tense or serious (*khriat*) in the pursuit of money. Grandmother Sa laughed and exclaimed, "All I see is McDonalds!"

In a post-crisis interview published in the *Bangkok Post* (November 16, 1997), Sulak was asked, "What can the middle class do to improve the [economic] situation?" He responded: "They should go back to their roots. They should go back and join hands with the lower class. Under this economic system, the Thai middle class are cut loose from their own roots. There are those who are embarrassed by . . . a grandfather because he is a farmer. There are things that teach us to be embarrassed because we are Thai." Asoke members who advocate their way of life in order to preserve Thai cultural identity agree wholeheartedly with Ajaan (Professor) Sulak. Ah Payasin lists a few elements of Thai culture that can be found at Srisa Asoke:

> This community can build good Thai culture by dressing Thai—not wearing shoes and wearing Thai-style shirt and *phathung*. And we build houses that are Thai form. Then the things we use are Thai, for example, clay water jars, stoves that use charcoal and wood—we don't really prefer to use gas stoves, na ka.

Other aspects of "traditional" Thai culture rescued by the Asoke group are an agrarian livelihood, music and dance, and etiquette such as the *wai* greeting.

Always the critical thinker, Ah Ai wonders how "traditional" can be pinpointed when culture is always changing:

> What they're always talking about is they want to restore the nation—what you call—to not be like America—to [not be] dominated by other nationalism. Because they say this is a cultural community. But I think we can keep our culture while we receive other culture—this has happened to Thailand since the past. If they want to keep Thai culture, they must have long hair and do something like this like in Sukhothai period [pantomimes winding hair into a topknot]. . . . I think culture is not [for] keeping. It should grow. Something better, you receive it and modify it. So if you play guitar [a Western instrument], you play Thai songs—why not? Even language . . . so if you want to keep Thai culture, you have to get rid of Pali and Sanskrit language because it's not Thai; it's Indian. Even Buddhism is Indian.

Ah Ai makes a very good point in my anthropological opinion, but not one that is well received by many Srisa Asoke residents.

I should like to point out that while the Asoke movement articulates a particular "traditional" Thai cultural identity, they do not shut out things modern. The movement has a fleet of trucks and vans to transport goods and people across the country as well as state-of-the-art machinery for making and packaging natural medicine for the domestic market. Even the most "traditional" rural community, Srisa Asoke, has hi-tech computer, communications, and sound equipment. Moreover, the Asoke movement has made use of foreign ideas such as natural-farming techniques from Japan and Western marketing and environmental concepts. Thus, Asoke people are being selective about what they receive from the global flow of goods and ideas.

Political Reform

Lastly, the Asoke movement may help Thai society in the political arena as well. Asoke member and former Bangkok governor Chamlong Srimuang declares, "In our system, a candidate buys votes, then has to steal to get the money back. The greatest enemy we have is not communism; it is rotten politics" (*Time*, March 23, 1992). In addition to vote buying and misappropriation of funds, relations of patronage common throughout Thai society also breed corruption in the political arena. Suvit Suvit-Swasdi states, "Image, influence, and flattery reflect the vanity of the bureaucratic system in which close ties to superiors are the bridge to power. . . . It is this system that allows politicians who lack ethics to come to power and abuse it" (*Bangkok Post*, December 1, 1996). According to Amaret Sila-On, chairman of Thailand's Financial Sector Restructuring Authority, the four "social evils"—cronyism, corruption, collusion, and complacency—are now on the rise (*Newsweek International*, July 12, 1999).

In the late 1980s and early 1990s, members of the Asoke movement had a brief foray into politics, serving as "watchdogs" against corruption in Governor Chamlong's Bangkok offices and campaigning with Chamlong's Force of Dharma Party for seats in parliament. Chamlong and his Asoke volunteers aimed to clean up Thai politics, particularly vote buying and bribery. Asoke members were not successful in their run for Members of Parliament (MP), nor was Chamlong in his effort to become prime minister. Regardless, this political activity was potentially threatening to the establishment and was effectively stopped short by the court case mentioned in chapter 2, in which Samana Bodhirak and his followers were charged with impersonating monks.

Now that the dust from the decade-long court battle has settled, Asoke members are once again considering politics as a forum for spreading Dharma. Recently, a columnist from the *Roth Thai* newspaper handed over to the Asoke movement a cooperative social party called For Sky and Earth. Mr. Nitipum obtained only 20,000 of 50,000 signatures needed to register the party, so he hoped the Asoke group could secure the rest. Ah Peum, the former village head of Srisa Asoke, is listed as the leader of the For Sky and Earth Party. She laughs, dismissing it as "only on paper." However, since Ah Peum ran for MP in the late 1980s, it is not a far stretch to imagine her running for prime minister.

If and when this political party becomes active, Ah Peum may have some competition for the position of prime minister. Bier is a twenty-year-old former Asoke student who now volunteers at Srisa Asoke when he is not helping his uncle run a convenience store in Kanthalak, cultivating straw mushrooms out back, or studying law. Bier is not shy about his aspiration to be prime minister in twenty-five years. Until that time, he will earn his law degree, work hard, and live a moral life. Bier also revealed that he has "500 friends all across Thailand" who also hope to serve their country in the political arena. Bier declares that they will be a "new kind of politician" who is honest and hardworking.

These are individuals—not the Asoke movement as a whole—who seek to help Thai society through political influence. Nonetheless, Samana Bodhirak has publicly expressed his idea that the Prime Minister of Thailand should not receive a salary—that people working for the government and for the country should sacrifice and work for free. At present, it is primarily Asoke members who are willing to forfeit money for the common good.

An Ideal Society

Since Asoke members are working actively to build their own society as well as Thai society in general, it follows that the movement has formulated a theoretical model for their ideal society. In their self-told history, Srisa Asoke leaders describe this model:

> *Conditions Leading to Utopia*
> Pau Than Bodhirak laid down five conditions for a Buddhist social system. They are *freedom, fraternity/sorority* [state of being brothers and sisters], *peace, efficiency,* and *integrity.* Intertwining these conditions is complicated but enables the system to function. For example, freedom means free from defilements. First of all, one must be free from attachment to materials—physical property, personal belongings, jewelry, and so on. This will lead to sharing and giving away without wishing it to be paid back. Sharing or giving away causes fraternity/sorority. Givers are always loved. The feeling of love among brothers and sisters who are born from the same "uterus of hearts" or "relatives in Dharma" will lead to peace. Peaceful living and love among brothers and sisters will last long and cause cooperation and harmony. No competition, no fighting, no taking things from each other, no policemen, no soldiers, and no weapons are necessary. Efficiency in humankind will be improved because people cooperate, share, and help each other. Creativity, technology, and new discoveries will be shared and used to better the environment and human lives. Standards of living of people will be improved and integrity will be maintained. The people with integrity are usually constructive but not attached to what is created. Instead they value charity. They give things away. By this practice, a new cycle of freedom, fraternity/sorority, peace, efficiency, and integrity will roll over again and again. Can a utopia be possible? The answer is up to the people.

When I asked Srisa Asoke residents, "What is the perfect society like?" none articulated this model, although most touch on at least one of the five concepts (freedom, fraternity/sorority, peace, efficiency, and integrity). Some residents gave a clearly Buddhist answer:

> Ah Kaenfa: The perfect society is a society that has people who are perfect. It is a society in which people are empty of defilements. They don't have defilements at all. . . . The perfect society is the society of the Noble Ones because they are not wicked, they are not greedy, they do not gather in. They sacrifice for society. There is only giving, not taking. This is perfect.

> Ah Wichai: The perfect society is—every person just thinks about giving and—just giving is all. If you give your time, if you give your life, your money, if you give your—just all. [He laughs.] It's very easy!

A few individuals like Mae Pranee focused on economics:

> The perfect society is capable of depending on itself by having a sufficient economy, and then capable of helping other societies. For example, like the society Srisa Asoke [she laughs].

Others emphasized human relationships and only basic material development:

> Ah Komwai: The perfect society, in my thoughts, the perfect society doesn't have anything much, na krap. It can help itself. It is not necessary to have many materials. People are smiling and cheerful; they are *phii nong* together. We even refuse some materials for ourselves. . . . But actually, my dream is to be able to depend on ourselves and have everyone be *phii nong*, to depend on ourselves so we don't have to depend on society—we don't have to have lots of cars and computers, we weave our own cloth, use our own fertilizer, and whatever, use our own. This is a big dream!

> Ah Chuan: It is likely to be a society that has loving-kindness toward each other, hospitality, has sympathy for each other, and tries to help each other. Also, that is, a society that exists together with peace and happiness. Then it is able to depend on itself and take good care of the environment so that it is possible to live well together, krap. Use the most benefits from nature; that is, live with nature more than using benefits from technology, but I don't mean resist technology. Some technology is good, but it can make many things become lost. We must choose the things that have usefulness. . . . I think it should be like this, krap.

Still other members such as Ah Sompan responded with general qualities:

> The perfect society has generosity, love, honesty, not taking advantage of each other. Even the poor can be perfect because we are not measuring numbers of the economy. We are measuring absolute peace that arises in that society.

And finally, Mua said it was not possible to say for sure:

> To say what is perfect is difficult. Sometimes a society that eats fully, sleeps fully, is *sabai*, and doesn't have to think much is not perfect because it is a so-

ciety that passively responds to wants. The society that has some conflict, some fighting, but tries to practice Dharma, doesn't look correct but has happiness. If I say perfect, what is it like? It's hard to say, because I haven't yet seen what is perfect—there is only developing little by little.

The ideal society as imagined by these Srisa Asoke residents sounds a good deal like the direction their community is heading. Clearly, they wish for all Thai people the kind of *Santi Asoke* (Peace without Sorrow) they seek for themselves.

Conclusion

One day while sitting on a bus in Bangkok, inching along through streets clogged with other buses, taxis, *tuk tuks*, Mercedes and Toyotas with lone drivers, and kamikaze motorcyclists, I occupied my time by observing my fellow passengers. Young women were adorned in pastel polyester suits with miniskirts, salon-styled nails and hair, and high heels. Men tried to look nonchalant in their hot, uncomfortable Western ties, slacks, and oxford shoes. Teenagers sporting platform tennis shoes and streaked hair clutched shopping bags full of goods looted during the siege on the mall. Many of these modern chic urbanites had cell phones or Walkmans attached to their ears. I thought despondently, these people are not remotely interested in what the Asoke movement is doing. Thirty years ago when the Asoke movement began, Buddhadasa Bhikkhu asked a similar question: "Who, in an expanding consumer society, is interested in enlightenment?" (Tambiah 1978:129).

Later, I described my frustration to the abbot at Santi Asoke and asked what we could do to encourage more Thais to have the "right view." He responded with typical Buddhist acceptance of the way things are: "Those with wisdom will come—the others, we cannot help." Back on the bus shortly after this conversation, I looked out the window as we crossed railroad tracks crowded with squatter shacks of corrugated tin and cardboard, and a hand-painted sign above a food stall caught my eye:

Help Each Other
IMF Era
Rice and Curry 10 baht

I felt a surge of hope. There *are* people outside the Asoke group who at least value cooperation and sacrifice, and who might be sympathetic to the Asoke movement's endeavors.

The Asoke movement aids Thai society in a wide variety of ways that coalesce into "right development" according to Buddhism. Unlike so many critics who pass judgment and do nothing, the Asoke movement has identified problems in its society and has taken action in culturally and environmentally appropriate ways. The Thai public's response to the Asoke movement has been mixed, but this is not discouraging to Asoke members. As one Asoke supporter at the New Year's Festival explained to me, "Everyone is looking for a *tang auk*, a solution or a 'way out.' Asoke is one solution. It is not right for everyone." Regardless of whether or not they can convert more outsiders to the Asoke movement, Asoke members will continue to make sacrifice, to help their *phii nong* in Thai society as a central element of their Buddhist practice.

Notes

1. The literacy rate in Thailand is quite high: 96 percent for men and 92 percent for women. However, the Asoke movement does make casette tapes of sermons so that their Dharma is accessible to people who cannot read.

2. "Right understanding" or "right view" is the first step of the Eightfold Path.

3. At the time of research, the exchange rate was roughly forty-two baht to one US dollar.

4. It seems that the need to sell large amounts cheaply overrode the distaste for produce grown with chemicals.

5. According to my observations, 500-700 is a more accurate number. They may use 1000 as an average since roughly 3000 people attend the Pleuksek festival at Srisa Asoke in April, and Srisa Asoke used to host the New Year's Festival as well before it grew too large. The number is also high because many people who attend the workshops are repeat visitors.

6. This information was taken from an unpublished Asoke pamphlet titled, "Three Professions to Save the Nation" given to me by the librarian at Santi Asoke, Bangkok.

Chapter 7

A Day in the Life of Four Women

As a more focused approach to participant observation, I "shadowed" four different women of Srisa Asoke, each throughout a single day. Ratana, Jantima, Siriwarn, and Tangbun are roughly the same age (between thirty-eight and forty), but they differ in geographical and ethnic backgrounds, marital status, motivations for joining Asoke, and participation in the community. By illuminating everyday life in Srisa Asoke Community, this ethnographic narration provides another vantage point to view how Asoke beliefs and practices build the individual, community, and (to a lesser extent) society. In addition, detailing the lives of women in an Asoke community reveals a greater degree of gender equality in Asoke lay and monastic life than in "outside" Thai society where women are expected to follow the path of marriage, not religion. The first section sketches this larger context.

Women and Gender in Thailand, Buddhism, and Asoke

These four days in the lives of Asoke women may be better appreciated in the broader context of women and gender relations in Thailand and Buddhism. There are two basic assumptions about women and gender in Southeast Asia: 1) There is complementarity in gender relations, and 2) women have higher status and more rights than in other parts of Asia (Atkinson and Errington, 1990). These assumptions bear some truth. Unlike women in more patriarchal societies, Thai women are not subject to arranged marriages; they may choose their own mates and set up their own households (though the new couple may live with the bride's family at first). Thai women also have more access to family wealth through bilateral inheritance. In fact, before wage labor became the norm, Thai women had even more socioeconomic and spiritual power since women's control of household resources made it their responsibility to give donations to the temple. In contemporary Thai society, women still tend to manage family budgets even though they are not the primary wage earners. Regarding access to education, another strong indicator of gender equality, an equal number of males and females are enrolled in elementary school through sixth grade (the national requirement). Access to education and control of wealth give Thai women substantial bargaining power in household decision making and thus bring balance to gender relations.

Nevertheless, relatively higher female status and complementarity in traditional agrarian gender roles do not imply gender equality. Exploitation of women and male bias are well-established in Thailand. For example, although prostitution is illegal, it is a common custom for Thai men to *tiaw phuying*—to frequent coffee shops, bars, and massage parlors where they may hire female sex workers (Sinith 1998). Admittedly, some women choose this profession for the urban, material lifestyle it affords; however, many more women from poor rural areas enter the sex trade to support their families or are sold as young girls by desperate parents (Pasuk 1982; Sanitsuda 1990). Young Thai women are also heavily exploited by industry as they are elsewhere in the developing world. Female factory workers suffer long hours, fatiguing work, unsafe conditions, and little pay (Enloe 1989).

Moreover, Thai women are generally considered subordinate to men. A popular Thai saying, "Men are the front legs of the elephant and women are the hind legs," suggests that men are leaders and women are followers. Men do in fact dominate Thailand's public sphere in politics and religion, as well as in other ways. On one occasion during my service as a Peace Corps community forestry extension agent in Thailand, I attended a seminar organized by the district agricultural extension office to which forty farmers were invited—all men. Women were present, but only to serve lunch. I knew women in the villages who ran their farms alone because their husbands had gone to work in Bangkok or had died. Yet these women were denied access to knowledge solely on the basis of their gender. When I brought this point to the attention of my female coworker (who had a degree from the provincial agricultural college), she responded passively: "That's the way it is."

Anthropologist Niels Mulder (1996) proposes an alternate interpretation of this Thai saying: female "hind legs" provide support without which the elephant would collapse. During my Peace Corps service, the women I saw everyday in rural Kamphaeng Phet worked incredibly hard. They were responsible for all domestic labor including child care, cleaning, cooking, and tending home gardens, as well as working in the fields and engaging in secondary income-generating activities. Too often I saw their husbands sleeping under the house, drunk or hungover. I am quite sure that without the wives' "support," these households would indeed fall apart.

So as not to give the impression of stasis, a growing feminist movement in Thailand is fighting female exploitation and legal discrimination against women. There are finally female judges and MPs (as well as male supporters) who are in a position to make changes. Although it is still the case that a man's adultery is not grounds for divorce but a woman's is, "minor wives" are now illegal, and husbands may no longer sell jointly owned property without their wives' consent. With respect to these changes, Thai scholar William Klausner quotes the "Thai male chauvinist pigs" as saying, "The elephant seems to be walking backwards these days" (2000:294).

When Buddhism is brought into the mix, gender relations in Thailand become more complicated. Although the Buddha taught that all sentient beings can attain enlightenment and trained both *bhikkhus* (monks) and *bhikkhunis* (nuns) including his own step-mother, the Thai Sangha is dominated exclusively by men. Bhikkhunis are not recognized by the Thai Sangha due to the belief that the Theravada bhikkhuni lineage died out; according to Buddhist law, the ordination of bhikkhunis must take place in the presence of bhikkhus and a minimum of five elder bhikkhunis. Nonetheless, the extinction of the Theravada order of bhikkhunis is debated. Chatsumarn Kabilsingh, a professor from Thaamasat University who has written forty books on Buddhism, traveled to Sri Lanka recently to be ordained. Her return to Thailand as a bhikkhuni in residence at a Bangkok temple has caused considerable uproar (*The Economist*, November 8, 2001).

This bhikkhuni is an exception. More common throughout Thailand are *mae chii*—religious women who wear white, shave their heads, and take eight or occasionally ten precepts. *Mae chii* occupy a liminal space of neither bhikkhuni nor laywoman (*upasika*). *Mae chii* are not an accepted part of the Sangha and therefore don't teach or hold rituals; rather their activities include cooking, cleaning, washing, and taking care of temple grounds in exchange for food, shelter, and a small stipend (Rattigorn 2001). In this way, *mae chii* are subservient to monks and do not command respect from lay Buddhists (Sulak 1992). Though not ideal, this is the position open to women who wish to devote their lives to Dharma. Moreover, staying at a temple as a *mae chii* is less demeaning than begging on the streets for old or widowed women who have no other means to support themselves. Regrettably, since temples will not accept children, this option is not available to mothers.

According to Thai Buddhist scholar Narumon Hinshiranan, the apparent "spiritual inequality" expressed through the absence of bhikkhuni and the relatively inferior status of *mae chii* in Thai society results from ideological influences. She explains:

> In doctrinal Buddhism, a woman can attain enlightenment by herself through meditation and moral discipline. Hence, she is religiously self-sufficient. Since the female image in doctrinal Buddhism is equal to the male, gender oppression is not an issue. However, in popular Buddhism, it is believed that women can attain ultimate merit by supporting her male kin, especially her son, to become ordained in a Buddhist monastery. Consequently, women are seen as dependent on men for making merit and thus not religiously self-sufficient. Hence, popular Buddhism manifests gender bias. (Narumon 1993:1)

Narumon further suggests that women have different potential for spiritual attainment in popular Buddhism because they represent worldly attachment. British anthropologist Jane Bunnag attributes the worldliness of women to their image as seducer: "In Thailand, as in other Theravada Buddhist countries, women are believed to be the inferior sex because they epitomize those sensual pleasures which form the chief obstacle to any man's spiritual advancement" (1973:11). Alternately, women embody worldly attachment through a different, positive image: "This image is of the mother who nurtures the religion by bearing sons who will one day enter the Sangha and by providing sustenance on a regular basis to those whose membership in the Buddhist order makes them a 'field of merit'" (Keyes 1984: 223).

While women may be "religiously self-sufficient" according to doctrinal Buddhism, it does not necessarily follow that women are equal to men. It is important to remember that doctrinal Buddhism is also culturally embedded; that is, it is influenced by India's hierarchical caste system and patriarchal gender relations in which it emerged. Bringing this theoretical discussion back to my empirical study, the librarian at the Santi Asoke center in Bangkok gave the following reasons why she believes men are superior to women: According to the Buddha, women have five kinds of suffering that men do not have: menstruation, serving their husbands, moving to be with the husband's family, pregnancy and birth, and raising children. She also informed me that according to Buddhist scripture, I was born a woman because in my past life as a man, I broke the third precept with adultery; if I had been a woman, I would have been reborn as a dog. The librarian also asserted that women are naturally weaker than men both physically and in self-control. When I offered the anthropologist's position that perceptions about women vary in different cultures (i.e., while this view might be commonly accepted for Thai women, it was not for American women), the librarian insisted it was true for all women. For additional proof, she pointed out that Christianity maintains the same ideas: Eve was made from Adam's rib and she was the first to succumb to temptation by taking an apple from the Tree of Knowledge.

As I told Sikkhamat Chinda about this conversation, she made a sour face. She does not support the librarian's perspective. She allowed, "*Maybe* if there are two *types*—masculine and feminine—where masculine is strong and wise and feminine is weak and foolish, then I might believe in that theory." Sikkhamat Chinda declared that the librarian has this idea because someone else gave it to her, not because she has proven it for herself, and she dismissed what the librarian said as "just words." I then asked what Samana Bodhirak might say on the subject of gender equality. Sikkhamat Chinda recalled Pau Than saying publicly that women and men both can end suffering and work for society and that all people equally must die.

In contrast to outside Thai society, the Santi Asoke Buddhist Reform Movement provides women with more lifestyle options with higher status. Women who want to practice religion may enter an Asoke community as laywomen or enter the temple as *khon wat* or nuns (*sikkhamat*).[1] The status of *sikkhamat* in Asoke society is significantly higher than that of *mae chii. Sikkhamat* teach Dharma, give council to lay members, and participate in community decision making in the same ways Asoke monks (*samana*) do. In fact, female Asoke members may seek out nuns before monks. Many women expressed excitement when they learned that Sikkhamat Chinda was moving to Srisa Asoke since they are embarrassed to consult monks on certain issues and feel another woman would better understand their problems.

Still, the stations of Asoke *samana* and *sikkhamat* are not equal. First, there is disparity in the strictness of their practice: nuns uphold 10 precepts while monks abide by the 227 rules of the *Vinaya* code. Second, there is a forced ratio of four monks to one nun, and women are required to spend a longer amount of time than men at each stage approaching ordination. This means that once a woman passes forty years of age, she has little chance to ordain since she will have to wait for the appropriate number of monks to ordain first. Sikkhamat Chinda's explanation of this ratio is that it is harder to control women's behavior because women and men are raised differently in Thailand. Boys must be brave and not cry; if a girl cries, the adults let her carry on as if it is natural. Furthermore, if a girl has much confidence in something, they say it is "too much," and if she follows, they applaud.

In addition to having ordination privileges, single, separated, divorced, and widowed women with or without children may lead fulfilling and unstigmatized lives within the Asoke group. Whereas women wishing to reside at a conventional temple are not permitted to bring their children, mothers may live with their children in an Asoke community—or even within the temple domain as *khon wat* like Roun and Ah Plekuan. A few women who separated from their husbands confessed to me that they would have chosen the path of religion rather than marriage had they known it was possible. Ah Tangbun states plainly, "If I had met Asoke before, it is likely that I wouldn't have married." Ah Plekuan is another of countless Thai women who married following the social norm despite their perception of hardship:

> I was interested [in Asoke] because of the basic point that family life, of women, is suffering. She has to serve her husband. . . . Women—Asian women—must take care of their husbands, whether it has to do with sex, na ka, or washing clothes, cooking, taking care of the house, raising children, na [said in a singsong way]. . . . I don't like it. But nobody said to me, why do you have to get married? Nobody said that. [It is commonly believed that] for the perfect life, you have to get married. . . . Before, I didn't have faith that I could exist [alone]. I would have to have someone to protect me, so I'd have to find a man to marry.

When Ah Plekuan came to Srisa Asoke, she found a different "Buddhist" norm concerning marriage. Ah Plekuan explains, "The perfect life that is above marriage is like this: You have to be able to live by yourself—to be able to depend on yourself." Even though the Asoke group tends to encourage members to remain unmarried so they have more time and energy to practice Dharma and sacrifice to society, adults at Srisa Asoke are evenly split between single and married people. Ah Warn is one of several residents who disagree with the view that marriage is suffering. Her opinions on the Buddhist views of family and suffering are as follows:

> I have said that some parts of Buddhism, I don't yet agree. I think . . . for life to be perfect, we must have a family. If we don't have a family [in which we relate intimately with others], how will we know what problems we have? I think it's necessary, na; I think a family is necessary. Because I myself have not yet seen suffering. I have passed through these [five kinds of suffering] and I have not seen hardship. . . . I am a person that likes service; I like to help like this. I feel that being able to serve is something that gives me pride. I want to do it. And getting married, moving, and having a new family—this is testing to a higher level. If we live with a new family—can we go in with them? How is my husband's mother? If they come and act like this, how will we act with them? It also might be good luck, to encounter good parents of my husband. . . . Then they say childbirth is a hardship. I was lucky just the same. My childbirth was easy. They say raising a child is hardship, but raising a child is easy. He listens and he is good. There might be some stubbornness that is normal for a child. . . . We want him to have his own thoughts.

The contrast between the perspectives of Ah Warn, the librarian, and Ah Plekuan may be attributed to different social backgrounds, Ah Warn's good relationship with her husband, or personality. In any case, views and experiences of womanhood and marriage vary widely within Asoke society.

My own observations of gender relations at Srisa Asoke indicate a generally higher degree of equality than in outside Thai society. Women and men work equally hard together in every task, and women are not excluded from particular jobs except where dictated by Buddhist law (e.g., only men may serve food to monks due to the taboo against monks touching women). Women also have prominent leadership roles as nuns (Sikkhamat Chinda, soon to come), head of the village (Ah Oi), and the community liaison to the Kanthalak District Department of Welfare (Ah Peum). Furthermore, both men and women take an active, vocal part in decision making at community meetings. Cultural perceptions about women and men may persist in individual minds, but the Asoke movement itself has made some structural improvement in the status of women and gender relations.

The remainder of this chapter describes four days spent with four women at Srisa Asoke, prefaced with selections from their life history and motivations for joining Asoke. I "followed" other women as well, but I chose these four in particular because of their differences in backgrounds, marital status, activities in the community, and personalities, in addition to interesting events that occurred during our day together. While the narratives offer a glimpse of women's status and gender relations in Asoke society, the primary focus is how four specific people—who happen to be women—spend their days in an Asoke community.

Ratana

Ah Ratana is a pleasant but shy forty-year-old, single *khon wat* from central Thailand. Ah Ratana speaks with few words and moves without hurrying. The calm she exudes may be her personality or the effect of living in a Buddhist temple for fifteen years as a *mae chii*. Ah Ratana moved to Pathom Asoke near her home in Supanburi after deciding that Asoke's practice was truer to the Buddha's teachings than what she had been following in the conventional temple. She stayed at Pathom Asoke for a year as a *khon wat* before coming to Srisa Asoke a year ago. Ah Ratana is a rather private person, and she did not offer much information about her life history. Following are her brief responses to my questions concerning her initial interest in Asoke and her reasons for moving to Srisa Asoke:

> Before I knew about this place [Srisa Asoke], na ka, somebody suggested I go to Pathom Asoke to study, so I traveled to Pathom Asoke. I went many times to listen to the monks' sermons. I listened; then I understood well—I understood the sermon well—that eating vegetarian is merit, and eating meat is sin. So I stopped eating meat. At that time, I was ordained as a *mae chii*, learning from *mae chii*, so I just went to stay at Pathom Asoke. I wore a suit like this [she's wearing an indigo short-sleeved Thai farmer shirt and *phathung* with a small indigo scarf over her hair] and was a *khon wat*, with eight precepts.
>
> *JE: Why did you come to Srisa Asoke rather than stay at Pathom Asoke?* I read in a magazine, an Asoke magazine, na ka. They said here [Srisa Asoke] they have natural agriculture—they plant vegetables in large quantities. So I wanted to come and see, and I wanted to plant vegetables. I read in the magazine, they have rice farming too and harvesting and threshing. I was interested because before coming I never farmed rice. I eat rice, but I've never planted rice! So I intended to come here and while here, plant rice. And I did come, and after coming, I planted rice, and after planting, I harvested and threshed the rice. I felt I had happiness. I was happy to be a rice farmer.

Ah Ratana does not aspire to ordain as an Asoke nun, partly because she would not be able to keep money in a personal bank account since the tenth precept disallows the handling of money. Instead, she states, "My target is to reduce defilements, reduce things that are luxury, things that exceed necessity in life, like that. [To have] a life that is content with little, content with what one has, simple. To have happiness like this."

Tuesday, January 16, 2001

At 3:30 a.m. I reluctantly crawl from my sleeping bag into chilly air and splash cold water over my puffy eyelids. Outside, it is completely dark except for the stars, porch lights shedding dim light on paths, and cooking fires glowing from the kitchen. As I join other warmly dressed residents walking quickly to the Common Hall, we greet each other and comment on the cold. I have arranged to meet Ah Ratana for *tom wat chao*, the morning program of chanting and preaching. I arrive first, so I take two mats from a pile and kneel with the other early risers. There is quite a commotion as about 100 secondary students enter and seat themselves in long rows facing the monks. The sleepy students shuffle their feet and rub their eyes. They typically sleep for another hour and a half, but on Tuesdays they attend all temple activities as part of their education in morality. As I watch the students settle, Ah Ratana kneels quietly beside me. We smile and *wai* each other.

To begin *tom wat chao*, we *graap* three times in unison toward the museum where the sacred relics are housed. The first half hour of the program is devoted to chanting Pali prayers. Sitting position is important during this period: We kneel with backs straight and palms pressed together at chest level. After the monks introduce or begin each prayer, the laypeople join in. New members and guests who are unfamiliar with the prayers may read from a pamphlet printed in Thai script with Thai translations of the prayers. The easiest prayer, "Homage to the Buddha," has three lines repeated three times:

namo tassa bhagavato	(Homage to the Incomparable Blessed One)
arahato	(The Worthy Undefiled One)
samma-sambuddhassa	(The Perfectly Self-Awakened One)

The chanting's slow cadence and resonant intonation has a lulling effect, yet concentrating on enunciating the prayers sharpens one's focus.

For the sermon portion of *tom wat chao*, we settle into a more comfortable seating position: legs tucked to one side and arms relaxed. A common format for sermons at Srisa Asoke allows each monk a turn to speak. They generally do not collaborate on a single topic but address issues relevant to Asoke community life based on their observations. This morning, the resident monks talk to the students about the importance of discipline, cooperation, and being prepared. Here are a few snippets from their lessons. Monk one says: "Asoke means building a new society; daring to be a good thing; having more self-discipline, not just letting oneself go. When it's time for morning lineup—lineup. When it's time to work—work; time to stop work—stop. If not, you might not have time to eat. Be on time." Monk two says: "If you want to be on time, come early. If you are making food for 100 people, make for 101. If you see a yellow light, stop." Monk three says: "Older ones watch out for the younger ones." Monk four says: "Everyone must help plant vegetables." The last monk, the abbot, selects a folded piece of paper from a bowl, reads a question submitted by a student, and answers it. He continues with a few more questions, and the other monks add their thoughts as well. By 5:20 a.m. the students are quite restless. In response to commands issued by student leaders, they *graap* in unison to the monks, then to the adults, and file out row by row. After the students leave, the adults similarly show gratitude to the monks for their teachings and head out to work.

Outside the Common Hall, Ah Ratana and I speak to each other for the first time that morning. We ask if the other slept well and comment on the cold weather. Neither of us is much for small talk, so we walk in silence until I ask her what we will do today. "Work in the Cooperative Merit Garden" is her reply. We stop at the hand-tool shed for hoes and meet three others—Ah Chuan, Ah Tangbun, and Ah Jaenjop—on a bare plot of land next to the auto repair shop. We all attended the "Intensive Human Development" training over the weekend, and we are eager to literally "dig into" the new program for self-sufficient food production. Today's task is to plant seeds for tomatoes, yard-long green beans, and squash. After Ah Jaenjop marks along the edges so the spacing of holes will be even, we begin to dig eight-inch square holes, each in our own separate corner. We continue to dig toward each other throughout the morning with little conversation, pausing now and then to rest. Since this area had never been cultivated, the ground is as hard as cement, and our progress is slow. When the gong sounds at 8:45 a.m., we set our hoes aside and rinse our hands at a nearby spigot. Walking back to the Common Hall, Ah Ratana and I compare blisters.

Everyday at 9:00 a.m. residents receive Dharma before Eating. This might be a sermon by the monks or a special activity such as "how to vote" in an upcoming election.[2] This morning while we worked in the garden, Ah Tangbun convinced me to give a talk on the "4 Rs" to the students. Although I am not thrilled about public speaking—especially spur of the moment, in a foreign language, into a microphone, over a loudspeaker—it would be un-Thai, un-Asoke, and simply ungracious to refuse. Actually, I am well prepared for this morning's mini-lesson since I led several environmental education seminars in secondary schools as a Peace Corps volunteer. Ah Peum approaches me with a bucket of trash for visual aids and offers to assist. I first teach the students relevant English vocabulary such as *recycle, reuse, repair, reject* (the "Four Rs"), *plastic, paper, glass, pollution,* and *biodegradable* (this last word is a bit of a challenge). As Ah Peum pulls items out of her bucket, the students shout out, "Paper!" "Plastic!" or the name of the object in Thai, and then identify whether the item is "pollution" or can be "recycled." In this way, the students have an English lesson while they learn how to separate waste.

At 9:50 a.m. pots and dishes of food are loaded on trays with casters and offered to the monks sitting in their usual places on the platform. The first monk serves himself and passes the trays along to the next monk. A man at the opposite end takes the trays off the platform and sends them between our two rows of adult men and women seated facing each other. The children line up to serve themselves from a table at the back of the hall. Once everyone has dished up food, a student leads the meal reflection. We eat while watching a National Geographic special on giant reptiles. It is indeed "graphic" with its fighting and birthing scenes, but it does not seem to lessen anyone's appetite except my own. By 11:30 a.m. Ah Ratana and I are well nourished and well rested. We both need to brush our teeth, wash a few clothes, and tidy our living space, so we agree to meet again shortly at the garden-to-be.

At 12:15 p.m. the five diggers reassemble at the Cooperative Merit Garden. Our work areas are close enough to each other now to allow conversation. Among the three women, the discussion turns to marriage. Ah Tangbun asks if I think it strange that someone like Ratana never married. I respond that many American women choose to have a career instead of marrying, or perhaps they never find the right person, but can still support themselves with their jobs. We talk about the high rate of divorce, both in the United States and Thailand. I am surprised to learn that the divorce rate is increasing in Thailand, with more than 50 percent of marriages splitting up. Ah Ratana comments, "Women want help supporting themselves and their parents, but many men are out of work." Ah Tangbun adds, "Too many people hurry to get married. They don't think first—they see movies and want that life, but it is not real."

At last, there are no more holes to be dug. I am hot and sore and need a break; judging by the way Ah Jaenjop bends stiffly with a hand on his back, I am not the only one. We squat in the shade for a bit, have a drink of water, and plan the remaining work. We decide on a production line: Ah Tangbun goes first with one bowl of homemade fertilizer per hole, Ah Ratana and I follow with four to five seeds, Ah Jaenjop covers them with the dirt we had loosened, and Ah Chuan spreads rice hay over top. As we put the seeds in the ground, I notice that they are covered with pink powder. I ask Ah Ratana if she knows what it is, and she replies in the negative. I then ask her if it is a chemical, to which she responds, "Yes, I think it is a chemical." She frowns and then adds, "That's not good, eh?" I surmise it is a pesticide to keep insects and animals from eating the seeds before they germinate, and Ratana nods, indicating the possibility. When our store-bought seed cans are empty, I volunteer to water everything with a hose. With such a system, we complete our work rapidly, demonstrating the value of cooperation.

After Ah Ratana and I put our tools away and wash our hands thoroughly with soap, we stop to rest on a wooden platform in the shade. The time is just past 4:00 p.m. and we are in no hurry to go anywhere. We chat for a while about farming-related topics that Ah Ratana has seen in the news. Though Ah Ratana is reticent to talk about herself, she is happy to share opinions on issues that affect the community or the world. She asks if I heard about the concern for mad cow disease in Thailand. By coincidence, my husband had just sent me an article on this subject, so I give her a synopsis. We agree that being vegetarian when such a disease threatens the world's meat sources is a good thing. Ah Ratana then asks if I saw the news story last week on chicken farms. Since I had not, she describes how the chickens are kept in tiny cages all in a row. To Ah Ratana, the fact that the chickens are not free to move around is "pitiful" and "ugly." Ah Ratana next turns the conversation to Christianity and how I, a Christian, feel living in a Buddhist community. I assure her that I feel quite comfortable because each religion teaches people to live a good life and because Srisa Asoke residents have warmly welcomed me. Some time later, Ah Ratana and I part company for our much-needed baths. I also intend to eat dinner with the students since Ah Ratana does not eat after noon. Before I leave, we make a date for 6:00 p.m. to watch the students practice a "cultural show."

When we arrive at the Common Hall, it is already filled with colorfully costumed students warming up instruments, going over dance sequences, organizing props, and testing sound equipment. At this evening's rehearsal, the monks are "censoring" the show for anything that is not in line with Asoke morality since it will be performed in public. (The students are scheduled to perform at the new location of the Lemon Farm, the organic shop in Bangkok where Kwang and other Asoke members work). In this cultural show, male and female students perform folk dances to demonstrate "ancient" activities, accompanied by a band of fifteen students playing traditional Thai instruments. Four university students introduce and explain each dance, imitating popular comic variety show MCs. The dances portray farming, rice processing, cotton production, courtship, and games such as tug-of-war and dragon's tail. As the MCs introduce the finale about Srisa Asoke Community and agriculture that will "save the nation," the students line up and face the audience. They sing without accompaniment this time—just the ringing of clear, young voices. They have practiced well. After the gaiety of all that preceded, this serious exhibition of pride has a profound, uplifting effect. When the song ends, the audience claps enthusiastically. The monks approve this show with no modifications. It is now almost 8:00 p.m., so Ah Ratana and I end our day together on this high note.

Jantima

Ah Jantima is a thirty-eight-year-old rice farmer from Roi Et. She has the open, obliging nature of Isan folk, and she is earnest in her desire to better herself and her surroundings. She also loves to sing and dance. Ah Jantima came to Srisa Asoke three years ago with her two children, though her husband stayed home. The following paragraphs from Ah Jantima's life history point to her hardships, aspirations, and motivations for joining Srisa Asoke.

> Before I knew Asoke, I feel I was a tense person. I am the youngest child, and my mother died when I was thirteen. I had to help myself a great deal because my father had a new wife, and when he went to live at his sister-in-law's, the sister-in-law saw the family and felt it was a burden. I watched them make a living, [and I thought] there should be more development than this, I should learn more than this. So I went to Bangkok to continue school at Ram Kamphaeng [University] for one year. . . . But I didn't graduate according to what I had hoped. I felt like what I learned, I didn't bring it into use. . . . Just then, my father wanted me to come home, so I went home.
>
> So there was a person that I knew—
>
> *"A father of a child. We came to know each other. He said he was going to go set up a family in the countryside. He had a tiny baby, a*

> *warm family, someone I knew what was in his heart. I wanted it"* [she is singing a song].

I thought this life should have a house, rice and crop fields, have a reasonable place to work and eat, and have people who know what's in each other's hearts, live reasonably, close to each other, living together, good-naturedly. This much—family life—should be enough. But as I went on, this wasn't so, because problems arose later on. There were a great many. . . . It wasn't the genuine happiness of humans. Sickness came due to tenseness related to the economic state in the family—you have to take responsibility for the children, take much responsibility in the family. . . . I need to develop; I need to work outside as well as in the family. But he needed me to only watch over the family, not go work outside, go train, go work for the community because just our family, this is good already. These are thoughts that were never equal.

I went to the field to harvest rice and I heard—I listened to reports—friend to friend—reports of every life problem. I listened to reports of curing of sickness and disease by eating natural food.[3] Our life is like what we eat. So I brought [this information] to follow in practice—I ate vegetarian to see first—would my health be better? . . . And then I made snacks from brown rice and sold them; I made soy milk and sold it; I made whatever was not made from meat and sold it—after I listened to some Dharma and I was afraid of sin increasing [by killing animals]. Before, I wasn't very afraid. If you go to the temple, you have to kill fish—a good piece of meat, a big fish—to respect the monks, and so my mother who had died could eat some. . . . Really, this was not right—When I listened to sermons by Asoke monks, [I understood] it was not true. Things that have died cannot eat. It was clear so I did not continue to do it. But I gave food to the monks to eat so I could continue to do goodness.

At the time, I fought with outside society and my husband, who did not yet have "right view." It was difficult. I had conflict with many things. . . . I endured little by little until my children—I had begun to know Asoke in the year 1996. At the beginning of [1998], my father died. The time before that I couldn't come because my father was still living.[4] . . . That year, my son lived at the temple by himself. My daughter and I were at home with his father. In 1999, I let my daughter . . . enter the new school here, third grade. Her father gave her permission to come. He did not oppose—he did not oppose, but he still could not come. But it didn't matter. I asked for one thing—to let my daughter and me come to the temple and be able to practice Dharma that was good, be able to go to a school that was good.

Nowadays, I go home at times of rice harvest and transplanting to help my husband, to be obliging in the things he is lacking. He still wants to keep the family, but our family—the target is, I want it to be a family that practices Dharma, all of the family. I don't want anyone to slip out. I want everyone to come to have the same line of thought and help in the [Asoke] group because this group has few people. *JE: Do you think your husband will follow you to live here?* I hope so. It would be a great thing if he would come for sure. He has said that he will come when he is ready.

Ah Jantima has come to Srisa Asoke so that her children will learn about morality, sacrifice, and the Three Professions to Save the Nation. She asserts that if they must return to Roi Et, they will continue to develop in these aspects. Along with this personal goal, Ah Jantima adds, "I would like our group of Asoke people to be strong, to be the axis for the way farmers practice—rural people who are trying to depend on themselves without hardship. This is my target."

Wednesday, January 17, 2001

At 4:00 a.m., Srisa Asoke residents assemble at the Common Hall for the weekly community meeting. I sit down cross-legged on the mat Ah Jantima saved for me, and we greet each other with a *wai* and "*Jalern thaam, ka*" ("May your Dharma progress"). For warmth, Ah Jantima is wearing a ski cap and an old cream-colored cardigan sweater over her usual gray short-sleeved shirt and gray and maroon striped *phathung*. As the meeting starts, I glance around and count twenty-nine women and seventeen men, plus five monks.

Ah Oi, speaking into a microphone, facilitates the meeting. We first amend and approve last week's minutes and then move through old business printed in the agenda. The microphone is passed to each speaker.

1. Ah Plekuan announces that many student groups are coming in the next few weeks for training.
2. Ah Jing Jing presents the plan drawn up at the "Intensive Human Development" training to increase self-sufficiency in food production. It was approved unanimously. He then urges anyone interested in helping with the planning to meet this evening.
3. Em reports the students' progress with their Lemon Farm show and announces the date and time of the actual performance.
4. Mootao reviews last year's finances. The meeting was going smoothly until this point. Even though Mootao had drawn tables on a blackboard to illustrate expenditures and income in different areas, some numbers are wrong and Mootao becomes horribly confused. Ah Kaenfa finally gets up to help, but after an hour, everyone is anxious to move on.
5. Ah Din Pieu gives a brief year-end report for the Goodwill Store.
6. A member from a national Asoke organization for "product development" makes a pitch for this activity as a way to develop oneself through work, to get income from better products, and to exist as a sign of successful Dharma practice.

By the time we finish with old business, it is already after 6:00 a.m. Ah Oi asks the presenters of new business to limit themselves to two minutes. She skips over the first three points printed in the agenda, but requests reports about 4) the amount of rice at the community mill and 5) a fair taking place next month at Sima Asoke. In the last portion of the meeting, "Subjects to Consider,"

Ah Oi calls for people to help receive training participants on the 23rd and 25th, requests additional help in the kitchen for the trainings, and asks community members to consider a proposal that the students lead a training in the next month.

At 6:45 a.m., an hour later than usual, the meeting is finally adjourned. Ah Jantima gives me a wobbly ride on the back of her bike over to the trash recycling center. Inspectors from Santi Asoke arrived the night before, so we hurry to help Ah Tangbun tidy this area. When we arrive, we discover that the dozens of bags of unsorted trash, here just two days prior, are gone. Ah Tangbun is already there sweeping, and she tells us blandly that Ah Peum had the students take everything to the city dump. Ah Peum deemed it too much work to do—we would never catch up, and she wanted everything to look clean for the inspectors. We share our thoughts while we sweep, straighten piles, and separate the trash collected yesterday evening. Ah Jantima expresses irritation: "We were doing *too well*, so it was taking too long." Ah Tangbun says thoughtfully, "Dumping the trash fixes only the face of the problem, not the heart. The problem is there is too much work and not enough people to do it." She sighs, "This is the problem all over the world; we cannot keep up." I say, "It's a shame. If the community is trying to promote the Three Professions to Save the Nation, then perhaps garbage ought to be more important." I also suggest that if everyone had come and worked for an hour, the entire garbage mess would have been eliminated.

At 8:40 a.m. the gong sounds for Dharma before Eating. Ah Jantima and I leave Ah Tangbun and stop at the kitchen to wash our hands. Reun (Ah Jantima's friend from home) greets us and asks for our help with an aluminum tub heaped with green onions. They must be stripped down to two or three shoots so the greens can be used for cooking and the bulbs replanted. We agree without hesitation and settle on the cement-slab floor to work. While we peel, we have an English lesson at Ah Jantima's request. Reun tries the basics for a few minutes before leaving us with a laughing "*Oiy*! I can't!" Around 10:15 a.m., Reun and her student assistants bring bowls of food to the middle of the kitchen floor and sit around them to eat. Since Reun and the students are all from the Northeast, the food they prepared for themselves is typical Isan fare—*nam prik* with raw vegetables, curried eggplant, and sticky rice. We join them, and Ah Jantima easily switches to her native Isan (Lao) dialect. When Reun asks if I can speak their language, I smile innocently and say, "I can't speak Lao"—in Lao, of course. Thais always find this enormously funny. When the burst of laughter subsides, the group quizzes me on my knowledge of Lao words for different food items and common phrases.

After a half hour, Ah Jantima balances the aluminum tub of green onion stubs on the back of her bike and takes them to the garden. Since the onions have taken my seat, I borrow Ah Warn's bike and ride over to meet her. While we are planting the onion stubs, Ah Jantima asks if I miss my husband. We commiserate about how hard it is living away from our husbands, and how it feels as if we are living in two separate worlds simultaneously. By asking if I am afraid that my husband will find someone new, she vocalizes her own fears about her relationship. Ah Jantima says being at Srisa Asoke with her children is the next best choice to living together as a family, but (unlike some women in the community) she hopes her husband will soon join them, and that one day they will buy a house in the community.

We finish with the onions around noon. Ah Jantima invites me to relax at her place while she washes clothes. I feel guilty sitting idly while others work, so I decide to sweep the floor and stairs. Just as Ah Jantima hangs the last item to dry, Ah Din Pieu (the assistant chair of the new farming committee) arrives to enlist Ah Jantima's aid in scouting out new spots to plant vegetables. I still have Ah Warn's bike, so we take a leisurely ride through the community searching for suitable areas. Roughly an hour and a half later, we pass by Ah Daeng's place. She and Ah Tangbun are working at a table in the shady space under the house, so we go over to investigate. They are making posters to instruct the students how to make herbal medicine. Ah Jantima has some knowledge of natural medicine, so she offers her input. Ah Daeng and I have only exchanged small talk before this, so the conversation is dominated by her curiosity about me. As we chat, they jot down directions on notebook paper and Ah Tangbun—who has the neatest writing—copies everything onto poster board.

When we hear the hourly time announcement "1500 hours" over the loudspeaker, Ah Jantima jumps up and excuses herself. It is time to instruct the elementary students in the Three Professions to Save the Nation. The children are already gathering under some shady trees in the village, and when Ah Jantima arrives, the student leaders issue the lineup command. Organization is no small task for thirty 6- to 11-year-olds. They shuffle themselves around, shortest to tallest, outstretching arms for proper spacing, pushing and teasing each other, until Ah Jantima admonishes them to hurry. When the students are seated, Ah Jantima prepares them for this afternoon's chores. She explains to the children that they are doing important work: garbage feeds fertilizer, fertilizer feeds plants, and plants feed people. She then requests volunteers for the tasks of watering, recycling mushroom cultivation bags, and mixing fertilizer. Since Ah Peum is overseeing the fertilizer processing, Ah Jantima and I spend the next two hours going back and forth between the waterers and recyclers. In addition to teaching the children, we also act as referees, calling fouls and time-outs.

After Ah Jantima sends the students to the kitchen for their dinner, we head back to the house she shares with Ah Tangbun and their three daughters.[5] We putter in her garden for a bit, weeding, watering, and collecting vegetables for dinner. The two older daughters arrive with rice from the kitchen, light the small charcoal cooker, chop our vegetables, put them in a pot of slowly boiling water, and flavor the soup with soy sauce. When Ah Tangbun emerges from the bathroom with her freshly bathed three-year-old, we sit down to eat. Afterward, I help clean up and then return home for my own bath.

At 6:30 p.m. Ah Jantima and I attend the farming committee meeting at the unfinished guest facility next to the Common Hall. Roughly twenty-five people are ready to settle the details of the new plan for self-sufficiency in food production. Ah Jantima suggests the new planting areas she and I investigated earlier in the day; everyone agrees upon areas to cultivate first as well as who should be the caretakers of each plot. We also discuss the cultivation methods to be used. At the "Intensive Human Development" training, natural-farming expert Ajaan Udom had talked about the Japanese method developed by Fukuoka, which stipulates no plowing (or hoeing), no chemical fertilizers nor insecticide, and no weeding.[6] Ah Jaenjop is experimenting with this method in the fields away from the community. While he is having success, Ah Jaenjop points out that initially, preparing the soil without digging may take a month or longer. The group concedes that in order to reach the goal of 5000 kilos of food by the festival in April, they would have to forgo this aspect and prepare the soil in the conventional way (hoeing). By 7:45 p.m. everyone seems satisfied with what was decided. Ah Jantima lingers to chat with a friend who just returned from visiting her family, so I say goodnight and thank her for a terrific day.

Siriwarn

Ah Warn is a vivacious thirty-nine-year-old Thai-Chinese woman who spent her younger years in Bangkok's Chinatown attending school and helping in her parents' noodle shop. She and her husband Ah Wichai (an "unemployed land developer" whom she met in Chinese class) have one ten-year-old son. Ah Warn came to Srisa Asoke primarily for her son's benefit. They intend to try living at Srisa Asoke for two years before deciding as a family whether or not to stay permanently. In our interview, Ah Warn spoke about why her nuclear family chose to join the Asoke group and move to Srisa Asoke:

> We went to many places, to know each temple, and their practice. . . . Monks that are very good, they might have them. But the monks that we saw . . . mmm . . . came, came to religion to make a living. Even a person I'm close with, my neighbor who used to buy and sell medicine, he said he worked but didn't have money, didn't have savings. But about three years after he ordained as a monk, he has loaned out 100,000 baht at interest [about US$2380]. Being a monk like this is good! It's not heavy work, and you can make a lot of money too! [said with sarcasm] We see this and think, aw, religion is like *this*? . . . About precept three, about relations with women—they have them. Some [women] might ask to stay in the monks' hut. It's an activity that's—that's ugly. . . . Such that I don't respect, I don't have faith in this business. Right? It's about the monks. I don't respect them as monks. They're the same as people all over the world. . . .
>
> We read [about Asoke] in a newspaper—we saw it in the paper just like [the other temples]. We went to Santi Asoke to see what the temple was like. . . . As soon as we entered, my heart said, "Eh? This temple doesn't have a donation cabinet! And the monks sleep in tiny huts!" I didn't see that they had any wealth—fans, refrigerators—none of the things we had seen before. They didn't have the things that afford convenience. Little tiny huts, like that. Uh, these monks are *good*. They don't use money, don't wear shoes, nothing. Eve-

rybody who lives in this community, Santi Asoke, dresses alike. . . . The fabric was not fabric like, oh ho! so fine, costing several hundred [baht] a meter. . . . Oh! This is so great, being frugal. This way, they had money left over for sure.

We went to donate money to them, but they would not take our money. We were surprised! What?! Other places ask for money first! Here they said, "If you do not come seven times and do not read seven books, if you do not have understanding about what we do here, we will not take donations. At least, you will know when you donate what they are going to do with the money. If you don't know what they're going to do with your money, why will you donate?" . . . These were distinct points—their dress and receiving money.

Then we went in to see the school because we think that the teaching of children is an important issue in a community. We went in to see their education, how they studied, and what "*sin daen, ben gnan, chan wicha*" meant. We had one child and we wanted our child to be this way. So we started to send our child to study on Sundays. . . . We started to become more intimate [with the temple]. That is, we love our child, na, and wherever our child is, we must be there too. There were many families who wanted their children to be good, but the parents did not come. The children might do well, but when they returned home, if their parents hadn't gone to study, they would not be able to tell their children about the knowledge the teachers taught. . . .

So we talked. In our family we have meetings, discussions. . . . Wichai, my husband, he studied and he understood Dharma more than us. He understood Asoke much more than us. He started to meet with our family: "Is this a good place to live?" I think in Asoke there is much that is very interesting. Even its culture, customs. What is important is that it is building society for our child as well. So we were interested. We consulted each other and studied. We went to see many [Asoke] places. . . . We studied each place and talked about Srisa Asoke, that we should come.

JE: What target do you have in living here? Personally, for myself, religion is not profound, na ka. . . . I myself have not yet decided to live as a person in the community. I have business; I have parents; I believe that I must have responsibilities on the outside. That is, for myself, if it is not good, I am prepared to leave. But living here—what will our child receive? The principal target is our child. We would like our child to be a person of resource who does well for society. We do not want him to be like teenagers all over, that is, study high, but not be able to give anything to the earth, to help anybody—even themselves, they can't help.

Ah Warn had four reasons for choosing Srisa Asoke over other Asoke communities: 1) There was an American English teacher (now gone); 2) the leaders have higher education and progressive thoughts; 3) the community is safe; and 4) the natural environment gives children a "gentle heart."

Thursday, February 8, 2001

At 5:00 a.m. Ah Warn gets her son Chim up and ready for school, and then goes right back to sleep. I know this because I am sleeping in the next room. (Kwang and her friends are visiting from Bangkok, so I vacated her house to give them more room.) I hear Ah Warn stirring again around 7:00 a.m., so I get dressed, roll up my bedding, and come downstairs. Ah Warn is squatting next to her "kitchen sink"—a spigot over a plastic tub on the ground—scrubbing out a few pans she left to soak the night before. She is wearing a Western-style light blue denim short-sleeved shirt and an indigo *phathung* someone in the community recently gave to her (she had never worn one before but finds it quite comfortable). When she sees me, she says "Good morning" in English and offers me coffee. Coffee is not drunk at Srisa Asoke, possibly because it is a luxury or because caffeine is an addictive drug. Ah Warn admits coffee is one thing she has not yet given up, so she hides her water heater and drinks coffee in private. While Ah Warn rinses out the pans, I squat on a low stool, hands wrapped around my steaming mug of Nescafe, sugar, and non-dairy creamer. Ah Warn sets the dishes aside to dry and mixes herself a cup. We sit and chat about the newly elected Prime Minister Thaksin, places we have visited in Thailand, and how we met our husbands.

Just before 8:00 a.m. Ah Plekuan stops by for some "supplemental food." Ah Warn offers her a substantial drink made from dry cereal powder and hot water. Without much cajoling, Ah Plekuan also shares what is left of a special Chinese New Year cake. Chim also comes home for breakfast at this time. He pours the same cereal powder into a bowl and eats it dry with a spoon. Chim tends to be a moody child, but this morning he is excited. With his mouth full, he tells his mother how he was praised for being hardworking during the morning work period. Ah Warn expresses great pleasure and then tells her son to keep his food in his mouth. Chim dances around and blows cereal powder out of his mouth to annoy his mother. Ah Warn calmly warns him to stop a few more times until she loses her temper and scolds him for acting in an "ugly" way. When Chim realizes he has pushed his mother too far, he gulps down the last spoonful, gives Ah Warn an exaggerated smile showing his powder-covered teeth, hugs her, and runs off to class.

If Ah Warn's kitchen had a door, it would be a revolving one: As Chim races out, he collides with Ah Jantima who has come to inform Ah Warn that community members are making dinner for the students that night. Ah Plekuan greets the new visitor before excusing herself to return to work. Just then, Ah Tangbun's twenty-year-old son Witthiyu stops in to use Ah Warn's phone. He needs to page his friends over the loudspeaker because they are going into town. Ah Jantima continues on her message errand as Witthiyu's friends arrive in a pick-up truck. Ah Warn gives the boys money to buy noodles while they're in town so she can make *radna* for the students' dinner.

As the truck pulls away from the house, Ah Warn and I escape before anyone else appears. We take her water heater over to the old ladies, three of whom are working at looms in front of their house. They drink the hot water plain, declaring it is good for the health. The old ladies resume weaving, one in solid indigo, one in plaid for *phakhoma* (a cloth used for a man's sarong, headwrap, baby sling, etc.), and one in an intricate *matmee*, the traditional diamond design of Isan. Ah Warn and I take turns on a loom strung with natural colored thread. As we fumble with the foot pedals and shuttle, we marvel at the skill of our grandmothers who so quickly and confidently weave pre-dyed thread into beautiful patterns. Our next stop with the water heater is the clinic. We make herbal tea for four sick students and stay awhile to cheer them up.

Around 10:30 a.m. we make the short walk back to Ah Warn's house, passing Ah Porn (Ah Jaenjop's wife) sweeping her front walkway. Ah Warn invites her neighbor to join us for a lunch of *guaytiaw* (a generic term for Chinese noodles). We get started chopping garlic and chilies, and soon Ah Porn brings over some vegetables to add to the mix. Two other women, Ah Jap Jai and Ah Daeng, stop by on some business and stay for lunch. These three visitors squeeze in around the tiny low table and begin to gossip in Lao. From what I could follow in the conversation, I learn that Ah Ai's wife wants a divorce and is taking their daughters back to Bangkok and that Ah Jantima is so sensitive that when someone criticized her the day before for snacking all day long, she cried. Ah Warn seems occupied with her cooking and does not enter the discussion. As we eat, the topic turns to raising children since all women present (except me) are mothers.

About an hour and a half later, the visitors leave Ah Warn and me to clean up alone. Ah Warn had not been her usual animated self through lunch; now she reveals that she does not like that kind of talk gossiping about other people's personal business. Furthermore, she does not like it when everyone speaks Lao because it excludes others (like the two of us) who are not native Lao speakers. At around 12:30 p.m. Ah Plekuan reappears hungry for *som tham* (unripened papaya salad, a staple of Isan). We completely forgot that we talked with Ah Plekuan that morning about making *som tham*. To save face, Ah Warn lightly scolds Ah Plekuan for coming too late as we had already eaten; then she gathers the ingredients for *som tham* and we begin our second lunch. Ah Plekuan asks if Ah Warn could take her and her daughter into town for a dentist appointment at 2:00 p.m. Ah Warn is glad for any excuse to go into town and "open her eyes," so she agrees readily. In the meantime, Ah Plekuan returns to her station at the information desk, Ah Warn finishes some paperwork for her husband who is away on Asoke business, and I catch up on field notes.

When the children get out of class, the five of us—Ah Warn, Chim, Ah Plekuan, her daughter, and I—climb into Ah Warn's truck and drive five kilometers to town. We park near the dentist and split up. Ah Warn, Chim, and I go across the street to the computer center where Chim plays video games and I check e-mail. Ah Plekuan and her daughter emerge from the dentist about an hour later, and we all walk up the block to a bakery. Ah Warn lets Chim pick out a few sweets, joking, "Don't think this is for your birthday!" She explains to me that giving birthday gifts is not a Thai custom and then teases Chim, "You should give gifts to your mother on your birthday because she could have died giving birth to you!" Chim is paying less attention to his mother than he is the goodies in the case in front of him. We each (except Ah Plekuan) point to what appeals to us most and we buy two of each. Ah Warn and I split the bill since no one else has money. Before going home, we stop at the shop owned by the uncle of Bier (the "future prime minister") to pick up *radna* sauce. On the ride back to Srisa Asoke, we eat our sweets and play a rhyming game, the rules of which elude me.

We arrive home at 4:00 p.m. to learn from someone riding by on a bicycle that there is a fire out past the cremation site. Ah Warn and I grab some old towels and hop on bikes to help. As we near the cremation site, we meet a crowd of people with empty buckets, singed blankets, and sooty faces. They report that the fire has been completely extinguished. In this abrupt end to our excitement, we never discover what started the fire. Ah Warn and I walk our bikes back to her house to start the *radna*. My jobs are to cut the fresh noodle sheets into one by three inch strips (the noodles Witthiyu and his friends bought in town) and shred cabbage. A couple high-school-aged boys who come looking for food at 5:00 p.m. are put to work as my assistants. Unfortunately, we do not finish the *radna* in time for the students to eat. At 6:00 p.m. the gong calls everyone for a special holiday service. Ah Warn says she needs to clean up first, so I go ahead of her.

Today is Magha Puja Day (also known as Sangha Day or Fourfold Assembly), one of five major Buddhist holy days. It commemorates the gathering of 1250 monks to listen to the Buddha speak. The Fourfold Assembly consisted of four factors: All 1250 monks were saints, all of them were ordained by the Buddha himself, they assembled by themselves without any prior call, and it was the full moon day of Magha, the third lunar month. Srisa Asoke celebrates this holiday by gathering to admire the moon in their lovely park landscaped with flowers, a green lawn, trees, and a reflecting pool. A solitary monk leads the chanting of Pali prayers and gives a sermon about the meaning of the day and the power of nature to transmit Dharma.

Ah Warn does not make it to the service. When I return an hour later, she has already taken a shower and has just finished cleaning up the kitchen. I help her carry the large pot of *radna* out front so that hungry students will see there is food. The first students approach empty-handed, and Ah Warn admonishes them to get their spoons and bowls because things are missing from her house. She then tells me that while we were in town, someone broke into the storeroom and stole dry noodles and a new battery-operated toothbrush. Ah Warn takes me into the storeroom to show me how things were in disarray. "See? At first I thought it was mice." She then points to the space where the wall stops short of the ceiling, indicating that a child could crawl over from the bathroom. She knew it was Mick and his friends because this was not their first offense. Stealing has become a problem in community, and Ah Warn is frustrated that nothing is being done about it. The students reappear with their bowls and spoons. Ah Ai and Ah Komwai also join us for dinner, and Ah Warn relays her story about the theft. At

7:45 p.m. I excuse myself to take a shower. When I come out, the students and Ah Komwai have left, and Ah Warn and Ah Ai are talking quietly together. Judging by the gossip I heard over lunch, I suspect Ah Ai may have some things he would like to talk over with his good friend in private. I plead sleepiness, say goodnight, and go up to my room to read by flashlight.

Tangbun

Ah Tangbun is an intense forty-year-old rice farmer from Ubon Ratchathani. Her given name is Dara, but like many Asoke members, she has been renamed by Samana Bodhirak. Her new name meaning "way of merit" fits her quite well, as Ah Tangbun's life is focused on traveling the road to sainthood. Ah Tangbun separated from her husband three years ago and brought her three children to Srisa Asoke. She now keeps five precepts, but she is trying to advance to *khon wat*. Ah Tangbun has a lovely smile, yet she tends to be serious, especially when it comes to morality. She told me that having the burden of children is her *wibaaggaam* for breaking the third precept. Now, Ah Tangbun covers herself with long sleeves and a polka-dotted scarf around her neck to protect herself from sexual desire. Ah Tangbun reveals through a life history mixed with sadness and hope how she finally found a home with Asoke:

> Before I came, actually, I'll explain from when I was born. I had a heart that thought "I do not like action that is violent, I do not like sinning, I don't like killing animals, I don't like oppressing, [and] I don't like exploiting." So I thought, eh, what should I do? I felt, if I'm the only one that thinks like this, I am crazy. Crazy for merit! . . . It made me not dare to talk to anyone. My heart looked deep, but there was no answer. There is no society, na, that would have people with morality, that do not oppress, and do not kill animals and life, that do not destroy nature by building great big houses and other big things. . . .
>
> There wasn't [a society like this], so it ended there and I just lived on. I worked until I was 18-19 years old and my mother wanted me to marry. . . . Actually, I wanted to ordain, na ka. But I didn't see any religious thought or principle that made me confident that there was a path. . . . If I had met Asoke before, it is likely that I wouldn't have married. My mother wanted me to marry, so I married and I . . . started to do according to what I had thought. I built a very small house—not big at all. Then I planted different vegetables and fruits. And I continued to do this.
>
> But deep in my heart, it still wasn't right. I was still thinking about how to build a new community. I didn't have friends—every way I looked, they did not think the same as me. Just then, in the year 1993, I planted a great deal of squash. I got a lot of money, too. Here, a person from Kanthalak bought [some squash] but was drunk and did not pay for it all. She swindled me [she laughs]. I followed her to ask for what she owed, and I passed the way here, to Srisa Asoke. I invited her to go and be my companion. . . . So we came to see, and

> oh! When we saw the students—the first time, I was very impressed with how Teacher Oi brought the children to say, "*Samneuk dii, ka*" ("Good thoughts," an Asoke greeting), I was surprised—I had never seen this kind of behavior by people in the world, in this era! It doesn't exist. There is only disinterest. . . . I started to have a sense of being family, and I started to feel more good-natured. . . . Oh, this society, this is the society I dreamed about! Here it is, truly. So I thought, I must come live here. I must find a way to be able to stay here. I quickly returned home and told my husband about it. "I'm going to live there—what are you going to do? Will you go?"
>
> So I came here to study. There was someone who . . . gave me books to read. They were *Saan Asoke* and *Dauk Yaa*. I read them and oh! I saw . . . [that] I haven't been going alone—there have been many people going together. . . . From there, I started to do things that would make me have more morality. . . . I made the intention to eat vegetarian food in 1993. . . . What I intended to do, I did. That is, to build nature, in order to make the area green, without pollution; do it for the world, for when we die, these things will still be here. . . . My friends who used fertilizer and pesticide were confused. "How can you do it?" I could even plant watermelon without chemicals. I could plant everything. But before, eh, why before did I not dare plant [without chemicals], but when I practice Dharma, I dare? "Dare to be poor" in order not to break the precepts, not to sin. I was a poor person who did not break the precepts, did not ruin the soil, did not destroy nature. . . . It fit in well with what Asoke and Pau Than taught: to make nature for humanity. So I planted more. We had everything to eat from vegetables that were young to plants that were mature. I felt we could not eat it all. . . . Mostly I brought [the fruit and vegetables] to make merit, and I sold a little. . . . Now, mangoes and whatnot completely filled the land. I only had to watch over them. . . .
>
> Now when I had done this, I thought, there is still better than this. I have made nature well, but one day when I die, who will continue to practice according to my intention? If the ones who come to continue do not have morality, they will destroy it. The things I have planted they will surely destroy because they are greedy, na. . . . If my child marries someone who does not have morality, they might do like capitalism because capitalism has strength. So I thought, if I live like this for a long time, it is likely that I will die free [of burdens]. . . . But when I die, I will not be free of suffering in my heart. For example, reducing defilements, greed, anger, misunderstanding, grasping at the things we have done, this is suffering just the same. It's better to find the way to enter the temple. . . .
>
> So I came to the temple to get better and better. When I came to the temple, it was clear I was finally dwelling with good things.

Ah Tangbun's "highest dream" is to become a nun. She says even if she does not ordain, she will continue "to act according to what the Noble One did."

Sunday, February 11, 2001

In the chill and darkness of 3:30 a.m., Srisa Asoke residents and I make our way to the Common Hall for *tom wat chao*. I see Ah Tangbun already seated to the side, so I pick up a vacant mat and kneel next to her. We exchange smiles and Asoke greetings. As usual, we begin by prostrating to the monks and relics and then chant prayers for a half hour. This morning, instead of a sermon, residents give a "summary" of what they were impressed with at the Phuttha Phisek festival that took place last week at Sali Asoke. Phuttha Phisek is an annual national Asoke festival during which participants keep eight precepts for seven days, listen to Dharma talks by Samana Bodhirak, monks, nuns, and other noted speakers, and take part in various activities relating to Buddhism and Asoke life. Through summaries, adults who did not attend the festival may hear about what they missed. Summarizing is a common Asoke activity that gives people the opportunity to reflect on their experiences and feelings, practice public speaking, and learn from their peers. In this morning's summaries, one man exclaims he was impressed with himself for sitting so long because it made his legs and back ache. A woman who listened to Pau Than speak about the Three Professions to Save the Nation thought that was impressive. Ah Jantima who remained at Srisa Asoke professes that those who stayed behind could go to the temple and listen to similar sermons about meritism. Than Din Thai observes that all participants ate only one meal a day during the festival. With regard to the eight precepts, he says, "People must always progress; you must fight." Ah Tangbun announces that after the festival, she is ready to take the eight precepts.

At 5:45 a.m. *tom wat chao* concludes. Ah Tangbun, Ah Jantima, and I walk down the path together away from the Common Hall. When I ask what work we will do this morning, Ah Tangbun hesitates. She would like to go to the kitchen to prepare some medicinal food to offer the monks. However, it is too difficult to concentrate when she has to watch her three-year-old in a dangerous environment full of knives, fire, and pots of boiling soup. Her elder daughter took care of the little one throughout *tom wat chao*, but Ah Tangbun must now fetch her because it is time to start school. Ah Jantima solves the dilemma by volunteering to babysit.

At the kitchen, we bid Ah Jantima, "*Jalern thaam, ka,*" as she continues home. While Ah Tangbun gathers her ingredients, she informs me that the monks at Srisa Asoke are not healthy due to old age, cold weather, and, for Than Din Thaam, an accident. It is especially important now for the monks to take medicine and healthy food because they exerted themselves at the Phuttha Phisek festival. The food she is making is called *kaoyaku* and contains brown rice, green beans, sesame seeds, and some kind of nut. It takes about an hour and a half to roast the nuts, cook the beans, and combine these together with rice and seeds in a large pan. We actually spend a third of that time mixing in the fifth ingredient: good thoughts. Ah Tangbun instructs me in the correct way: "You stir it up like, having concentration, make your heart good, do good things, so the person who eats it will have good health." To convince me of this food's medicinal capabilities, she declares that she has made it for wage laborers who became ill from insecticides in the rice fields, and it made them stronger.

We cover the pan with a cloth, carry it to the Common Hall, and set it on the food table where it will remain until mealtime. We then walk back to the large garden area in the middle of the community to pick fresh greens that accompany every meal. There we encounter Ah Cheun, a *khon wat* who lost an arm ten years ago in an accident. Ah Cheun would like to be a nun; unfortunately, she is ineligible because her body is imperfect (this is a general Buddhist law, not specific to Asoke). As we join her in gathering leaves, she points to each plant and recites its medicinal value: this one has vitamin C, this one gives you energy, this one solves constipation, this one in a tea soothes a sore throat, and so on. I ask her how she came by this extensive knowledge, and she replies that her father "knew everything about plants that heal," but she also studied on her own.[7] The gong sounds for Dharma before Eating, so we exit the garden and take our baskets of greens to wash at the old ladies' house. We dump our harvest into a large aluminum tub, and Ah Cheun fills it with water from a spigot and rinses the leaves. When she is satisfied, Ah Tangbun and I help her drain off the water since it takes more than one hand to ensure no plants escape. We then organize the leaves according to type and lay them on a round plastic platter. I am familiar with only a few: cilantro, mint, *cha-om*, and *keelek* (the last two are strong-tasting leaves, the latter bitter, from perennial shrubs). The others came from a mix of naturally occurring and cultivated plants. I carry the platter to the Common Hall accompanied by the two older women.

We arrive a bit late. The students are present and in the progress of summarizing what impressed them about the Phuttha Phisek festival. Only the high school students (ninth grade and up) were permitted to go. The students who remained behind are quite interested and ask what it was like to keep eight precepts. Ah Jantima comes in just as we are dishing up food so Ah Tangbun can feed lunch to her daughter. After we recite the meal reflection, we turn to face the television and eat while watching an American movie dubbed in Thai, starring Robert DeNiro and Sean Penn as priests. The movie is a treat for the students who "endured hardship" at the festival the previous week. At about quarter till noon, Tangbun excuses herself to take care of personal business. She suggests we meet again in an hour at the recycling center so we can collect trash while the sun is too hot to water vegetables.

Later, Ah Tangbun and I get a pushcart from the recycling center and roam around the community collecting trash from separation stands. These covered stands have six large hanging bags (three on each side) labeled for paper, plastic bottles, other plastic, milk boxes, glass, and cloth, and four tins underneath labeled for metal, batteries, "contaminated with bodily fluids," and other (see fig. 3.8 in chapter 3). We only take the bags and tins that are more than half full.

That morning I wished I had had my tape recorder while Ah Tangbun and Ah Cheun talked at great length about the medicinal qualities of certain foods and plants. I put the recorder in my bag after lunch, and I am rewarded with a lengthy diatribe about how pollution is destroying the world. Here is a portion of Ah Tangbun speech during garbage pickup:

> People who understand this work are hard to find. For example, in doing the garbage, there must be detail. What can be used we keep. Some people discard everything like it doesn't have benefit. . . . We have to try to recycle, reuse. People did not see the benefit in this shirt of mine. I got it from the trash. It's still good. . . . Glasses, metal spoons, many things that children and many people, na—sometimes guests come and I see them throw away—I see they are good things so I save them. If someone works in garbage, they must see these details. It's true that it uses time but it must be done. It is a necessary issue.
>
> All the same, I sympathize with people who discard trash. Sometimes in just one bag, there is *everything* [she laughs]—wet garbage, dry garbage, paper. It must be separated. We have to make our hearts understand them, that it is probably hard. They probably don't have time, na. . . . So make our hearts not angry with them. I think we can practice Dharma by being patient, making ourselves see the ill effect—If these people do not practice truly and do not reach true Dharma, they will not see these details. . . .
>
> I see this garbage as the index pointing out that the world is going to break apart. Because people create pollution, create much garbage. For example, I go to the market and get, I don't know, lemongrass or other ingredients to put in food. People have embarrassment in things they should not be embarrassed about. If I bring a food carrier to put it in [rather than take a plastic bag from the seller], they are likely to be embarrassed by this sight, right? But making trash and building pollution, they are not embarrassed. . . . If people continue like this, the world will break apart. Like styrofoam—it has to be burned, right? Batteries—this is pollution, right? Packaging, and even cosmetics, oh! it is more than what is necessary. I see people who like beauty, but on the inside there is nothing. And giving gifts like this [she picks a fuzzy bear key chain out of the "other" tin]—it's just a decorative thing. These are social preferences that are wrong, that ruin society very much.
>
> When I see it, I think, I think to myself, but I do not criticize other people. I have been direct with them before, but when you are direct, they are not happy [she laughs]. . . . It's pitiful, this world, and people do not understand.

Ah Tangbun seems happy just to have a sympathetic ear, so I nod in agreement now and then.

We drop off the bags of trash at the recycling center at around 3:00 p.m. Now that the air is cooler, we water vegetables we planted a month ago in the Cooperative Merit Garden. I am pleased to see how much the plants have grown. Someone had erected three-legged frames made of sticks over the beans so the vines would have something to wrap around; the squash vines are creeping over the ground. We also water another new immense plot of watermelon behind the mushroom-cultivating area. On the way back to Ah Tangbun's house, we pass her older daughter walking her little sister toward the kitchen for dinner.

At the house, we water vegetables and plant seedlings until the light starts to fade. I suspect that Ah Tangbun is not going to have dinner, so I leave her with a promise to return after I eat and bathe.

I return some time after 6:30 p.m. and find Tangbun sewing a button on a shirt with her young one snoring in her lap. When she finishes, she rearranges her sleeping child in her arms, and we walk to the Common Hall for morality check. Throughout morality check, the mood is light. No noteworthy sins had been committed in the past week. Nevertheless, it takes over an hour to get through eight precepts. The monk is about to go on to the ninth, but someone asks if it is really necessary since no one present keeps more than eight precepts. As usual, it is past the old ladies' (and the anthropologist's) bedtime. The monk dismisses us, and the crowd walks out together. At the point where our paths home separate, I thank Ah Tangbun for sharing her day with me and wish her a sincere "*Jalern thaam, ka.*"

Conclusion

This chapter meant to present additional ethnographic information about Asoke beliefs and practices and give a rhythmic sense of daily life at Srisa Asoke. The narratives highlight individual variances in thoughts, interests, activities, and aspirations, but they also demonstrate how these different individuals come together as a community. These narratives further serve as a reminder that the research subject is not merely a development model, but actual people engaged in the pursuit of a better life.

Of secondary importance, this chapter offered a limited comparative analysis of gender relations and women's status in Thai versus Asoke society. While Asoke society offers women more lifestyle choices, higher status, and improved gender relations, members' individual perceptions range widely. At one end is the Santi Asoke librarian who believes we were born as women because we violated the third precept in our past life. At the other end is Ah Warn. In our discussion of women and Buddhism, Ah Warn asks what I would like to be in my next life, a man or a woman. Skirting the issue of whether or not I believe in reincarnation, I reply simply that I like being a woman. Ah Warn grins and nods emphatically: "Me too!"

Notes

1. The Asoke movement uses the alternate terms *sikkhamat* and *samana* as a result of the court case against them, in which it was decided that the Asoke movement could not use the same terms as used in the Thai Sangha.

2. In the voting lesson, Ah Peum passed out sample ballots and the residents practiced the mechanics of voting. Ah Peum did not tell residents who to vote for but suggested they watch the news, read the paper, and decide in their own hearts who is the best candidate.

3. It is not clear, but I suspect that the "reports of curing sickness and disease by eating natural food" Ah Jantima heard in the fields are both Asoke and non-Asoke. There is a long tradition of herbal medicine in Thailand. Yet since she speaks of a vegetarian diet and later of Asoke monks, it is likely some people working in the fields were familiar with Asoke. In fact, at least two other adults and several students at Srisa Asoke come from Ah Jantima's district in Roi Et.

4. As the youngest daughter, it was Ah Jantima's duty to care for her father in his old age.

5. Female students live in the community either with their parents or five to a house. Male students all sleep in one large dormitory.

6. The Fukuoka method is meant to be as close to nature as possible with little human intervention. Hoeing or plowing is actually not desirable because it destroys the soil's structure.

7. In Thailand's ancient tradition of herbal medicine (*ya samoonphrai*), herbalists typically learn their trade through apprenticeships with an established mentor, or through a school of traditional medicine such as the one at Wat Pho in Bangkok. The number of herbalists in Thailand had drastically decreased as deforestation made finding plants more difficult and as the younger generation sought more "modern" professions. In recent years, however, there has been renewed interest stimulated by the growing organic movement in Thailand.

Chapter 8

Building the World: Lessons in "Right Development"

If [the aid agencies] were doing a proper job of promoting development in the Third World, then, presumably, they should have put themselves out of business by now. (Hancock 1989:74)

Buddhists might call the Asoke way of life "right development" because it promotes the development of morality, wisdom, and concentration—the Way of Dharma, not the worldly way. Development scholars and practitioners might also call it "right development," pointing to the Asoke movement's success in raising the quality of life for ordinary people. To do so, I argue that development must be 1) culturally/locally situated, 2) focused on livelihoods instead of macroeconomic growth, 3) environmentally "sustainable," and 4) endogenously inspired, implemented, and maintained. Asoke beliefs and practices as enacted at the Srisa Asoke Buddhist Center clearly illustrate this kind of development. Thus, this final chapter situates Asoke-style development within contemporary development discourse, suggesting reasons why the mainstream international development industry has not brought prosperity to the majority of the world's population and expounding on this alternative approach.

A History of the Development Industry

The concept of development implies positive change, and it is clearly an ideal toward which individuals, groups, and nations strive. The Western world's conceptualization of development—unilinear growth, evolution, or maturation toward an ever more perfect form—has its roots in evolutionary theories of the nineteenth and early twentieth centuries as well as the Enlightenment view of unending progress (Fagerlind and Saha 1983). Development as a *global project* emerged in the aftermath of World War II. At this time, development became synonymous with economic growth, and the ideal was modeled in the likeness of industrialized nations, particularly the United States. Anthropologist Riall Nolan succinctly describes the technicist paradigm that took shape early on: "The *ends* sought were primarily material, *strategy* was derived from Western economic theory, and the *means* consisted of Western capital combined with Western technology and know-how" (Nolan 2002:45). This configuration of ideas still informs policy and practice within the multibillion-dollar development industry that exists today.

The Bretton Woods agreement signed by financial leaders of forty-four countries toward the end of World War II instituted the economic approach to development. This agreement established mechanisms—including the International Monetary Fund (IMF) and the International Bank for Reconstruction and Development (IBRD, now part of the World Bank)—to rebuild the economies of Europe and reassert political stability. Through the Marshall Plan, the European economies received large infusions of capital to stimulate rapid economic growth and were soon thriving again.

After the war, poverty was "discovered" as a global phenomenon (Escobar 1995). Western leaders felt that extending the Marshall Plan's program of development to former and transitional colonies could help these nations "catch up" with industrial nations, while simultaneously stopping the flow of communism. Indeed, President Kennedy declared in 1961, "Foreign aid is a method by which the United States maintains a position of influence and control around the world and sustains a good many countries which would definitely collapse or pass into the communist bloc" (cited in Hancock 1989:71). In the 1950s and 1960s, development in the newly labeled "Third World" emphasized macroeconomic planning and large projects for sector growth (particularly in industry), infrastructure, and large-scale agriculture. In Thailand during this time, Prime Minister Field Marshall Sarit (a US ally) followed precisely this model of modernization in order to promote national security against the communist insurgency growing in the region.

The language and assumptions of this early development era were reminiscent of colonial days. Setting the standard for economic development, President Truman declared that the degree of "civilization" in a country could be measured by the level of its production (Sachs 1990, 1993). And like the colonial era, the developers would be the United States, Great Britain, and other prosperous European nations, which had "superior knowledge" and resources. The early modernization school of development proposed that in order to promote true economic development, the obstacle of "traditional" culture (which lacked the necessary Western values of gain and achievement) must be overcome. In Arthur Lewis's modernization model, the market sector would expand through the eradication of the "traditional economy," whereby the "backwards sector" (i.e., subsistence agriculture) would provide labor at below-market cost to the swelling capitalist sector. When labor was no longer abundant, wage rates would rise, signaling the complete absorption of the subsistence sector by the market (Gudeman 1998). This process was hailed as development. Though this modernization approach of the 1950s and 1960s has fallen out of popular development discourse, such ideas do not seem wholly out of place in today's market-centric environment.

By the early 1970s, development planners realized that some economies simply were not "taking off" as projected by development economists (e.g., Rostow 1960); in cases where growth was occurring, there were problems in distribution of the benefits. When Robert McNamara became president of the World Bank in 1968, he brought with him a new concern for equity issues and the needs of the very poor (Nolan 2002). In 1976, the International Labor Organization (ILO) formalized the basic needs approach introduced by McNamara. Ivan Illich observes that through this approach, "Needs became a powerful emblem in spite of the fact that, for the mainstream economist, 'need' is a non-word" (1992:88). During the 1970s, women, communities, and small farmers all posed new problems to be tackled with special strategies. Development was continually repackaged as it met with failures, absorbed criticisms, and endeavored to appease donors (Escobar 1995). This was a decade of tremendous innovation in alternatives for local-level development, but there were rumblings that development agencies were straying from the financial and technical aspects of development for which they had expertise.

Trouble hit the development industry with the debt crisis of the early 1980s. Aid to developing nations over three decades had come in the form of loans at or near market rate that became increasingly difficult to repay. In 1984, several Latin American countries defaulted. Furthermore, due to burdens of loan repayment (compounded by continued population growth and the global oil crisis), efforts in poverty alleviation were not progressing as hoped (So 1990). Under the Reagan administration's trend toward privatization and market reform, the IMF and the World Bank designed and implemented structural adjustment programs (SAPs) to assist economies faltering with debt. To receive bailout loans, national governments were required under SAPs to cut spending in social sectors like health and education, focus resources on private-sector export production, and institute democratic reforms. In theory, these governments would then be able to repay their loans with an influx of foreign capital attracted to political and economic stability. These reforms would in turn open new markets for Western nations. On the downside, developing nations increased their dependency on fickle foreign capital and global markets, and the poorest people in these nations felt the worst effects of macroeconomic reform (Harrison 1997). By necessity, local-level development projects that began in the 1970s continued through the 1980s and 1990s in order to help poor people adjust to the burdens of SAPs.

Criticisms of the development industry have always come from academics; in the 1990s, growing public outcry expressed dissatisfaction with five decades of development that exacerbated rather than alleviated poverty and inequality.

For example, Fifty Years Is Enough, an NGO established in 1994, has called for an end to IMF and World Bank dominance of international development efforts.[1] Other popular protests over the last few years have included the boycott against Nike for employing sweatshop labor and large demonstrations at the World Bank and IMF meetings in Seattle in 1999 and again in Genoa the following year, as well as the fight for global debt relief led by international pop star Bono of U2.

The field of development is now poised for a major shift in policy and practice. During the World Bank and IMF spring meetings in 2002, President Bush announced his intention to increase foreign aid by $5 billion a year (within three years)—the largest increase in thirty years. In this new development era, the question remains how best to deliver aid (*The Economist*, April 22, 2002). The following sections outline a theoretical yet grounded development approach founded on criticisms of and alternatives to mainstream development put forth by anthropologists and other social scientists.

Culturally/Locally Situated

The conventional development industry operates on the notion that all nations of the world will develop similarly if given the opportunity through monetary and technical aid. This approach assumes that other social groups can, want, and should develop like Western industrialized nations. To the contrary, many scholars and development practitioners recognize that raising the quality of life for ordinary people requires attention to the specific culture and place where development is to occur. A culturally/locally situated approach may be more successful than conventional "cookie-cutter" development because it accounts for diversity in people's histories, resources, capabilities, and aspirations for development. In support of such an approach, the following section critiques the mainstream development model for its historical and cultural construction and then surveys more culturally/locally sensitive perspectives emphasizing appropriate technology and local knowledge. Lastly, a more comprehensive consideration of culture and locale is demonstrated by the Asoke movement.

The Historical and Cultural Construction of Development

The creators of the global development industry regrettably failed to consider what post-structuralists now take as self-evident: The Western development model is historically and culturally constructed and as such cannot be reproduced globally with satisfying results. The rapid development of US and European economies was made possible by a specific, unrepeatable moment in history called the Industrial Revolution. According to Maria Mies (1993), the "myth of catching-up development" is based on an evolutionary view of history that does not allow for alternate beginnings, trajectories, or end points. Neo-Marxist dependency theorists further argue that Third World nations can *never* follow the West's path. The dependency school's core/periphery model suggests how exploitation was structured into the colonial relationship, such that the development of one necessarily leads to the underdevelopment of another (Frank 1967; Dos Santos 1971). Many contemporary scholars such as liberation ecologists Peet and Watts also reject mainstream development as an academic and governmental enterprise "inseparable from the process by which the 'colonial world' was reconfigured into a 'developing world' in the aftermath of WW2"[2] (1996:19).

In terms of its cultural construction, the mainstream development model is driven by the Western belief that a high material living standard indicates a high quality of life. Because the market is the dominant mechanism for determining value, material possessions have become global symbols of success. The occurrence of this phenomenon in Thailand was discussed in chapter 2. Gérald Berthoud explains the assumption underlying the conventional development goal: "Being human is thought to be motivated by a constant search for material well-being . . . somehow transcending all the particulars of culture and society" (1992:82). To development planners who seldom leave Washington, D.C. (physically or ideologically), it is a non-issue that social groups have varying views on progress and poverty, and, consequently, about development.

Divergent conceptions of development may stem from religious beliefs, as illustrated by the Asoke development model. The Asoke group's aim is not a Western ideal—to accumulate high levels of material comfort—but a Buddhist ideal—to release attachment to the material world and attain spiritual freedom. Asoke members' efforts to develop themselves, their community, and the society around them thus reflect this Buddhist ideal. Thai social critic Sulak Sivaraksa also advocates "true development" from a Buddhist perspective:

> Development must aim at the reduction of craving, the avoidance of violence, and the development of spirit rather than of material things. . . . The goal of increasing the quality of life is understood differently. From the materialist standpoint, when there are *more* desires, there can be further development. From the Buddhist standpoint, when there are *fewer* desires, there can be further development. (1990:171; emphasis added)

Ajaan Sulak has been influenced by Gandhi, who similarly felt that focusing on industrialization and economic growth was not in line with India's aspirations for a spiritual way of life based on Hindu tradition.

In addition, small-scale subsistence economies may also have different development objectives than large-scale market economies. For example, Gudeman and Rivera (1990) observed in Columbia that swidden agriculturalists aim to "sustain" rather than "gain." These economic anthropologists theorize that subsistence-based economies strive to achieve a level of production sufficient for the continual reproduction of their system; what is left over (the surplus) is progress. The predominant value is frugality, to economize or minimize the means to a certain end. Asoke communities work in a similar way toward a "sufficiency economy" (*setagit pau piang*);[3] but the surplus is sacrificed to society for "spiritual progress."

Since many people who have become accustomed to a materialistic existence commonly misconstrue subsistence livelihoods as impoverished and in need of "development," ecofeminist Vandana Shiva would make a distinction:

> It is useful to separate the cultural conception of subsistence living as poverty from the material experience of poverty that is a result of dispossession and deprivation. Culturally perceived poverty need not be real material poverty: subsistence economies which satisfy basic needs through self-provisioning are not poor in the sense of being deprived. (1988:10)

To illustrate Shiva's point, Srisa Asoke looks like a poor rural village when compared to the modern development of Bangkok, yet while the Asoke movement has a slogan, "Dare to Be Poor" in the eyes of materialistic outsiders, they do not intend deficiency in basic needs. Thus, different values and objectives such as subsistence, wealth accumulation, or spiritual enlightenment may determine development's form.

Culturally/Locally Appropriate Alternatives

Many alternative development efforts have sought to make development more "locally" appropriate by taking into account "local" capabilities, resources, and knowledge. One such alternative is the appropriate technology (AT) approach that emerged during the 1970s Small Is Beautiful movement (following E. F. Schumacher). According to Warren and Bourque, AT aimed "to attack Third World poverty and underdevelopment by increasing local productivity without reinforcing patterns of dependency on industrial nations" (1991:284). AT offered an improvement over the mainstream development approach in its realization that capital- and technology-intensive industrialization is not feasible—or necessary—in some places. AT targeted small-scale subsistence needs by introducing technology such as mud ovens that reduce fuel consumption (subsequently reducing the time women spent collecting wood) as well as low-cost storage facilities to keep animals and insects out of harvests, thereby increasing available food.

Though well intentioned (and at times quite effective), AT's predominantly "top-down" approach replaces local innovation with foreign technology, thereby locating the power of knowledge and control over change with outside development agents. Emma Crewe observed that when international development agencies became involved in the production of cookstoves in the South in the late 1970s, users and artisans were displaced from the center of the technical innovation process. She states, "Cooks, despite their daily practice of cooking, apparently have less technical knowledge in their perceptions, than designers in laboratories do in their findings" (Crewe 1997:68).

Stephen Marglin (1990) explains that the prevalence of Western knowledge in development activities is due to the privileging of *episteme* (abstract analytic knowledge) over *techne* (tactile practical knowledge) in Western culture. Michael Dove comments, "The idea that the villager, the peasant, the tribesman is an expert is old hat to anthropologists" (1988:6), but it is not so apparent to development planners. In Dove's experience of development in Indonesia, the typical, highly educated and highly paid development expert finds it unlikely that the typical, poorly educated and poorly paid villager knows far more about his/her own local economy and environment than the "expert" knows or is likely to learn. The advanced formal education of development planners is regarded as a guarantee of the validity of their observations and conclusions.

By contrast, anthropologists maintain that local knowledge-based change, or innovation-on-the-ground, allows flexibility to find the most appropriate solutions and constitutes people as potential agents. Local knowledge is not a closed system but a dynamic array of beliefs, values, and practices that may encompass survival and livelihood skills; familiarity with the immediate environment; spiritual ideas about the relationship between humans, nature, and the supernatural; cultural practices of resource management and dispute resolution; and so on. The contributors to Mark Hobart's edited volume *An Anthropological Critique of Development: The Growth of Ignorance* (1993) in particular stress the value of treating local knowledges seriously and examining what they may contribute to people's material, intellectual, and general welfare.

The work of anthropologists Michael Dove and Daniel Kammen illustrates how the use of local knowledge may bring success in development efforts where Western scientific knowledge does not. In a positive story about cookstove innovation, Kammen and Dove (1997) state that in Kenya, problems of design and expense were overcome using "mundane science," that is, by working them out in real-life situations (rather than in a lab) with the help of local craftspeople and likely users.

Anthropologists generally recognize that culture is dynamic and thus do not romanticize a return to "tradition," unlike many alternative-development efforts that facilely privilege "native wisdom" or "indigenous knowledge" over Western "expert" knowledge. In a study of development intervention in Ecuador, Bebbington (1996) observed agricultural programs that differed from state-fostered modernization as well as proposals by intellectuals and activists who suggest that appropriate rural development should build only or primarily on farmers' own techniques and innovations.[4] The Asoke development model similarly draws from "traditional Thai culture," Western environmental concepts and marketing techniques, Japanese methods of natural farming, and so on. In reality, people select from a wide variety of ideas and techniques available to them from global, regional, local, and historical sources. In the imaginative combination of these elements, something entirely new is fashioned.

The Asoke way of life represents a culturally and locally situated approach to development, at the very least because it is based on Buddhist and Thai values. Moreover, the agrarian livelihood practiced at Srisa Asoke is appropriate for its up-country location and, more generally, for a country whose population is over 60 percent rural. Yet a culturally/locally situated approach to development requires more than merely incorporating local knowledge, beliefs, and practices and recognizing local resource constraints. These aspects are indeed important, since treating each community in its own terms allows a better understanding of people's particular needs and goals than a pre-fabricated development project. However, the Asoke development model offers a more holistic approach in the way members assert their rights to autonomy, territory, identity, and their own vision of the future (Escobar 1995). This form of culturally/locally situated development is more empowering and can have longer-lasting effects, and thus has greater potential to raise the quality of life for ordinary people.

Livelihoods, not GDP

Countless scholars, activists, and practitioners take issue with the development industry's tendency toward "growthmania"—its blind faith in economic growth as the solution to poverty (Daly 1996). The previous section touched on criticisms that the "development equals economic growth" model is based on Western values of material accumulation and excludes other cultural configurations of development. This section is concerned with two additional arguments. First, macroeconomic strategies implemented to foster economic growth (e.g., export production and trade liberalization) are not designed with the welfare of ordinary people in mind and frequently have negative affects on the poorest. Examples from India, Jamaica, and Thailand are provided below. Second, the standard measure for economic growth—the gross domestic product (GDP)—is a flawed indicator of development since it does not measure accurately either economic growth or human welfare. Instead of development geared toward raising the GDP, a "livelihood model" of development is favored here.

Problems with Macroeconomic "Development"

From the 1980s onward, international development agencies sought to stabilize flailing economies and spur growth by increasing connections to the global economy. While opening access to foreign capital and markets made sense to international financiers, scholars and activists fault macroeconomic structural adjustment programs (SAPs) of export-led growth and trade liberalization for their lack of attention to the lives of ordinary people.

Vandana Shiva asks, what should be the global economy's primary objective: freedom for trade or freedom for survival?

> "Free-trade" in agriculture as construed in GATT [General Agreement on Tariffs and Trade] terms aims to create freedom for transnational corporations (TNCs) to invest, produce, and trade in agricultural commodities without restriction, regulation, or responsibility. This freedom for agribusiness is based on the denial of freedom to rural women to produce, process, and consume food according to the local environmental, economic, and cultural needs. (1993:231)

Shiva criticizes India's SAP that prescribed the removal of food subsidies (that provided cheap food to the public) and urged import liberalization. She states that in 1991, India exported 672,000 tons of wheat, but the next year after liberalization, India *imported* 2.5 million tons of wheat—half of which came from the United States. The cost of importing wheat was more than the subsidy the government had paid to Indian farmers. As neither the Indian government nor Indian people benefited from these transactions, Shiva declares that SAPs transfer the benefits of economic activity from the poor (India's farmers) to the rich (US agribusiness).

In observing declining conditions in a Jamaican ghetto over a fifteen-year period, Faye Harrison blames the same macroeconomic "development":

> The debt constrained, export-led, and free-trade-based development path that the Jamaican economy is following has failed to deliver the masses of Jamaican people from the dilemmas of persistent poverty and underdevelopment. Benefits from this development strategy have not trickled down the socioeconomic ladder. However, what have trickled down are the adverse effects of drastic austerity measures, which are the strings attached to aid from the IMF and World Bank. (1997:456)

Like countless others who criticize the social affects of SAPs, Harrison asserts, "These policies have sacrificed ordinary people's—especially the poor's—basic needs in health care, housing, education, social services, and employment for those of free enterprise and free trade" (451).

During the recent Southeast Asian economic crisis, Thailand did not suffer so badly under the stipulations of the IMF's $17.2 billion bailout loan. A strong local lobby of journalists, academics, public intellects, and NGO workers informed the government that the crisis's social impact "weighed heaviest on the poor" and pushed for action. The king supported this lobby in his December 1997 speech: "Being a tiger is not important. What is important is to have enough to eat and live, and to have an economy that provides enough to eat and live" (cited in Pasuk and Baker 2000:73). According to Pasuk and Baker, the combination of NGO reports, the king's speech, and warnings by other "establishment figures" (like former Prime Minister Anand and Dr. Prawase Wasi) has forced the government "to make policy with one eye on the issue of the poor"

(74). Nevertheless, since the crisis began, poverty has tripled in Thailand (*Bangkok Post*, December 9, 2001).

Problems with GDP

Structural reforms for export-led growth and trade liberalization aim to expand a country's GDP, which the development industry hails as development. There are other human development indexes such as literacy and infant mortality rates, but the GDP far outweighs them all as the indicator of a nation's development. Conversely, numerous scholars (including some economists) reject the GDP as an indicator of development since it does not measure accurately economic growth or human welfare. Members of Redefining Progress (a non-profit organization) assert that the GDP is a faulty indicator of progress because it is "simply a gross tally of money spent—goods and services purchased by households or government and business investments, regardless of whether they enhance our well-being or not" (Cobb et al. 1999:1). That is, the GDP does not distinguish between productive and destructive activities. For example, the destruction of old growth forest for timber adds the market value of the wood to the GDP but does not subtract the cost of diminishing assets. Pollution is a "double gain" since the production of oil that creates pollution as well as clean-up costs add to the GDP. Similarly, car accidents, disease, crime, and divorce all generate income for the GDP through money spent on auto repairs, hospital bills, home security systems, and legal fees.[5] A steadily growing GDP may therefore hide real social and environmental problems that detract from people's well-being. "In short," say the people at Global Exchange (an international NGO), "the GDP values growth at all costs over the things that really matter to people such as clean air and water, a healthy and safe community, and free time to enjoy them."[6]

Development economist Amartya Sen (1988) adds that since the GDP measures per capita "income," it is possible to have an average growth of GDP per head while distribution becomes more unequal (i.e., there is a decline in the real income of the poorest people). As stated in chapter 2, Thailand's economic boom in the late 1980s following IMF structural adjustment recommendations was in fact limited to Bangkok. Geographer Chris Dixon (1996) remarks that for Thailand, NIC ought to signify "newly industrializing *city*" rather than "*country*" since Bangkok so thoroughly dominates the country's economy. The contributors to *Uneven Development in Thailand* maintain that the majority of Thailand's population in rural areas did not benefit from their country's remarkable economic growth. In fact, "Some have benefited at the cost of others and, more generally, a minority has enjoyed the lion's share of the spoils of growth" (Parnwell and Arghiros 1996:27). Since the economic crisis, the income disparity in Thailand has worsened even though the economy's annual growth rate is steadily climbing. At a forum for poverty reduction strategies late last year, former Prime Minister Anand stated, "Currently, the increasing gap between the rich and poor has created an inequality that leaves little hope for those striving for a better future, which is also causing other social problems" (*Bangkok Post*, December 9, 2001).

More generally, Sen (1999) counters the narrow view of development as growth in the gross domestic product with the notion of "development as freedom." By "freedom" he means "the 'capabilities' of persons to lead the kind of life they value—and have reason to value" (18). In Sen's view, the GDP does not measure people's *ability* to use their income to live well; thus, it cannot be used as an indicator of actual well-being. Sen contends that while growth in GDP may be an important means to expanding capabilities or "freedom," there are other contributing factors. He states, "What people can positively achieve is influenced by economic opportunities, political liberties, social powers, and the enabling conditions of good health, basic education, and the encouragement and cultivation of initiatives" (5). The narrow view of development as growth in GDP might ask if these social and political freedoms are "conducive to development," but Sen argues that this phrasing of the question misses the point that these freedoms are "constituent components" of development. There is, in fact, a mutually reinforcing relationship. Rather than focusing on any one particular means to development (such as growth of GDP), Sen calls our attention to the overarching objective of development—the enhancement of economic, social, and political freedoms that allow people to live a life they value.

Livelihoods

"Free trade" may increase the GDP, but it does not feed people. Thus, focusing development efforts on livelihood security rather than macroeconomic growth will help raise the quality of life for ordinary people. Like a culturally/locally situated approach, the livelihood approach is small scale. At this level, it is possible to see social and environmental problems that the GDP hides, as well as the multitude of factors (besides money) that influence well-being.

Feminist economists Grown and Sebstad describe livelihood systems as "a mix of individual and household survival strategies, developed over a given period of time, that seeks to mobilize available resources and opportunities" (1989:941). These strategies may include market and subsistence activities, borrowing, social networking, changing consumption practices, technical innovation, and so on. Livelihood systems are most successful when people diversify their strategies in order to optimize economic, social, technological, and environmental resources. Grown and Sebstad state that for the poorest people, survival is the utmost goal. Once survival is assured, the goal changes to security, and then may advance to growth. These economists contend that too few development planners realize the distinction between these three goals—most collapse everything into growth.

Development practitioners Robert Chambers and Gordon Conway (1992) direct their work toward establishing sustainable livelihoods. They conceive of livelihoods as comprising people, their capabilities, and their means of living (including food, income, and assets). Chambers and Conway's goals for developing livelihoods include enhancing capabilities, improving equity, and increasing sustainability. As mentioned above, Amartya Sen is responsible for the concept of "capabilities" (1984, 1988, 1999), referring to what a person is capable of doing and being. Equity may be defined in terms of relative income distribution (another of Sen's concerns) or more broadly, equal distribution of assets, capabilities, and opportunities. Lastly, both social and environmental sustainability are sought. Social sustainability is the ability to cope and recover from stress and shock as well as provide for future generations. A livelihood is environmentally sustainable when it maintains or enhances local and global assets on which livelihoods depend and has beneficial effects on other livelihoods.

Livelihood development may occur through complicated models constructed by dedicated development practitioners such as Chambers and Conway, or it may transpire through trial and error by individuals endeavoring to craft their own lives. The Asoke development model is as much about building and securing a "right livelihood" as it is about spiritual advancement. In fact, material and spiritual development are mutually supportive. The strategies used by the Asoke movement to promote livelihood security for members and outsiders alike include education in morality, vocation, and applied academic subjects; trainings in the Three Professions to Save the Nation; the daily practice of "working hard and consuming little"; equitable distribution of resources and opportunities via the meritism system of public property, communal labor, and participatory decision making; and the refinement of efforts to achieve self-sufficiency through meetings and experimentation. The fact that the thirty-year-old Asoke communities continued to thrive throughout Thailand's economic crisis is a strong indication that developing livelihoods rather than the economy is the key to improving ordinary people's lives over the long term.

Environmental "Sustainability"

"Sustainability" has emerged in the last decade as a key concept in development thought and practice as negative environmental consequences of rapid economic growth have become glaringly apparent. The central question in mainstream sustainable development (SD) seems to be, how can we sustain economic growth considering finite resources? Conversely, a development approach that aims to raise the quality of life for ordinary people might ask, how can we sustain livelihoods considering widespread environmental degradation? Environmental concerns figure largely into the alternative development approach offered here since people's well-being and that of the environment are interrelated. This section gives an overview of international dialogue on SD, presents critiques of the mainstream SD approach made by scholars in the social sciences and the development field, and offers alternatives in the form of social movements.

International Dialogue on SD

At the 1972 UN Conference on the Human Environment in Stockholm, the phrase "sustainable development" was proposed to smooth over the dichotomy between economic growth based on industrialization and the associated adverse environmental impacts. Much later, the World Commission on the Environment and Development's (WCED) *Brundtland Report* popularized a general definition of SD: "development that meets the needs of the present without compromising the ability of future generations to meet their own needs" (WCED 1987:43). Whereas past definitions were vague about how SD would be implemented, the *Brundtland Report* is much more elaborate about operational objectives:

1) reviving growth;
2) changing the quality of growth;
3) meeting essential needs for jobs, food, energy, water, and sanitation;
4) ensuring a sustainable level of population;
5) conserving and enhancing the resource base;
6) reorienting technology and managing risk;
7) merging environment and economics in decision making; and
8) reorienting international economic relations. (WCED 1987:49)

The emphasis is clearly economic, with related global developmental concerns of basic human needs, population control, technology, and managing resources. Documents produced at the UN Conference on Environment and Development at Rio de Janeiro in 1992 (particularly *Agenda 21*) added little to previous thinking about SD (Adams 1995). They did, however, highlight ongoing disputes between Northern and Southern countries over the environment and development. There is difference of opinion on key problems: For industrialized countries, global atmospheric change and tropical deforestation are pressing issues; and for unindustrialized countries, poverty and problems which flow from it are paramount. There is also conflict over responsibility for finding solutions (Redclift 1987).

The failure to ratify the Kyoto Accord on global warming is a telling example of these disagreements. The Kyoto Accord was a pact signed in 2001 by eighty industrialized countries to decrease greenhouse-gas emissions over the next fifteen years. President Bush refused to sign not only because cutting emissions would "hurt the US economy"—and thus was not in US interests—but also because the agreement did not include major developing nations. Since the United States produces the largest amount of greenhouse gas, many other countries felt the accord would fail without the United States, and as a result, it was

Critiques of Mainstream SD

The mainstream SD approach has not been successful in reconciling environmental and developmental concerns for several reasons. The first issue is SD's conceptual and operational ambiguity. SD is generally thought to mean "environmentally sustainable development," but it could also refer to "sustained growth" or simply "successful development." More importantly, the objectives of sustainability are continually under debate: What is to be sustained, for how long, and for whom? Anthropologist Victor King (1999) observes that the overall problem with SD is that a particular policy deemed "sustainable" for certain interest groups often undermines sustainability for others. For example, hydropower projects—though promoted as renewable energy sources and therefore suitably "sustainable"—may force local communities to abandon their homes and livelihoods (Parnwell and Bryant 1996). The World Bank's Pak Mun Dam in Thailand, which affects 25,000 villagers, is under popular protest for decimating fisheries the villagers depend on for their livelihood. The developers, talking on cell phones as they drive their Mercedes through Bangkok traffic, claim that the dam will benefit the villagers by providing electricity (which they already had). The question remains how the villagers will now pay for electricity since they can no longer earn a living (*Christian Science Monitor*, August 9, 2000).

Furthermore, anthropologist Virginia Nazarea (1999) observes that ideas about the environment and sustainability are culturally constructed. In an ethnoecology study conducted in the Philippines, Nazarea sought culturally relevant indicators of sustainability and quality of life. Her central question was, "How do people arrive at decisions about levels of exploitation and rightful distribution and access that permit certain strategies and disallow others?" (93). She discovered culturally shared dominant themes (e.g., usefulness, diversity, and beauty of the environment) that were more salient for the local population than economic value. Similarly, Srisa Asoke residents value nature as a conduit of Dharma as well as for the cool shade it provides. In place of Western "scientific" measures of sustainability, a culturally/locally situated development approach would work with these non-quantifiable concepts, which are more meaningful to the users of that environment.

Arturo Escobar (1995) extends the anthropological critique of mainstream SD by faulting its privilege of global ecosystem management (e.g., of deforestation and global warming) over people's livelihoods and for the facile link it makes between poverty and environmental degradation (i.e., poor people cause environmental degradation). For example, in the late 1970s, ethnic minorities in Northern Thailand who had occupied marginal forest areas for at least two generations were displaced by national forestry policy following Western models that establish preservation areas where settlement and use of forest resources are forbidden (Leungaramsri et al. 1992). The Thai government has blamed deforestation in the northern mountain regions on these ethnic minorities who farm and forage there; however, swidden agriculture and gathering non-timber forest products pose little environmental threat when land is abundant. At present, the added pressures of increasing population, commercial logging (partly sponsored by the Thai government), and permanent cash crop cultivation by large agribusinesses disrupt the balance of short-cultivation and long-fallow reforestation cycles necessary for sustainable swidden agriculture. According to David Gow (1995), ecosystems analysts seldom recognize that the "degrading" activities of "the poor" are rooted in such complex development processes.

Last but certainly not least, mainstream SD reproduces the central problem of conventional development: unwavering confidence in economic growth. Although the *Brundtland Report* is praised for its comprehensive examination of environmental problems, it is criticized by grassroots environmental organizations, social activists, scholars, and alternative development practitioners in both the North and the South who maintain that is impossible for accumulation to continue without unacceptable environmental costs (Goodland and Daly 1992; Redclift 1987). The *Brundtland Report* asserts that environmentally sustainable economic growth is possible through improving and managing technology and social organization; however, Paul Ekins (1993) contends that the scale of the technological challenge required is inconceivable. Ekins states that the environmental impact of each unit of consumption (which captures changes in technology) would have to fall by 93 percent in the next fifty years (assuming a population of 10 billion and a moderate growth rate of 2 to 3 percent) in order to meet the conservative definition of sustainability that has been adopted by organizations such as the Intergovernmental Panel on Climate Change.

Sulak Sivaraksa underscores the idea that underdeveloped or developing nations "cannot and should not aspire to quantitative development on a par with that of Europe and America" (1990:170) due to real limits of the world's resources. He quotes Gandhi as saying, "God forbid that India should ever take to industrialism after the manner of the West. The economic imperialism of a single tiny island kingdom [England] is today keeping the world in chains. If an entire nation of 300 million took to similar economic exploitation, it would strip the world bare like locusts" (*Bangkok Post*, February 5, 1998). Similarly, Srisa Asoke's leader, Ah Oi, observes that if everyone followed the modern "social preference" to consume, all the world's resources would "flow away." Hence, Asoke members accept their responsibility to "consume little."

Alternative Approaches to SD

Grassroots and NGO movements that strive for just, equitable, and sustainable livelihoods may succeed in uniting developmental and environmental interests where mainstream efforts have failed. Liberation ecologists Richard Peet and Michael Watts observe, "Indeed, it is striking how indigenous rights movements, conservation politics, food security, the emphasis on local knowledges and calls for access to and control over local resources (democratization, broadly put) crosscut the environment-poverty axis" (1996:35). These liberation ecologists propose that social movements offer diverse "visions of those forms of social and individual practice which are ethically proper and morally right with regard to nature" (1996:263). They also suggest that these "environmental imaginaries" are prime sites of contestation. The Asoke movement's Three Professions to Save the Nation may be considered such an environmental imaginary, as their Buddhist ethics of chemical-free agriculture and waste management stand in opposition to conventional, environmentally harmful, export-oriented agriculture in Thailand.

In a similar vein, studies by feminist political ecologists clearly demonstrate the interconnection between people, their environment, and development. According to Rocheleau, Thomas-Slater, and Wangari (1996), the SD of everyday lives emphasizes survival; the rights to live and work in a healthy environment; the responsibility to protect habitats, livelihoods, and systems of life support from contamination, depletion, and destruction; the determination to rehabilitate what has already been damaged; and the social organization needed to accomplish these things. Examples of "everyday SD" include Spanish women demonstrating against dumping toxic waste in ethnic minority regions (Brú-Bistuer 1996), social movements in tropical rain forests bringing their own cultural models of appropriation and conservation to biodiversity debates over territorial control and intellectual property rights (Escobar 1999), and the Asoke movement advocating a way of life appropriate to and conservative of Thailand's environment.

In sum, the "everyday SD" approach is an improvement over conventional SD for a number of reasons: 1) sustainability is an issue of particular people-environment-development problems rather than abstract global management; 2) it does not prioritize economic growth; 3) it accounts for cultural conceptions of the environment; and 4) it is more empowering to ordinary people.

Endogenously Inspired, Implemented, and Maintained

The last stipulation of this "right development" approach, that development be endogenously inspired, implemented, and maintained, is perhaps the most challenging. What comes closest is participatory development, the most recent strategy to address problems incurred by the development industry, from specific project failures to the broad-sweeping negative effects of macroeconomic reform. The United Nations designated the year 2000 as the People's Millennium, valorizing the voices of people whom processes of colonization and development have historically silenced.[7] The intent was to "put a human face on development," that is, to be more responsive to people's needs as well as more empowering. This section surveys the implications and shortcomings of "participation" in the development context, considers one mainstream participatory development strategy (participatory rural appraisal—PRA), and vies for alternatives that are endogenously inspired, implemented, and maintained.

Adnan et al. (1992) classify "participation" into three broad categories. The first refers to the process in which information about a project is made available to the public. In this type of participation (which can hardly be considered so), views may be solicited from local leaders, but control remains in hands of outside planners. The second category comprises project-related activities in which community members contribute their labor or make a long-term commitment for maintenance. This form of participation allows local people more involvement but still no direct control. The third class includes people's own initiatives that fall outside projects sponsored by development agencies. Some scholars and activists (e.g., Bebbington 1996; Norberg-Hodge 1991) contend that this third category is the only true form of participation because it is not imposed from outside.

While Michael Woost (1997) applauds the emergence of a participatory element in authoritative discourses of development, he agrees with Adnan that "participatory development" has many different connotations, only some of which allow for a more bottom-up debate. Woost claims that mainstream use of participatory rhetoric in Sri Lanka offers little in the way of alternative development. On the contrary, the notion of participation has been "laundered and reshaped in official discourse to fit the mould of an increasingly ruthless drive to implement market-led development strategies intended quickly to turn Sri Lanka into a NIC [newly industrialized country]" (Woost 1997:230). This case seems to validate Dianne Rocheleau's fear that participatory-development methods may serve as "Trojan horses to bring a new level of global economic and environmental restructuring processes directly to rural communities" (Rocheleau 1994:4). In other words, development planners pay "lip service" to participation but continue on with development as usual.

According to Philip Hirsch's observations in rural Thailand, power and control are fundamental to the evocation of participation in the development context. He states, "There is a constant tension between development as a *liberating force* giving people more control over their own lives and access to a better standard of living, and development as a *constraining influence* in the sense that decisions affecting people's livelihoods are made at an ever more remote level" (Hirsch 1990:1 emphasis added). Participation in the "liberating" sense is inspired from within the community and structured around internally identified needs and objectives. Participation in the "constraining" sense is dictated by the agendas of national governments and international organizations, which often supersede the aims of village-level participants. Hence, the idea of participation is ambiguous in its implications for the role of villagers and the degree of control they have over change in their communities. Like Rocheleau, Hirsch ponders whether participation is merely a hollow redistributive measure to include villagers—a means of making villagers more amenable to change desired by outside developers.

Anthropologist Mark Hobart (1993) points out that since development discourse often construes people as ignorant, passive victims of forces over which they have no control, the agency for change must come from someone else: development planners who have "superior" knowledge and power. Hobart's statement ties in with the discussion in the "culturally/locally situated" section above, concerning the privileging of *episteme* (abstract analytic knowledge) over *techne* (tactile practical knowledge) in Western culture. Tariq Banuri (1990) is quick to point out that the dominance of Western knowledge comes not from its inherent superiority, but from the political advantage of those who *believe* in its superiority. Though many development agents have honest "participatory" intentions, this relationship of "outside experts bringing development to the locals" is reminiscent of "colonizers civilizing the savages." The possibility exists that people's rights to autonomy, identity, and their own vision of the future will be tred upon in the process of externally imposed development, no matter how participatory.

Robert Chambers, a leading figure in participatory rural appraisal (PRA), is more optimistic. He declares, "A massive shift in priorities and thinking has been taking place, from things and infrastructure to people and capabilities" (Chambers 1997:9). Chambers summarizes the PRA approach as follows:

> PRA describes a growing family of approaches and methods to enable local people to share, enhance, and analyze their knowledge of life and conditions, to plan and to act. . . . PRA has sources in activist participatory research, agroecosystem analysis, applied anthropology, field research on farming systems, and rapid rural appraisal (RRA). . . . Dominant behavior by outsiders may explain why it has taken until the 1990s for the analytical capabilities of local people to be better recognized and for PRA to emerge, grow and spread. (Chambers 1994:953)

In Chamber's opinion, PRA is really working—it is truly participatory.

While PRA is an improvement over Anand's second category in which people's labor is considered participation, PRA stops short of Anand's third category in which development is endogenously inspired, implemented, and maintained. Anthropologists Katy Gardner and David Lewis cautiously agree that PRA has "begun to challenge the assumptions of development practitioners trained within bureaucratic, status conscious and quantitative research based institutional cultures" (1996:114). Nevertheless, they state that it can easily be used within existing top-down frameworks. "For example, villagers can be routinely consulted, maps and charts can be drawn, games can be played to reveal local realities, but experts may well go off and implement their project much as planned. Like 'participation,' PRA is easily abused in practice" (ibid.:115). The degree of participation thus depends on the agent.

Development practitioners may continue to improve their participatory models, but feminist political ecologists Rocheleau, Thomas-Slayter, and Wangari (1996) maintain that local organizations and grassroots movements are key to effective social change. The Asoke movement clearly falls into Adnan's third category of participation—through their own strength and intellect, the Asoke movement has rejected conventional (worldly) development and are charting their own (Dharma) path. "Participation" facilitated by outside development agents has had mixed success in raising the quality of life for ordinary people; however, shifting the locus of power and creativity in this way can better address particular problems with more lasting effects.

Clearly, this last component is an ideal: it is not realistic to believe that all development can spring forth spontaneously and be carried on flawlessly from within localized communities. In many cases, people simply need some encouragement and external resources to begin. However, a more pressing concern than merely giving development a jump start is that communities or organizations are rarely homogeneous, and conflicting ideas are dealt with according to existing power structures, such that what emerges is not necessarily representative of all members' aspirations. Thus, the need still exists for sensitive and committed development agents who use participatory methods to uncover experiences that differ according to social location, empower participants as central actors and holders of knowledge, and mediate power differentials within the community and between the community and external parties involved in the development process. This, however, is a subject for another book.

Conclusion

This ethnography was designed to frame the Asoke way of life as a development approach that is culturally/locally situated, focused on livelihoods instead of economic growth, environmentally "sustainable," and endogenously inspired, implemented, and maintained. The Asoke development model itself is not intended as a new meta-strategy for global development, nor even one that may be readily duplicated throughout Thailand. On the contrary, this project underscores the need to investigate and encourage diverse methods of dealing with particular social, economic, and environmental dilemmas. The reason, quite simply, is that different problems require different solutions. Ultimately, the transformation of development will come from the manifestations of alternatives by grassroots movements such as Asoke—as well as by ethnographic inquiries into communities that have created their own version of "right development" as evidence of what is possible.

In closing, it must be stressed that while the Asoke movement has had great success in raising the quality of life for ordinary people, there is more to this story than material development. As the abbot of the Santi Asoke Buddhist Center in Bangkok stated, if people come for purely economic reasons, they come for the wrong reasons and soon leave. At Srisa Asoke and other Asoke communities, the atmosphere is one of genuine effort to be a better person, to fulfill the human potential by following the (Asoke) Buddhist Path. Thus, for Asoke members who endeavor to be "good people"—to be self-dependent and make sacrifices to mend society's problems—material and spiritual development are inextricably intertwined.

Notes

1. www.50years.org/about/index.html

2. President Truman introduced the term "underdeveloped" in his 1949 inaugural speech.

3. The Asoke movement takes this term "sufficiency economy" from the Thai government, which since the economic crisis has been promoting to its populace this type of development over cash cropping.

4. Akhil Gupta (1998) observed similar "hybridity" in agricultural development in Northern India.

5. As an alternative, Redefining Progress has created the Genuine Progress Indicator that subtracts these costs, allows for income distribution, and adds the value of domestic, community, and volunteer labor that does not pass through the market. Thus, they "redefine progress" to bring people and their environments into the economy.

6. www.globalexchange.org/economy/econ101/gdp.html

7. Nilifur Chagatay, United Nations Development Program, personal communication.

Epilogue

At the end of each interview with Srisa Asoke residents, I asked if there was anything else important that I had not asked, that the individual would like to add. Some individuals gave a general summary comment while others "entrusted" me with a message for Americans, academics, people of the world, or other Asoke people. It seems fitting that Srisa Asoke members should have the last word here.

Ah Wichai:

> The most important and interesting thing about Asoke to know is that Asoke is not perfect now. The world has nothing perfect. Asoke is just on the way, practicing ourselves. So don't be hopeless when we have some mistakes. I think if everyone knows and believes the thought of Asoke—the target of Asoke—and can do it, Asoke society will be perfect—in 500 years [he laughs]! I think—I don't like it when someone says, "Oh, Asoke is very good, very good!" Because Asoke is not perfect now—it's just on the way. Don't have the expectation about Asoke [that it will be a certain way] because it [hasn't] arrived yet.

Ah Ai:

> I entrusted a lot already! Okay. I thank you for the effort of people in Asoke. I believe they are good. I believe their goal is good. I believe they don't have any goal for themselves, especially the key man. Phra Bodhirak is very good. If I have to trust anybody, I will trust Asoke people and my Mormon people—the ones that show me they follow the Way, really follow the Way, because sometimes I know they are Asoke or Mormon but they don't practice.

Em:

> What is important is—in the future, if it happens that the Asoke leader is no longer here, that is, he dies, how will Asoke be? This is important. Because, for myself, my thoughts are not there yet. I can't yet get a picture of how it will be, but I know it's important. If it happens that Asoke does not have a leader, will it be the same? Will it break apart? Will we believe what we hear just the same? Will we believe the monks and the adults? JE: *Yes, if the leader is not*

here, if he dies, how will it be? Asoke people must take responsibility themselves. They must believe. . . . They must have confidence.

Ah Komwai:

I don't really have anything, na krap. But the society here is a society in which everyone has the same intent, the same spirit, in that we came to develop relating to the spirit. Everyone came here in order to be close to religion. Everyone has the feeling that being near the temple, the opportunities to develop our spirit is higher than 100. In the morning we can listen to sermons or meetings or whatever will polish us. Therefore, any community anywhere that Asoke people established, the temple is the pillar, in our work, in whatever we do. That is, the principle that is most important is religion—in the carrying out of work of Asoke people. We take religion to be the pillar.

Ah Kaenfa:

The thing that is most important in what I have said is things that are hard for humans to do. They are difficult things for humans to do, but they can do it. . . . It is really a subject that tends to be difficult for people who don't yet understand. But it will be easy for people who will begin to know how to do it. . . . At the beginning, we must understand about the precepts first. . . . When we uphold the five precepts, reduce *abayamook*, eat vegetarian, we take another step—we must depend on ourselves completely. We must reduce, yield this, na krap. We reduce things to ornament the body, we reduce other things, and diligence increases. This is the way of proceeding. But new people must start with this point first—five precepts and yield *abayamook*, and eat vegetarian—they have to rise from here first.

Ah Tangbun:

I don't know what else to say, I have said it all. Everyone who has come here, including me, everyone in the world only wants to be good. But they only think that far. . . . They do not look at the details. . . . I believe that people of this era are lazy even in thought. If they are diligent in thought, diligent in review, they will not sin. They will see, oh, this person does this and gets this result. They don't have to look far—around their house, there. People these days . . . are confused; their heads are mixed up. They do not have time to be with themselves; they don't have time to review themselves—what they have done wrong. People on the outside, if they review themselves, where they had walked incorrectly, and then fix it, adapt and change, they will get results—they will begin to be good; they will search for things that are good, like I search. I think I have found it. I have found it and I will not go anywhere else. But I will not stop in doing good. So I would like everyone, I would like to entrust to everyone, to review themselves, the things they have done, and the results. Everyone look at other people, sympathize with other people, like your heart and their heart is a single heart. Understand each other—they are like us and we are like them. Then people will have loving-kindness toward each other. Society will have peace and happiness. I think it must be like this, na.

Ah Jaenjop:

I entrust to you that, I don't know at the present time what kinds of thoughts you have about practicing Dharma here. But I would like to entrust to you, as you are doing your thesis, the things that you study here, I would like for you to study so that it enters your heart, until you see the value and take it into your own life to practice and be an example [to others].

Ah Sompan:

Something important that I would like to say is that everyone has freedom in deciding[(how to] proceed in one's own life. If you, Juli, think to help society, help the nation, help humanity, help people in the world, I would have you decide to do just one thing that you think can help other people.

Mua:

I entrust to you that America must encounter *wibaaggaam*, such that one day America must encounter a condition of being the most tread down, in trouble, helpless. I entrust to you, that you should hurry and leave America! [Mua laughs, making light of his serious words.]

Ah Payasin:

I want to speak to the subject of protecting the resources of the world, na ka. In the world now, our resources are decreasing—for example, forests. We are using too much and it gives rise to harmful substances that ruin our health, the life of animals and people, na ka. If we reduce our use of energy, use fewer resources, and adapt to find a life that is more with nature, and we don't use too much technology—more than what is necessary, it will make our world not anxious, harmful substances will decrease, and vying, competing for resources will be little. We will not have robbing from each other in order to compete for food or raw materials. We will have peace and happiness.

Ah Oi:

I would like to entrust, na ka, to you and your thesis, I would like each society in the world to think very much about humanity. Especially ones who study high [degrees], I would like them to see the ones who study less, who do not have the opportunity—I would like [societies and learned people] to think of them very much so that we can live together with happiness. That's all.

Ah Chuan:

I think the foundational thought of Americans, and ours in the East here, are different, by the foundation that is different. I think that if the Western way takes into consideration the state of being *phii nong* [elder and younger siblings] of the world, that is, sees everyone in the world—the whole world, not just this single country—as *phii nong* together, and then do not try to, like, want benefits from other countries for themselves, it will help this world be more livable. This is good for now.

Ah Peum:

I would like you to know my feelings, na ka. I think that people in the world are *phii nong* together, na ka. Regardless of what country. I would like people in the world to think this way. If people think like this, they will not think to divide up, to be good at conflict, taking what is others to be their own, na ka. Pau Than Bodhirak teaches that. He teaches us that if we are excellent, we won't think that we ourselves are the principal [ones]. We will give to this country and that country, na. But these days, people are harsh; they are greedy, very greedy. They are very greedy and infringe on different countries, such that they don't think they are *phii nong*. They think [the others] are lower and they exploit them, like that. I think, I think I would like to change their heart. I think if we can change their heart, [to feel] that every nation, every united group of people are *phii nong* together, they will see them with hospitality. I would like to entrust, na, I would like to entrust, having the opportunity to talk with foreigners. I would like to say, I would like you to see people, like, suppose they have less—how can you help them, na ka? People who have less are the same, how can we help them? Giving shelter, hospitality between nations. I would like it to be like this. I would have [everyone] be *phii nong* together truly.

Ah Jantima:

I entrust [you with a message] to Americans, to look at every country of every level to be the same people: ones who are proceeding to fight difference just the same, ones who will come to be friends in old age, sickness, and death, all the same. Therefore, we must depend on each other; then everyone will find happiness. This life, I understand that finding happiness is very difficult. People don't know where happiness is. Happiness is little suffering, that is all. Do you agree? [We laugh at the simplicity of this idea.] If there is little suffering, it might be happiness. But in the condition that there is very little suffering—we know the truth, we catch up with reality—the suffering is not much . . .

Than Din Thaam:

If everyone lives above the world like this, it is certain that if we feel that we want to develop ourselves, we must know the problems, both our own and society's. Living in any society and trying to know the problems: What problems does this society have? What problems does the household have? What problems do people have? What problems does our community have? And knowing the problems, then helping each other to solve the problems. When we want to help each other solve the problems, it gives rise to wisdom. It is also developing ourselves. Then society will exist in the most peace and coolness. It is certain. . . .

Appendix A: Cast of Characters

Table 1

Name	M/F	Age	From Where	City/ Rural
1. Ratanaporn Pumpothaung	F	47	Srisaket	rural
2. Somrak Pansiri	F	25	Ubon Ratchathani	city
3. Gert Thaisatuen	F	84	Srisaket (Kantalak)	city
4. Gesom Petak	F	44	Srisaket	rural
5. Wiroj Apaisom (Roj)	M	23	Srisaket	rural
6. Keer Habut	M	70	Srisaket (Kantalak)	rural
7. Warangkana Saekow	F	49	Batguapkerekan	rural
8. Songboon Chaohinfa	F	71	Srisaket (Kantalak)	rural
9. Glanporn	F	52	Surin	city
10. Seethaam Tombun	F	63	Srisaket	rural
11. Brakaung Sareentaw	F	59	Ubon Ratchathani	city
12. Pairat Arsanok	F	23	Sakaew	rural
13. Jap Jai	F	43	Supanburi and Bkk	city
14. Raud	F	23	Srisaket	rural
15. Reun Thurapan	F	31	Roi Et	rural
16. Siriwarn Vimonsiriparn (Warn)	F	39	Bangkok	city
17. Ratana Suddtho	F	40	Supanburi	rural
18. Plekuan Pullap	F	36	Roi Et	city
19. Pranee Nantwang	F	53	Srisaket	city
20. Leyam Kongkapan	M	69	Ubon Ratchathani	rural
21. Sa Kanya	F	74	Ubon Ratchathani	rural
22. Pichai Vuttigunparnid (Em)	M	22	Chiang Mai	rural

Continued on next page.

Table 1—Continued

Name	M/F	Age	From Where	City/ Rural
23. Mootao Singkam	F	24	Srisaket (Kantalak)	rural
24. Wichai Jaim	M	43	Bangkok	city
25. Sompan Boontachit	M	37	Srisaket	rural
26. Khaundin Singkum (Ah Peum)	F	45	Srisaket (Kantalak)	city
27. Kaenfa Sanmuang	M	45	Masarakam	city
28. Apichat Silakam (Mua)	M	20	Srisaket	rural
29. Jaenjop Pumpothaung	M	46	Srisaket (Kantalak)	city
30. Komwai Raiymau	M	37	Srisaket (Kantalak)	city
31. Nuankod Suwan (Ah Oi)	F	44	Ubon Ratchathani	rural
32. Dara Gaunsuwan (Ah Tangbun)	F	40	Ubon Ratchathani	rural
33. Chuan Dthandthuawangpun	M	52	Bangkok	city
34. Paiyasin Siriwathana	F	43	Kanchanaburi	city
35. Than Din Thaam	M	38	Chaiyapum	rural
36. Akanit Sapprasert (Ah Ai)	M	48	Bangkok	city
37. Jantima Palapol	F	38	Roi Et	rural

Table 2

Former Occupation	Work at Srisa	Yrs @ Srisa	Educ. Level	Marital Status*	# Kid
1. vendor	help with anything	1 yr	B. 5	M	1
2. student	administration	12 yr	BA	M	0
3. none	housewife	25 yr	B. 1	M	7
4. farmer	elderly care, anything	3 yr	none	S	0
5. student	Goodwill Store	8 yr	M. 6	S	0
6. rice farm, sales	vegetable garden	3 yr	B. 4	M	9
7. selling	help with everything	2 yr	B. 6	S	0
8. practice Dharma	hand-tool shed	13 yr	B. 4	M	3
9. artist	artist and cook	2 yr	M. 6	D	3
10. rice farmer	sew bags	13 yr	B. 4	W	5
11. none	vegetable garden	4 mo	B. 4	S	0
12. student	herbal medicine	7 yr	M. 6	S	0
13. univ. admin.	Goodwill Store	10 mo	assoc.	M	2
14. student	assistant to Ah Peum	7 yr	BA**	S	0
15. rice farmer	head of kitchen	3 yr	B. 6	D	1
16. shopkeeper	husband's secretary	10 mo	M. 3	M	1
17. *mae chii*	agriculture	1 yr	M. 3	S	0
18. shopkeeper	info/PR, teacher	3 yr	M. 6	D	1
19. teacher	teacher, cook	4 yr	BA	M	5

Continued on next page.

Table 2—Continued

Former Occupation	Work at Srisa	Yrs @ Srisa	Educ. Level	Marital Status*	# Kid
20. soldier	vegetable garden	25 yr	B. 4	M	6
21. farmer	vegetable garden	14 yr	B. 1	M	3
22. student	teacher, herbal medicine	3 yr	assoc.	S	0
23. student	accountant	11 yr	BA	S	0
24. land developer	teacher, trainings	10 mo	BA	M	1
25. teacher	asst. to village leader	4 yr	BA	M	3
26. teacher	teacher, comm. liaison	11 yr	BA	S	0
27. engineer	admin. leader, teacher	12 yr	BA	S	0
28. student	mushroom cultivation	8 yr	BA	S	0
29. sell *kanom*	farming and training	1 yr	B. 4	M	1
30. driver	rice-mill manager	4 yr	B. 7	M	1
31. teacher	teacher, agric., leader	15 yr	BA	S	0
32. rice farmer	garden, trash	2 yr	B. 4	D	3
33. family business	agriculture, help monks, serve meal	2 mo	assoc.	S	0
34. teacher	librarian, cook, teach, gardener	1.5 yr	MA	S	0
35. student	monk	2 yr	BA	S	0
36. phys. Ed. teacher	math teacher	1 yr	MA	D	2
37. rice farmer	farmer, child care	3 yr	M. 5	M	2

*M=Married, S=Single, D=Divorced, W=Widowed
**BA in progress.

Appendix B: Interview Questions

A. Personal History and Aspirations

History of life before coming to Srisa Asoke
Why were you interested in Asoke and why did you choose Srisa Asoke?
How long will you stay here?
What is your target here at Srisa Asoke?
Do you want to be a monk/nun (*nakbuad*)?
What do your friends and family think about Asoke?

B. Personal Practice

What do you usually do in a day?
How many meals a day do you eat? Where do you eat?
How often do you go to the Common Hall?
Did you choose the work you do? Would you prefer to do something else?
How do you meditate?
Do you own the house you live in? Do you own a car or bike?
Do you have personal money? Where? (bank, on person, family, etc.)

C. Asoke Concepts and Practice

In your view, what is most important about Asoke thoughts and way of life?
How important is it to: (Describe and then list top three most important)

- Eat vegetarian
- Eat once a day
- Use little
- Wake up at 3:30 a.m.
- Not drink alcohol
- Wear the Asoke uniform
- Not have a family

How are the Three Professions to Save the Nation related to Buddhism?

D. Srisa Asoke Community

What is the target of the community? How successful is it?
What problems does this community have?
Is there anything you do not like about this community?
Is the way of life at Srisa Asoke congruent with Asoke values?
What do you think about the school/monks/Asoke people here?
What will Srisa Asoke community be like in twenty years?

E. Asoke Group and Society

How does the larger Asoke group help Thai society? How could it help more?
In your opinion, what is a perfect society like?

F. Last Words

Do you have anything to add, a message to entrust?

Appendix C:
External Funding Received at Srisa Asoke

Amt of Funds	Sponsor	Project	Year
7,000,000 Baht	Healing Art Division, Ministry of Public Health	Collection and Propagation of Herbal Plants	
1,500,000 Baht	Concrete/Cement Funds	Rice Barn	1997
790,000 Baht	Community Development, Srisaket Province	Mushroom House	
1,300,000 Baht	Cooperative Promotion Dept.	Grain Dryer	1996
5,000,000 Baht	Ministry of Internal Affairs	Rice Mill	1997
500,000 Baht	Center for Development of Herbal Raw Materials, Institute of Thai Medical Doctors, Dept. of Medicine, Ministry of Public Health	Herbal Medicine	1997
500,000 Baht	Center for Development of Herbal Raw Materials	Herbal Medicine	1998
500,000 Baht	Center for Development of Herbal Raw Materials	Herbal Medicine	1999
9,500,000 Baht	Office of Social Investment		1999

Source: "Srisa Asoke: Buddhist Center of Srisaket," unpublished document

Glossary of Thai, Pali, and Sanskrit Terms

A

Aajan	Thai	Teacher
Abayamook	Thai	The six vices: alcohol, drugs including cigarettes, gambling, nighttime entertainment, laziness, and sexual playing
Ah	Thai	Aunt or Uncle
Ahimsa	Pali	Non-violence
Anatta	Pali	Non-self
Anicca	Pali	Impermanence

B

Bahn	Thai	House, home, village
Bhikkhu	Pali	Buddhist monk, member of Buddhist Order
Bhikkhuni	Pali	Buddhist nun
Bun	Thai	Merit
Bun-niyom	Thai	Meritism, lit. to prefer merit

D

Dharma	Sanskrit	Buddha's teachings, duty, laws of nature
Dukkha	Pali	Suffering

F

Farang	Thai	Foreigner, generally white skinned

G

Gaam	Pali	Sexual desire
Graap	Thai	To prostrate oneself
Gnan	Thai	Work, life-related activities

I

Isan	Thai	Northeastern region of Thailand

K

Kao taeow	Thai	Line up, lit. enter the line
Karma	Sanskrit	Destiny, volitional action, moral principle of the law of cause and effect
Karuna	Pali	Compassion
Khandas	Pali	The five causally conditioned elements of existence
Khon wat	Thai	Temple person
Kilesa	Pali	Moral defilements
Krengjai	Thai	To be considerate, reluctant to impose
Kuti	Thai	Monk's sleeping hut

L

Lokiya	Pali	Mundane, worldly
Lokuttara	Pali	Supramundane, transcendental

M

Mae	Thai	Mother
Maechii	Thai	Devout laywoman
Mak noi	Thai	To be content with little
Metta	Pali	Loving-kindness
Mudita	Pali	Altruistic joy

N

Nam jai	Thai	Goodwill
Nirvana	Sanskrit	Enlightenment, salvation

P

Pali		The Vernacular language of northern India in the Buddha's time. The original language for the Buddhist text. The canon of Buddhist writings.
Paññã	Pali	Wisdom
Paticcasamuppada	Pali	Doctrine of Dependent Origination
Pau	Thai	Father
Phathung	Thai	Traditional wrap skirt
Phii nong	Thai	Siblings

R

Rai	Thai	Measurement of land equaling 0.4 acre
Rap phit chaup	Thai	Responsibility
Riap roy	Thai	Proper, neat, orderly
Rongrien	Thai	School

S		
Sabai	Thai	Easy, comfortable, content
Sala	Thai	Meeting hall, usually without walls
Samana	Pali	Monk, recluse
Samãdhi	Pali	Concentration attained through meditation
Samsãra	Pali	The cycle of rebirth
Sandood	Thai	To be satisfied with what one has
Sangha	Pali	Community of Buddhist monks
Sanskrit		The language of Aryan peoples and of Hindu scriptures, also related to Greek, Latin, and Persian.
Santi	Pali	Peace
Sati	Pali	Mindfulness
Sikkhamat	Pali	Nun
Sila	Pali	Morality, the precepts
T		
Tanha	Pali	Craving, desire
Thammachat	Thai	Nature, natural
Than	Thai	Title for a monk
Theravada	Pali	"Doctrine of the Elders," the form of Buddhism practiced in Sri lanka, Burma, Thailand, Cambodia, and Laos, considered to be the original and orthodox form of Buddhism.
Tiaw phuying	Thai	To visit prostitutes
Thun-niyom	Thai	Capitalism, lit. to prefer capital
Tombun	Thai	To make merit
Tom wat chao	Thai	Morning religious services
U		
Upekkha	Pali	Equinimity
W		
Wai	Thai	Hands pressed together at chest, chin, or nose level as sign of greeting, prayer, apology, thanks, or respect
Wat	Thai	Temple
Wibaaggaam	Thai	The consequences of past evil deeds
Y		
Ya ba	Thai	Methamphetamine, lit. crazy medicine
Ya samoonphrai	Thai	Herbal medicine
Yai	Thai	Grandmother
Yatithaam	Thai	Relatives in Dharma

References

Santi Asoke Publications and Pamphlets:

2000. "30 Years of Work," video [in Thai]

1999. *What Do We Think?* 5, no. 109 (August).

1995. *Bodhirak, Enlightenment Activities.* Bangkok: Fa Apai [in Thai].

1992. "15 Minutes with Pau Than," *Saan Asoke* (August) [in Thai]

1989. *Insight Into Santi Asoke, part I.* Bangkok: Dharma Santi Foundation Press.

1988. "15 Minutes with Pau Than," *Saan Asoke* (January) [in Thai].

n.p. "House-Temple-School," [in Thai].

n.p. "Srisa Asoke: Buddhist Center of Srisaket," [two versions in Thai and English].

n.p. "Three Professions to Save the Nation," [in Thai].

Newspapers and News Magazines

Associated Press. October 27, 2000.

Bangkok Post. December 1, 1996; July 27, 1997; September 21, 1997; November 16, 1997; February 5, 1998; September 13, 1999; December 9, 2991.

Christian Science Monitor. July 24, 1998; August 9, 2000; May 29, 2002.

The Economist. November 8, 2001; April 22, 2002.

London Times. June 21, 1998.

The Nation. August 24, 2001.

Newsweek International. July 12, 1999.

Time. March 23, 1992.

Books and Articles:

Adams, W. M. 1995. "Sustainable Development?" In *Geographies of Global Change, Remapping the World in the Late Twentieth Century,* edited by R. J. Johnston, P. Taylor, and M. Watts. Oxford: Blackwell Publishers.

Adnan, Shapan, Alison Narret, S. M. Nurul Alam, Angelika Brushtinow. 1992. *People's Participation, NGOs, and the Flood Action Plan: An Independent Review.* Dhaka, Bangladesh: Research & Advisory Services.

Atkinson, Jane Monnig and Shelly Errington, eds. 1990. *Power and Difference: Gender in Island Southeast Asia*. Stanford: Stanford University Press.

Banuri, Tariq. 1990. "Development and the Politics of Knowledge: A Critical Perspective on Theories of Development." In *Dominating Knowledge: Development, Culture, and Resistance*, edited by F. Apffel-Marglin and S. Marglin. Oxford: Clarendon Press.

Bebbington, Anthony. 1996. "Movements, Modernizations, and Markets: Indigenous Organizations and Agrarian Strategies in Ecuador." In *Liberation Ecologies: Environment, Development, Social Movements*, edited by R. Peet and M. Watts. London: Routledge.

Berthoud, Gérard. 1992. "Market." In *Development Dictionary: A Guide to Knowledge as Power*, edited by W. Sachs. London: Zed Books.

Brown, Kerry. 1992. "In the Water There Were Fish and the Fields Were Full of Rice: Reawakening the Lost Harmony of Thailand." In *Buddhism and Ecology*, edited by M. Batchelor and K. Brown. London: Cassell.

Brú-Bistuer, Josepa. 1996. "Spanish Women against Industrial Waste." In *Feminist Political Ecology: Global Issues and Local Experiences*, edited by D. Rocheleau, B. Thomas-Slayter, and E. Wangari. London: Routledge.

Buddhadasa Bhikkhu. 1956. *Handbook for Mankind*. Bangkok: The Sublime Life Mission.

Bunnag, Jane. 1973. *Buddhist Monk, Buddhist Layman: A Study of Urban Monastic Organization in Central Thailand*. Cambridge: Cambridge University Press.

Chambers, Robert. 1997. *Whose Reality Counts? Putting the First Last*. London: Intermediate Technology Publications.

Chambers, Robert. 1994. "The Origins and Practice of Participatory Rural Appraisal." *World Development* 22, no. 7: 953-69.

Chambers, Robert and Gordon Conway. 1992. *Sustainable Rural Livelihoods: Practical Concepts for the 21st Century*. Sussex, England: Institute of Development Studies.

Cobb, Clifford, Cary Sue Goodman, and Mathis Wackernagel. 1999. "Why Bigger Isn't Better: the Genuine Progress Indicator—1999 Update." San Francisco: Redifining Progress.

Crewe, Emma. 1997. "The Silent Traditions of Developing Cooks." In *Discourses of Development: Anthropological Perspectives*, edited by R. D. Grillo and R. L. Stirrat. Oxford: Berg.

Daly, Herman. 1996. *Beyond Growth: The Economics of Sustainable Development*. Boston: Beacon Press.

Daly, Herman and John Cobb, Jr. 1989. *For the Common Good: Redirecting the Economy toward Community, the Environment, and a Sustainable Future*. Boston: Beacon Press.

Darlington, Susan. 2000. "Rethinking Buddhism and Development: The Emergence of Environmentalist Monks in Thailand." *Journal of Buddhist Ethics* 7.

Darlington, Susan. 1998. "The Ordination of a Tree: The Buddhist Ecology Movement in Thailand." *Ethnology* 37, no. 1:1-15

Dixon, Chris. 1996. "Thailand's Rapid Economic Growth: Causes, Sustainability, and Lessons." In *Uneven Development in Thailand*, edited by M. Parnwell. Aldershot, England: Avebury.

Dos Santos, Theotonio. 1971. "The Structure of Dependence." In *Readings in the U.S. Imperialism*, edited by K. T. Kan and D. C. Hodges. Boston: Extending Horizons.

Dove, Michael. 1988. "Introduction: Traditional Culture and Development in Contemporary Indonesia." In *The Real and Imagined Role of Culture in Development: Case Studies from Indonesia*, edited by M. Dove. Honolulu: University of Hawaii Press.

Ekins, Paul. 1993. "Making Development Sustainable." In *Global Ecology: A New Arena of Political Conflict*, edited by W. Sachs. London: Zed Books.

Enloe, Cynthia. 1989. *Bananas, Beaches, and Bases*. London: Pandora Press.

Escobar, Arturo. 1995. *Encountering Development: The Making and Unmaking of the Third World*. Princeton, N. J.: Princeton University Press.

Escobar, Arturo. 1999. "Whose Knowledge, Whose Nature? Biodiversity Conservation and Social Movements Political Ecology." *Journal of Political Ecology* 5:53-82.

Fagerlind, Ingemar and Lawrence J. Saha. 1983. "The Origins of Modern Development Thought." In *Education and National Development: A Comparative Perspective*. Oxford: Pragamon Press.

Frank, Andre Gunder. 1967. *Capitalism and Underdevelopment in Latin America*. New York: Monthly Review Press.

Fukuoka, Masanobu. 1985. *The Natural Way of Farming: The Theory and Practice of Green Philosophy*, translated by Frederic P. Metreaud. Tokyo: Japan Publications, Inc.

Fukuoka, Masanobu. 1978. *The One Straw Revolution: An Introduction to Natural Farming*. London: Bantam New Age Editions.

Gardner, Katy and David Lewis. 1996. *Anthropology, Development and the Post-Modern Challenge*. London: Pluto Press.

Goodland, Robert and Herman Daly. 1992. "Three Steps toward Environmental Sustainability" Parts I and II. *Development (Journal of SID)* 2 and 3:35-41, 64-71.

Gow, David. 1995. "Anthropology, the Environment, and the Third World: Principles, Power, and Practice." *NAPA Bulletin* 15, no. 1:46-59.

Grown, Caren and Jennifer Sebstad. 1989. "Introduction: Toward a Wider Perspective on Women's Employment." *World Development* 17, no. 7:937-52.

Gudeman, Stephen. 1998. "Banishing the Other from the Market: The Development Economics of W. Arthur Lewis." *Paideuma* 44:125-38.

Gudeman, Stephen and Alberto Rivera. 1995. "From Car to House (Del coche a la casa)." *American Anthropologist* 97, no. 2:242-50.

Gudeman, Stephen and Alberto Rivera. 1990. *Conversations in Colombia: The Domestic Economy in Life and Text*. Cambridge: Cambridge University Press.

Gupta, Akhil. 1998. *Postcolonial Development: Agriculture in the Making of Modern India*. London: Duke University Press.

Hancock, Graham. 1989. *Lords of Poverty: The Power, Prestige, and Corruption of the International Aid Business*. New York: The Atlantic Monthly Press.

Harrison, Faye. 1997. "The Gendered Politics and Violence of Structural Adjustment: A View from Jamaica." In *Situated Lives: Gender and Culture in Everyday Life*, edited by L. Lamphere, H. Ragoné, and P. Zavella. New York: Routledge.

Heikkilä-Horn, Marja-Leena. 1996a. "Two Paths to Revivalism in Thai Buddhism: The Dhammakaya and Santi Asoke Movements." *Temenos* 32: 93-111.

Heikkilä-Horn, Marja-Leena. 1996b. *Santi Asoke Buddhism and Thai State Response*. Äbo, Finland: Åbo Academis Forlag.

Hirsch, Philip, ed. 1996. *Seeing Forests for Trees: Environment and Environmentalism in Thailand*. Chiang Mai, Thailand: Silkworm Books.

Hirsch, Philip. 1990. *Development Dilemmas in Rural Thailand*. Singapore: Oxford University Press.

Hobart, Mark, ed. 1993. *An Anthropological Critique of Development: The Growth of Ignorance*. London: Routledge.

Illich, Ivan. 1992. "Needs." In *Development Dictionary: A Guide to Knowledge as Power*, edited by W. Sachs. London: Zed Books.

Jackson, Peter. 1989. *Buddhism, Legitimation, and Conflict: The Political Functions of Urban Thai Buddhism*. Singapore: Institute of Southeast Asian Studies.

Kammen, Daniel and Michael Dove. 1997. "The Virtues of Mundane Science." *Environment* 39, no. 6:10-15, 28-41.

Keyes, Charles. 1984. "Mother or Mistress, But Never a Monk: Buddhist Notions of Female Gender in Rural Thailand." *American Ethnologist* 11, no. 2:223-41.

Keyes, Charles. 1983. "Introduction: The Study of Popular Ideas of Karma." In *Karma: An Anthropological Inquiry*, edited by Charles Keyes and E. Valentine Daniel. Berkeley: University of California Press.

King, Victor. 1999. "Forest and Farms: Environmental Issues." In *Anthropology and Development in Southeast Asia: Theory and Practice*, edited by V. King. Oxford: Oxford University Press.

Klausner, William J. 2000 [1981]. *Reflections on Thai Culture*. Bangkok: The Siam Society.

Leungaramsri, Pinkaew and Noel Rajesh, eds. 1992. *The Future of People and Forests in Thailand after the Logging Ban*. Bangkok: Project for Ecological Recovery.

Macy, Joanna. 1983. Dharma and Development: Religion as Resource in the Sarvodaya Self-Help Movement. West Hartford, Conn.: Kumarian Press.

Marglin, Stephen. 1990. "Losing Touch: The Cultural Conditions of Worker Accommodation and Resistance." In *Dominating Knowledge: Development, Culture, and Resistance*, edited by F. Apffel-Marglin and S. Marglin. Oxford: Clarendon Press.

Mayer, Theodore. 1996. "Thailand's New Buddhist Movements in Historical and Political Context." In *Loggers, Monks, Students, and Entrepreneurs*, edited by B. Hunsaker. DeKalb, Ill: CSEAS, Northern Illinois University.

McCargo, Duncan. 1997. *Chamlong Srimuang and the New Thai Politics*. London: C. Hurst & Co.

Mies, Maria. 1993. "The Myth of Catching-up Development." In *Ecofeminism*, edited by M. Mies and V. Shiva. London: Zed Books.

Mills, Mary Beth. 1997. "Contesting the Margins of Modernity: Women, Migration, and Consumption in Thailand." *American Ethnologist* 24, no. 1:37-61.

Mulder, Niels. 1996. *Inside Thai Society: Interpretations of Everyday Life*. Amsterdam: The Pepin Press.

Narumon Hinshiranan. 1993. "The Case of Buddhist Nuns in Thailand." *Sakyadhita Newsletter* 4, no. 1 (Summer).

Nazarea, Virginia. 1999. "Lenses and Latitudes in Landscapes and Lifescapes." In *Ethnoecology: Situated Knowledge/Located Lives*, edited by V. Nazarea. Tucson: University of Arizona Press.

Nolan, Riall. 2002. *Development Anthropology: Encounters in the Real World*. Cambridge, Mass.: Westview Press.

Norberg-Hodge, Helena. 1991. *Ancient Futures: Learning from Lakakh*. San Francisco: Sierra Club Books.

Obeyesekere, Ganath. 1968. "Theodicy, Sin, and Salvation in a Sociology of Buddhism." In *Dialectic in Practical Religion*, edited by E. Leach. Cambridge: Cambridge University Press.

Ortner, Sherry. 1984. "Theory in Anthropology since the Sixties." *Comparative Study of Society and History* 26, no. 1:126-66.

P. A. Payutto. 1995. *Good, Evil, and Beyond: Kamma in the Buddha's Teaching.* Bangkok: Buddhadhamma Foundation.

P. A. Payutto. 1992. Buddhist Economics: A Middle Way for the Market Place. Bangkok: Buddhadhamma Foundation.

Parnwell, Michael and Daniel Arghiros. 1996. "Introduction." In *Uneven Development in Thailand*, edited by M. Parnwell. Aldershot, England: Avebury.

Parnwell, Michael and Raymond Bryant. 1996. "Conclusion: Towards Sustainable Development in Southeast Asia?" In *Environmental Change in Southeast Asia: People, Politics, and Sustainable Development*, edited by M. Parnwell and R. Bryant. London: Routledge.

Pasuk Phongpaichit. 1982. *From Peasant Girls to Bangkok Masseuses.* Geneva: International Labor Office.

Pasuk Phongpaichit and Chris Baker. 2000. *Thailand's Crisis.* Chiang Mai, Thailand: Silkworm Books.

Peet, Richard and Michael Watts, eds. 1996. *Liberation Ecologies: Environment, Development, Social Movements.* London: Routledge.

Queen, Christopher and Sallie King, eds. 1996. *Engaged Buddhism: Buddhist Liberation Movements in Asia.* Albany: State University of New York Press.

Rattigorn Rattanaburi. 2001. "The Life of a Maechee." *Seeds of Peace* 17, no. 2 (May-August).

Rahula, Walpola. 1956. *History of Buddhism in Ceylon.* Columbo: Gunasena.

Redclift, Michael. 1987. *Sustainable Development: Exploring the Contradictions.* London: Routledge.

Redfield, Robert. 1956. *Peasant Society and Culture.* Chicago: University of Chicago Press.

Rigg, Jonathan, ed. 1995. *Counting the Costs: Economic Growth and Environmental Change in Thailand.* Pasir Panjang, Singapore: Institute of Southeast Asian Studies.

Rocheleau, Dianne, B. Thomas-Slayter, and E. Wangari, eds. 1996. *Feminist Political Ecology: Global Issues and Local Experiences.* London: Routledge.

Rocheleau, Dianne. 1994. "Participatory Research and the Race to Save the Planet: Questions, Critique, and Lessons from the Field." *Agriculture and Human Values* (Spring-Summer): 4-25.

Rostow, W. W. 1960. *The Stages of Economic Growth: A Non-Communist Manifesto.* Cambridge: Cambridge University Press.

Sachs, Wolfgang. 1993. "Global Ecology and the Shadow of Development." In *Global Ecology: A New Arena of Political Conflict*, edited by W. Sachs. London: Zed Books.

Sachs, Wolfgang, ed. 1992. *The Development Dictionary: A Guide to Knowledge as Power.* London: Zed Books.

Sachs, Wolfgang. 1990. "On the Archaeology of the Development Idea." *Lokayan Bulletin* 8, no. 1.

Sanitsuda Ekachai. 1994. *Seeds of Hope: Local Initiatives in Thailand.* Bangkok: Thai Development Support Committee.

Sanitsuda Ekachai. 1990. *Behind the Smile: Voices of Thailand.* Bangkok: Thai Development Support Committee.

Santikaro Bhikkhu. 1996. "Buddhadasa Bhikkhu: Life and Society through the Natural Eyes of Voidness." In *Engaged Buddhism: Buddhist Liberation Movements in Asia*, edited by C. Queen and S. King. New York: State University of New York Press.

Schmithausen, Lambert. 1997. "The Early Buddhist Tradition and Ecological Ethics." *Journal of Buddhist Ethics* 4.

Sen, Amartya. 1999. *Development as Freedom*. New York: Anchor Books.

Sen, Amartya. 1988. "The Concept of Development." In *Handbook of Development Economics, Vol. 1*, edited by H. Chenery and T. N. Srinvasan. Amsterdam: Elsevier Science Publishers.

Sen, Amartya. 1984. *Resources, Values, and Development*. Cambridge, Mass.: Harvard University Press.

Seri Phongphit. 1988. *Religion in a Changing Society: Buddhism, Reform, and the Role of Monks in Community Development in Thailand*. Hong Kong: Arena Press.

Shiva, Vandana. 1988. *Staying Alive*. New Delhi: Kali for Women.

Sinith Sittirak. 1998. *The Daughters of Development: Women in a Changing Environment*. London: Zed Books.

Smith, Bardwell, ed. 1978. *Religion and Legitimation of Power in Thailand, Laos, and Burma*. Chambersburg, Pa.: ANIMA Books.

So, Alvin Y. 1990. *Social Change and Development: Modernization, Dependency, and World-System Theories*. London: Sage Publications, Inc.

Somboon Suksamran. 1988. "A Buddhist Approach to Development: The Case of Development Monks in Thailand." In *Reflections of Development in Southeast Asia*, edited by Lim Teck Ghee. Singapore: Institute of Southeast Asian Studies.

Somboon Suksamran. 1976. *Political Buddhism in Southeast Asia: The Role of the Sangha in the Modernization of Thailand*. New York: St. Martin's Press.

Stacey, Judith. 1988. "Can There Be A Feminist Ethnography?" *Women's Studies International Forum* 11, no. 1:21-7.

Sulak Sivaraksa. 1992. *Seeds of Peace*. Berkeley, Calif.: Parallax Press.

Sulak Sivaraksa. 1990. "True Development." In *Dharma Gaia: A Harvest of Essays in Buddhism and Ecology*, edited by A. Badiner. Berkeley, Calif.: Parallax Press.

Swearer, Donald. 1989. *Me and Mine: Selected Essays of Bhikkhu Buddhadasa*. New York: State University of New York Press.

Tambiah, S. J. 1984. *The Buddhist Saints of the Forest and the Cult of Amulets: A Study of Charisma, Hagiography, Sectarianism, and Millennial Buddhism*. Cambridge: Cambridge University of Press.

Tambiah, S. J. 1978. "Sangha and Polity in Modern Thailand: An Overview." In *Religion and Legitimation of Power in Thailand, Laos, and Burma*, edited by B. Smith. Chambersburg, Pa.: ANIMA Books.

Tambiah, S. J. 1976. *World Conqueror and World Renouncer: A Study of Buddhism and Polity in Thailand against a Political Background*. Cambridge: Cambridge University Press.

Tambiah, S. J. 1970. *Buddhism and the Spirit Cult in North-east Thailand*. Cambridge: Cambridge University Press.

Tambiah, S. J. 1968. "The Ideology of Merit and the Social Correlates of Buddhism in a Thai Village." In *Dialectic in Practical Religion*, edited by E. Leach. Cambridge: Cambridge University Press.

Taylor, Jim L. 1996. *Forest Monks and the Nation-State: An Anthropological and Historical Study in Northeastern Thailand*. Singapore: Institute of Southeast Asian Studies.

Taylor, Jim L. 1990. "New Buddhist Movements in Thailand: An 'Individualistic Revolution,' Reform, and Political Dissonance." *Journal of Southeast Asian Studies* 21, no. 1:135-54.

Taylor, Jim L. 1989. "Contemporary Urban Buddhist 'Cults' and the Socio-Political Order in Thailand. " *Mankind* 19, no. 2:122-25.

Warren, Kay and Susan Bourque. 1991. "Women, Technology, and International Development Ideologies: Analyzing Feminist Voices." In *Gender at the Crossroads of Knowledge: Feminist Anthropology in the Postmodern Era*, edited by M. di Leonardo. Berkeley: University of California Press.

Weber, Max. 1958. *The Religion of India: The Sociology of Hinduism and Buddhism*. Glencoe, Ill.: Free Press.

Woost, Michael D. 1997. "Alternative Vocabularies of Development? 'Community' and 'Participation' in Development Discourse in Sri Lanka." In *Discourses of Development: Anthropological Perspectives*, edited by R. D. Grillo and R. L. Stirrat. Oxford: Berg.

World Commission on Environment and Development. 1987. *Our Common Future*. Oxford: Oxford University Press.

Index

About the Author

For over a decade, **Juliana Essen** has pursued a better way of doing development that would actually raise the quality of life for ordinary people. This endeavor began at Michigan State University with a BA in Social Science International Studies specializing in International Development and an internship at Michigan State's Office of Women and International Development. She then gained practical experience in the development field as a United States Peace Corps Community Forestry Extension Agent in Thailand. Her studies continued as a MacArthur Scholar at the University of Minnesota, culminating in a PhD in cultural anthropology. She currently works as an adjunct at Soka University of America in Aliso Viejo, California, and is in the process of establishing a nonprofit organization to further her development ideals. When she's not trying to save the world, she enjoys kicking back with her husband and dog in the sunny, eclectic community of Laguna Beach.

www.ingramcontent.com/pod-product-compliance
Ingram Content Group UK Ltd.
Pitfield, Milton Keynes, MK11 3LW, UK
UKHW012040150926
475560UK00001B/100

9 780739 1093